Modern Archaeology and its Reflection in the Value System of Contemporary Culture

Based on anthropological/archaeological research conducted in Australia

Boris Deunert

BAR International Series 648

1996

Published in 2019 by
BAR Publishing, Oxford

BAR International Series 648

Modern Archaeology and its Reflection in the Value System of Contemporary Culture

ISBN 9780860548331 paperback
ISBN 9781407349565 e-book

DOI https://doi.org/10.30861/9780860548331

A catalogue record for this book is available from the British Library

This book is available at www.barpublishing.com

BAR Publishing is the trading name of British Archaeological Reports (Oxford) Ltd.
British Archaeological Reports was first incorporated in 1974 to publish the BAR
Series, International and British. In 1992 Hadrian Books Ltd became part of the BAR
group. This volume was originally published by Tempvs Reparatvm in conjunction
with British Archaeological Reports (Oxford) Ltd / Hadrian Books Ltd, the Series
principal publisher, in 1996. This present volume is published by BAR Publishing,
2019.

BAR
PUBLISHING

BAR titles are available from:

BAR Publishing
122 Banbury Rd, Oxford, OX2 7BP, UK
EMAIL   info@barpublishing.com
PHONE   +44 (0)1865 310431
FAX   +44 (0)1865 316916
www.barpublishing.com

To my parents and all

helpful supporters

LIST OF ILLUSTRATIONS

ACKNOWLEDGMENTS

There were an enormous number of people that showed interest in this study and were gladly willing to support me in various ways. It is not my intention to evaluate this support according to its helpfulness or to artificially create a "typology" of the respective people that benefited me, ordered, i.e., after grade of friendship, warmth or cuteness etc.. I would like to emphasize that the arrangement below does not reflect any of these criteria.

Two people, however, have to be mentioned separately. These are my doctoral supervisor Prof.Dr.Helmut Ziegert and my successful middleperson Shawn Buchanan.

Helmut Ziegert (Professor for pre- and early history at the University of Hamburg) agreed on my lousy proposal and the few unstructured ideas I had for my doctoral thesis. He probably gave his consent because of the fact that I did not do much better with my masters and it still turned out well. Not much support was possible in Australia, except a nice recommendation (was it me he was talking about?), but back in Germany he supplied me with everything needed.

Shawn Buchanan (Student at present) was my companion throughout the Australian continent. Not only was she a successful interviewer, but also a thriving pushstarter of our car that never wanted to run as it should. She had the honor to live through the most horrible time of her life for science's sake.

I am especially grateful to Phillip Alice and his life companion Agnes Young, who showed us around in the Alice Springs region and were never tired of answering our sometimes nerve-wracking questions. An unforgettable adventure was a weekend in the bush, even though guana shooting and the taste of kangaroo blood is not quite arousing in the authors point of view.

I also wish to thank Meriam and Roberta Alice for their kindness in inviting Shawn and me to their community.

Lena and Jack Calvanagh were most helpful in conducting stone tool experiments.

Special thanks shall be directed to the Arunda people dwelling in and around the Todd River. These people coming from several different Aboriginal communities in the southern part of the Northern Territory were willing and glad to have their say about the problem in question.
    Anewne Kangketje aneme marpe Santa Teresa arenheke and Todd River arenhe marpeke.
    Anewne thankem elheme anewne let em ilheke apmere le anhetjeke and kangketje anthurre anheme.

I wish to thank Prof.Dr.Robert Borofsky, of whom I intensely thought in Australia, but whom I never wrote. I would like to apologize for that, since some of the things he taught me are taken into consideration within the thesis.

MA Rainer Michel converted parts of the Ph.D. written in Word format into Winwrite format and helped me as much as he could.

Prof.Dr.Peter Hiscock, University of Darwin, built me up in a phase of frustration about administrative difficulties.

Prof.Dr.Vinx, University of Hamburg, conducted the mineralogical investigation of thin-sectioned sandstone, though he was overworked anyway.

The owner of the old camel farm camping ground, which is pitiably closed now, gave us the permission to camp almost for free, since she supported our doing and knew about our financial situation.

I am especially in debt to the staff of the TAFE college in Alice Springs. The friendliness of the staff in admission, library and computer lab, and the willingness to provide me with everything I needed was exemplary.

I am grateful to Sue, Sharon and Jim Halliday, who were the supplier of our daily firewood, tea and cookies, and family like warmth.

The Ainsly Village administration shall be thanked for letting us stay on the lowest tariff and for offering us the possibility to conduct first interviews, also with people in alcohol rehabilitation.

I would like to express my gratitude to Lucy and Marinus de Wolf, who accommodated us, fed us, and showed us Australian hospitality.

Geraldine Triffith and John Tarbath became our honest friends and were always good for a critical conversation. Their gift, a 40 liter water container, probably saved our lives several times.

I would also like to express my appreciation to the staff of the Australian Institute of Aboriginal Studies and Torres Strait Islanders for their kindness to mess with their meticulous order and much, much help.

Thanks to all the mechanics who kept our car running, mostly without any charge. Special thanks to the genius electrician Max Tate in Tennant Creek.

A Swiss couple, whose names I do not even know, towed us, when our car's timing chain ripped right in the desert, for which I am very grateful.

Jennifer Thompson, health worker in Alice Springs supported us with advice and unconventional help. Thank you very much.

I am grateful to a Maori family, which gave us shelter for a few days and helped us to recover from the loss of our car.

Thank you to David Blanasi, Eddy Ryon, and all the Interviewees, who willingly answered our questions and showed interest in the present work.

Last, but not least, I would like to thank my parents, who supported me throughout my education and did their share also in this adventure.

TABLE OF CONTENTS

1. INTRODUCTION

1.1 OBJECT ORIENTED PROBLEM

The main problems being investigated in this thesis can be phrased as follows: How can archaeologists work closely together with Aboriginal people and in a way that can mutually benefit both parties involved, concerning the research outcome for the scientist and giving Aborigines a proven base of the prehistory they are aiming to identify with, but are not willing to explore in detail themselves ? Since the author of this thesis chose archaeology as a major and anthropology & geography as minor subjects at the university in order to investigate European prehistory and the notion that this knowledge is an integral part of his cultural awareness, he did not understand why Aboriginal people "obviously" do not have the urge to explore their culture in detail. Knowing that such a conclusion is inadequate, if not proven through carefully conducted research or a representative general inquiry, a thorough search for this sort of information was the consequence.

Several pre-investigational steps had to be taken, in order to investigate these problems. A major precondition was the in-depth knowledge of the historical and up-to-date archaeological & anthropological interpretation of prehistoric Australia including all other major scientific branches involved. Although, numerous major works about partial aspects of Australian prehistory exist, they have not substantially included other science branches as was done in this thesis. Further information, such as references to authors are located in the outline. The need for this particular research becomes obvious when securely statable results of today's scientific research are evaluated and incorporated in Aboriginal dreamtime stories, as well as, supporting Aboriginal cultural awareness and assertiveness.

The second, but equally important investigational step was the clarification of the status of Aboriginal people in past and present times, as well as, their cultural awareness and identification with their own and forcefully obtruded culture. Researchers interested in studying Aboriginal culture have to be aware of the status of Aboriginal people in historic and today's Australian society in order to understand Aboriginal needs and ideological developments. Scientists, who take this pre-investigational step may be able to predict the aboriginal interest in his/her studies and the support to be received. Archaeologists, especially those, working in the field of stone technology or those who aim to interpret single findings need Aboriginal people stating the actual use of a tool. (For example, in a special manner) These scientists might want to structure their research program differently, including themes of Aboriginal interest, being directed towards the main research purpose. This author chose to examine the Aboriginal identification problem with their past, also including today's land claim processes as being closely related to the problems in question.

The questionnaire, which was used in the actual interview should not only incorporate solely archaeological questions, but also those explicitly investigating the Aboriginal identification problem. The initially prepared question catalog had to be expanded and altered, while obtaining in-depth knowledge about Aboriginal history & prehistory and their standing in today's society (sections II. and III.)

The actual interview, as well as, the stone technology section represent the main investigational tools in this thesis. Both parts are not thought to develop far reaching conclusions, but to exemplify the dilemma modern science has to face if working in a field, where not only the exchange of knowledge between two diverse cultures is questioned, but also cultural assimilation both ways. The aim of these investigations is to find a possible way of mutually beneficiary relations. (See also Smith/Briddle 1975:122)
[A similar discussion of the problem in question has taken place in the United States concerning the Native American and Polynesian cultures and is now slowly reaching the Australian continent. e.g. Borofsky 1987, Harding 1991, Lancaster, 1992, Lightfoot 1992, Pevar 1992, Pewewardy 1992, Ross 1992, Snyder-Joy 1992]

The close connection of the interview and the stone technology section was thought to enhance the outcome of the stone tool experiments. The author surely has to ask himself if the insight he will or will not experience actually reflects the interest of the Aboriginal people towards the main problem of the thesis rather than simply towards the stone tool experiments. It is anyway questionable if some research projects can benefit Aboriginal people at all and if the researchers' efforts are wanted or just tolerated. The main questions asked in this part can be phrased as follows:

Is it possible to use special stone tools as cultural markers or is this attempt inadequate ? Do multi-purpose tools exist, and, if yes, are they suitable for frequently moving groups concerning their handling, manufacturing and function ?

Replicative experiments of common stone tools, and an evaluation of their use and effectiveness shall establish a base for subsequent conclusions. A detailed use-wear analysis of several surface findings and material obtained from limited excavations shall support or deny the previous hypothesis.

Apparently these data were unobtainable (due to lack of references) or very difficult acquire through the internal library exchange program on an international level. When researching with Aboriginal culture in Europe one inevitably has to rely on research conducted in Australia and process and record the results so that it has a westernized style and appearance for the convenience of the interested reader. Information obtained about the authors made it obvious that they were either European, American or Australian of European descent. The decision was made to do further research in Australia with the aim being of finding out if the Aborigines were interested in their cultural heritage (1)

----
(1) considering both their dreamtime stories and the research results of modern scientists

and if everything the "white man" had written was correct, since the Aboriginal people seem not to contradict in writing. Arriving in Australia with the assumption that there was a research gap or large educational differences between researchers and Aborigines the author was quick to learn differently even during the first weeks of his stay. The originally prepared questionnaire had to be expanded to include either self-derived questions or questions derived with the help of a third party. (see section 1.4a/VIb) The research more and more revolved around the main question; is archaeological & anthropological research both needed and wanted by the Aborigines or is it is maybe conducted only for the researchers selfish interest ? Might it be that the Aboriginal groups or communities throughout the country are perfectly content with their dreamtime stories and handed down knowledge of ancestry and descent ? How, if possible at all, can archaeology & anthropology support Aboriginal interests ? How are archaeologists and anthropologists perceived and what is expected of them by the Aborigines ? Critically analyzing these questions, one becomes aware that these implied problems cannot be dealt with on a national Australian level, but have to be considered as a product of a fatal development in European and American research.

In a time when social science is discriminated in favor of other scientific branches in terms of financial support and when professorial positions are canceled or based on temporary employment, the study of those sciences is purposely made unattractive through the requirement of high grade point averages and the requirement of not only a doctoral, but also a masters and, in some countries, a BA Honors thesis. All the promising future scientists "enrich" our libraries or archives with another thousand books, manuscripts or pamphlets of rewritten and/or slightly altered but basically the same information (2). In order to meet the requirement of independent, analytical research, students spread out all over the world seeking the last unexplored secrets, if possible in connection with contemporary cultures. The most haunted culture seemed and seems to be the Aboriginal one. How, one might think, do the people react towards this flood ? Are they still honest (or have they ever been) if scientifically asked in order to answer research problems ? Do they care about the outcome ? Is the research worth conducting ? Do researchers have the responsibility to positively influence the Aborigines role and perception in society ? How is this role or status of Aboriginal people defined in a white dominated society ? Is the poor relation of Aborigines and white Australians solely based on a color problem or is the cultural component dominating ? All this is likely to be answered through this research.

1.2 THEME DELINEATION AND DEFINITION

a) factual

Modern archaeology and its reflection in the value system of contemporary cultures includes not only the questioning and study of the investigated communities, but also a critical self-reflection of one's own cultural values and the role of archaeology in one's own society. The immense pride of modern archaeologists, including the author, for the valuable achievements in theory and methodology over the last 30 years might stand in a huge contrast with, hitherto undiscovered, archaeological interests of the investigated ethnic groups. The notion that all the cultures, like ours, will be interested in the explicit explanation of their prehistory, could be a naive one. Ignoring this consideration, generations of amateur and professional researchers were eagerly aiming to give "those people" a history they could rely on, pointing out, their forefingers raised, that one day the explored cultures will be grateful for their doing. In order to prove or disprove the theory that Aboriginal people are fully content with their dreamtime stories and their own knowledge, whatever one might understand as such, about the past and also to answer the questions raised in part 1.1, basic information about the conducted research and its history had to be obtained. The "outline of the archaeological/anthropological interpretation of prehistoric Australia" as well as the "research level and history" is thought not only to sum up the research carried out (under special consideration of its outcome), but also to be used in abstract for question No. 8 in the questionnaire. The research level and history section will be characterized by an insightful look at the changing anthropological self-understanding with its convulsive attempt to ingeniously fulfill new demands towards this branch of science. Especially the anthropologist's role as expert witness in land claim court cases will further show that this duty does not only politically involves a foremost "innocent science" (3), but also divides researchers into two opposing groups and makes them into the most hated people in the Aborigines' view. The "evaluation of the sources and techniques used" section shall argue about the pros and cons of the usefulness of an either prepared and/or altered question catalogue. Personal experience as well as the literary work-up of this question will be considered, in order to choose the appropriate questionnaire to be used for the interviews. The literature used, their quality, diversity and accessibility, will be critically analyzed with point b) of the same section. This point in combination with the literature list might prove the authors carefulness concerning his research or give reason to critically argue about omissions. The use of a middleperson is a central point in the authors approach of different communities and individuals. This point stresses the usefulness, selection, and Aboriginals' perception (4) of the middelperson and the subsequently en hanced or

---

(2) comparable to ancient Greek excavations, where another 10.000 sherds are excavated, analyzed, published and stored without any historical value (Ziegert, Doctoral seminar 1990)

---

(3) See also comment No. 24
(4) Cross comparisons with the interview outcome without a middleman will be provided

similar information obtained. Another point tries to investigate the truthfulness of answer and the credibility of informants as far as this can be stated through the comparative analysis of the answers given. Literature concerning this problem will also be considered.

Point 1.5 indicates the inquiry method used for this thesis. The explanation of this method will enable the reader to test the authors conclusions and detect eventual absurdities, should they exist.

Section II shall acquaint the reader with the geological setting of the Australian continent, as well as the primary archaeological research history, common theories, and mainstream ideas. The geological part will deal with plate tectonics, the ice ages and the Pleistocene flora and fauna, always considering the possible impacts occurring through these factors or the feasible interactions of them towards early Australian settlements. Although the archaeological research conceptions in Australia will probably not be much different from the European ones, the unique characteristics shall be especially mentioned. Since the author often heard the saying that the Aborigines were always in Australia, he included the scientific derivation theories developed over the last eighty years. The scientific explanation of the ancestry of today's Aborigines will be threefold, considering biological, cultural/linguistical, and archaeological research. Each research conception and outcome will individually be analyzed and tested for validity. In the end, the results of the analyses of the three scientific branches might conclude a possible derivation theory. Settlement and subsistence patterns of prehistoric and contemporary Aboriginal groups might infer the accuracy or inaccuracy of previously stated derivational theories. If the traceable migrational routes within Australia as well as the living style and the modes of behavior, show similar or overlapping traces to the concluded ancestral cultures, then one or the other derivational theory seems to be more plausible. Four exemplary archaeological sites will be chosen in order to show the possibility of Pleistocene settlement and subsistence reconstruction based on concrete archaeological records. These sites should be dispersed over the continent, whereas the aquatic and/or terrestrial environment was preferably exploited. A thorough and critical analysis of the excavation method, realization, and outcome shall enable one to detect weaknesses, untenable conclusions or in-/adequate reconstructions. Stratigraphical perspectives will be a valuable tool to test time related statements and to eventually disprove far-reaching interpretations. The human impact on the environment, if through changing of the fire regime or excessive hunting, might be an indicator of the approximate time of early Australian settlement, as well as for the successful exploitation of the faunal and floral environment. It might even contradict the common view of the harmonizing relationship of Aborigines and nature. Special notice shall be directed to the relics of the material culture, as further needed for the stone technological experiments. The most commonly found artifacts, well preserved over thousands of years, are represented in the stone tools, more fragile artifacts have mostly perished. Prominence shall be given to classificational types considered to be cultural markers, in order to use these types to improve the special hypothesis developed in the stone tool replicative experi-

ments. Replicative experiments conducted by other researchers as well as use-wear considerations were noted and will also be of use for experiments conducted by the author. On the one hand, Aboriginal art might be an indicator of Aboriginal technology, behavior and antiquity, but on the other hand, it might show the cultural remoteness of the Aboriginal, and westernized living style, and the involved thinking processes.

The status of the Aboriginal people in today's society will be historically evaluated by the aid of literature, while interviews with Australians of European descent shall clarify today's conditions. This evaluation is extremely important since it shows the relation of the majority of land users to the minority of traditional land owners. The interviews shall establish if the Australians of European descent try to accept the Aboriginal culture as it is or if they definitely see a need to change it. The questions asked will target the problem of forced assimilation, the subsequent cultural pressure to change to a westernized lifestyle, and the involved stages of development (5) or degeneration (6). The section about the cultural awareness and assertiveness of the Aboriginal people tries to show how far the assimilation progressed and asks if there are movements either to reverse the process or to direct it more suitably in the Aboriginals perspective.

Section V will give a short excursion in the delicate venture of approaching and contacting Aboriginal communities. The reader will be acquainted with both the bureaucratic way over the land council and the direct, unbureaucratic approach of Aboriginal communities. The function, structure, use, and abuse of the institution "land council" will be critically analyzed. A theoretical model, developed by the author, will be opposed to the common procedure of handling the researcher's request to visit special Aboriginal communities. Concerning this, it will be investigated if Aboriginal people do have a strong sense of separateness, isolation, and suspicion of outsiders, or if this is just another of those stories created (by "white people") to justify their life on reservations.

The actual questioning and description of the interview situations will be evaluated in section VI. It is planned to interview at least 100 - 150 Aboriginal people and 40 Australians of European descent. It will not matter, in this instance, if someone is a full blooded Aborigine or partly mixed, or if an Australian of European descent settled in Australia in the 6th or 2nd generation. It is important, however, to get a wide variety of informants from the several different parts of Australia visited by the author. The majority of the interviewees of Aboriginal descent will be chosen from Aboriginal communities. The interviews will be conducted with or without a tape recorder (note taking, through memory practice enhanced debriefing), depending on the informant's wish. It is desirable to interview Aborigi-

----

(5) In Australians' with European descent perspective
(6) In Aboriginals' perspective

3

nes, as well as Australians of European descent in rural and urban areas, with completed university studies, desert school or school of the air absolvents. The respective ages of the informants will be considered in order to eventually examine age specific opinions.

The question catalogue itself will be introduced in its original, prepared form, as well as in its altered form, which was actually used for most of the interviews. Typical interview situations will be described supporting the decisions to alter certain questions or to add or cancel others. A critical reflection upon the question catalogue shall detect weaknesses and omissions that might be valuable knowledge for future researchers aiming to continue or disprove statements of the present thesis.

An evaluation of the interviews, combined with partial or full presentation of single interviews, shall be done in section VII. Through this procedure, the reader is able to test conclusions based on the interviews. Untenable statements and absurdities should be detectable, if present.

The stone tool analysis will acquaint the reader with the physical properties of certain basalt used in the replicative experiments. Although the masters thesis of the author was written about basalt tools and involved their replicative production, a certain unfamiliarity of the basalt found in Australia, as well as its flaking attributes, could not be denied. Several basalt modification experiments would be necessary before indigenous Australians could be asked to produce typical tools and the technique applied by them could be understood. Tools either found on the surface of an old chipping floor or those discovered through restricted excavations (7) in relatively recent habitation or manufacturing sites will be microscopically investigated. The main idea of these investigations is the detection of possible multi purpose tools that were predominantly used by frequently moving groups. This thesis tries to move beyond the theory that stone tools are cultural markers, which provide an indication of disparate cultures through often slight inventory differences/changes. Consequently, tool related theories about migrational routes or developmental stages of Aboriginal culture could be biased.

b) spatial

Roughly indicating the spatial restriction of the present investigation, the states of New South Wales, Queensland, Victoria, the Northern Territory, and the federal district Canberra shall be mentioned, even though several interviewees were visitors from Western Australia, several islands, and a few from Tasmania. The interviews took place in urban as well as rural areas, in universities, and in desertschools. The majority of the interviews, however, were held in self-governed Aboriginal communities or among Aboriginal

groups dwelling along riverbeds and resting areas along the main highways. The stone tool experiments took part in a more restricted area. Even though one stone tool worker was from Western Australia, he only used basaltic material from quarries around Katherine. The other experiments took place around the Alice Springs area or near Katherine.

c) temporal

In reading the title of this thesis, one might assume that the present research does not reach further back than the date that modern archaeology started, in Australia, for example, in the sixties. This assumption does not consider all the aspects involved in investigating the problem in question. Since modern archaeology presumably has its role in the process of better understanding Australians of European descent and indigenous Australians, the pre- and historical development has to be known, in order to set new standards in cross-cultural fieldwork. The question of whether modern archaeology intends or is designed to meet the requirements and eventually claims of the people it is investigating can only be answered through the historic evaluation of archaeology and the knowledge of pre- and historical Aboriginal culture. To make a long story short, the thesis covers the last 45.000 years of Australian pre-/ and history, with special consideration of the last 150 years.

----
(7) permitted by the respective Aboriginal community

1.3 RESEARCH LEVEL AND HISTORY

Intensive library research and the questioning of archaeologists and anthropologists largely working in the field of Aboriginal culture convinced the author that no one worked with the specific topic of this thesis. Since this thesis is built on a problem oriented approach, several sub-problems (questions in part 1) do find discussion in certain anthropological research. The general perception of Aborigines by researchers, varying over time, will be shown in the "outline of the archaeological...". The most recent 30 years of anthropological research work shall find particular mention here, as they were characterized by the critical self-reflection of the anthropological science. This process, already ongoing in Europe (8) and America (9) for several years, was critically analyzed in the second anthropological forum of the University of Western Australia. Elkin (1964:152ff), the father of Australian anthropological research, tried to give an overview of the past anthropological research in Australia. His, in the author's opinion, quite inappropriate enumeration might be shortened and altered, since Radcliffe-Brown (1913), who published his findings on the social structure of three Western Australian tribes, was the first modern anthropologist. His generalizations for Australia as a whole were noted in his later work about the "social organization of Australian tribes" (Radcliffe-Brown 1930-31). Especially his statements about land tenure became important for subsequent anthropological self-understanding. The patrilineal, patrilocal, autonomous groups, termed a horde by Radcliffe-Brown, clearly defined local land ownership. Whereas any member of the local group might hunt over the land that belongs to his/her respective group, he/she has to ask for permission if wanting to do so over the land of other groups.

He also mentioned that land ownership is spiritual in nature, which implies that the spirits of the ancestors occupy the land and will be worshipped in sacred places. Elkin (1938) and some of his students, like Stanner (1965) and Berndt R.M./C.M. (1964), first accepted his theory, but had to deny it with subsequent research (Hiatt 1962/Gumbert 1981,1984). The crucial point in this anthropological orthodoxy was the fact that Stanner and Berndt were subpoenaed to court as witnesses for the Aborigines in the Cove Land Right Case under the leadership of justice Blackburn, as will be mentioned later. Also in 1964 Catherine Berndt pointed out the possible uses and misuses of anthropology. Referring to the upcoming and intensifying reproach that anthropology is of no use, she saw the main function of anthropology to be in teaching and research rather than in political issues. Though everyone has to make personal decisions and has to set priorities, the possible misuse of anthropology would be most severe if working in political institutions. Collected anthropological material given in confidence and under the promise of secrecy by informants should not be misused through public display in any form. She even saw the danger that anthropological knowledge might be oriented towards commercial or personal prestige goals, which could lead to falsifying of information (since under disclosure) or corruption if facing court cases. Jaspan (1964), who historically analyzed anthropological commitment in political decisions, dryly commented that these anthropologists consequently "spoil" subsequent research by influencing the local group (Jaspan 1964:218). The code of ethics for applied anthropology, primary established by Tugby (1964), recognizes "the right of the anthropologist to function as a social scientist and to protect him against loss of self-esteem" (Tugby 1964:231). Noticing the influencing factors of working as an anthropologist attached to an agency (s.a.:226), he pointed out the need to remain a social scientist in the first place and not to be misused for institutional aims. An anthropologist should also recognize his/her irreversible influence towards the group studied and his/her obligation not to abuse the informants' confidence. Geddes (1964:193) on the other hand argued that anthropologists have to be involved in political issues if attempting to maintain a confidential status with the ethnicity, which would be essential for the success of his/her scientific investigation. The Cove Dispute, probably decisive for the awareness of the need for Aboriginal land right legislation, started out with a press announcement in February 1963. The Federal Government had approved of leases of land to the Cove Bauxite Corporation. Berndt, R.M. (1964:293) wrote about the dispute in its beginning and about the Aboriginal attachment to the land, based on several anthropological visits in this region. This work and several other articles made him qualified to be heard as a witness in the subsequent trial about land tenure on the Cove Peninsula. The trial came up because of the decision of the Conservative National Country Party government to transfer land on the Cove Peninsula to large mining companies. This land was traditionally claimed by the Aborigines of this area. The first time in history the anthropological science was asked to witness the claims of Aboriginal groups in court (10). Stanner and Berndt, influenced through Radcliff-Brown's models of "hords", could not convince the court of the legitimate Aboriginal land claim. The common law established in 1971 states that Aborigines have no recognizable right to land since they can not state their claim on the legal ground of the Australian court. The change of the government in November 1972 (11) and the "Aboriginal Embassy" encampment in front of the Australian parliament led to a new hearing in the Aboriginal Land Right Claim. The 1976 Land Rights (Northern Territory) Act was the consequence, and it acknowledged Aboriginal land rights. This act generally resembled Berndt's conception of Aboriginal land tenure, since traditional Aboriginal owners in relation to land means a local descent group of Aborigines who-

a) have common spiritual affiliations to a site on the land, affiliations that place the group under a primary spiritual responsibility for that site and for that land

b) are entitled by Aboriginal tradition to forage rightfully over the land. [Court definition]

----

(8) Lèvi-Strauss (Paris), Heine-Geldern (Wien), Helmut Petri (Köln)
(9) Margret Mead (New York), Ward H. Goodenough (Philadelphia)

----

(10) All the court members were white European can not state their claim on the legal ground of the Australian
(11) The Labor National government was elected after 23 years in opposition

In the following years a new discussion kindled over the question of whether anthropologists should be involved in the land claim procedure, and, if yes, what role should they play. Already in 1910 Friedman, facing the first Native American claims, notes the possible abuses of expert testimonies. He asked the fundamental questions, who should be considered as an expert, and who makes the final decision on what expert might be subpoenaed to court (12). Articles of Greenberg (1956:953-70), Rose (1956:205-18), and Wolfgang (1974:239-47) saw the increasing employment of anthropologists and sociologists in legal cases concerning environmental, familial, and race-related matters. Rozen (1977:577) summed up the uses or misuses of certain anthropologists in American law cases. Anthropologists "have testified on everything from racial segregation, miscegenation laws and child custody, to the blood types of putative fathers, the nature of religious communities, and the cultural background of criminal defendants. Their predominant role has been in cases involving American Indians" (Rosen 1977:556). The exemplary selection of cross-examinations of scientific colleagues supports his theory that anthropologists involved in such proceedings obviously have to testify on more than the simple presentation of objective data (13). Anthropologists today have to deal with the battles their own experts fight over definitions of some concepts, such as tribe or band. Since a law case requires clearly defined terms on which to base its conclusions, the subjective opinion of the chosen expert influences the judicial decision. Subsequent research might reduce their assessment to absurdity. One thing we always have to realize is that there is no such thing as absolute truth in anthropology. In Australia Aboriginal law cases accumulated especially in the beginning of the eighties. The role of the anthropologists in court was described by the first Aboriginal Land Commissioner Toohey as follows: "The Land Right Act is not an exercise in anthropology. Anthropologists are recorders of material and their capacity to collate it, and in its presentation to the hearing and comment upon it has proved invaluable" (Toohey 1980:paragraph 89). The Aboriginal Law. Bulletin was edited because of the feeling that the white-ruled legal system was repressive and racist against Aborigines. The bulletin commonly published by lawyers of the Aboriginal Law Research Unit and anthropologists tried to advertise the newest legal actions and its effects on Aborigines. One article in the bulletin concerned the legal protection of secret and sacred items of Aboriginal culture (Neate 1982). An amendment to the Aboriginal Land Rights (Northern Territory) Act 1976 has recognized the significance of many objects, designs, stories, ceremonies, names, and sites to the spiritual life of Aboriginal culture. Photos taken of people, sites, objects collected in museums, etc. may not be broadcasted

without the permission of the land owners, and earlier collected items have to be returned. A newly convened anthropological forum in 1983-84 dealt especially with the role of anthropologists in court and his/her scientific responsibilities. [Professional discretion for the social scientists in court and public] Bell (1983/84:176-81) enumerated the diverse employment possibilities that Australian Anthropologists will face in the future. Her employment forecast predicted well-paid positions available in legislation, consultancy, professional organizations, and the like, but the burn-out rate would be high. While other social science branches would place their graduates in an ever-shrinking labor market, the anthropologists studying Aboriginal culture would have a rosy future, since the supportive money flowing from the ACT seems to be secure. To meet all the requirements of being a consultant anthropologist for the Aboriginal Land Right Commissioner the respective anthropologist has to be qualified and experienced in the area of question, and has to be approved and appointed by the Land Commissioner's research officer, as Tonkinson (1983/84:187) noted. If accepting the role as a consultant, the anthropologist should be well aware that he/she will face an adverse relationship with his/her colleagues, and that responsible and well-balanced judgments have to be made. The main idea of an anthropological consultant is the witnessing of the claims and the established evidence, and to clarify, cross-check or possibly correct them. Tonkinson concluded that the anthropologist, if functioning as a consultant, should not try to decide on issues endlessly discussed in applied anthropology forums without ever being satisfactorily resolved. To further develop this idea, such a decision could become a precedent case, on which future decisions might be based. In 1983/84:221ff, Vachon firstly reflected over the Aboriginal responses to the anthropological enterprise. One, admittably radical, response was the notion that a consultant position in court has little, if anything, to do with academic qualification. Even though someone seemed to be qualified in the "White man's eyes", it would not imply that he/she understands the complexity of the matter and will be able to solve problems concerning Aboriginal claims. Anthropologists, if not the "pure", institutionalized kind, have meant to argue about political issues and have obtained success, but also failure. In any case, they were "only tools" (14) used to claim Aboriginal rights in the "westernized" court. Cromwell (1983/84:240-53) gave a visionary view of the anthropologist's role towards its clients. He pointed out that the anthropologist has the obligation to suit the client's needs and has to serve him/her as best as he/she can. Cromwell's quite futuristic picture of "new anthropology" imagined anthropologists role as advocates for the present and future needs of minorities (Cromwell 1983/84:252). The old approach of the institutionalized anthropology is becoming extinct or is only recessively held for reasons of nostalgia. In "paradigm lost...", or "neither justice nor reason", Gumbert (1981/84) argued that classical anthropological conceptions of Aboriginal local organizations and, consequently, of traditional land tenure are based on inadequate models, which render narrow and distorted

---

(12) The Indian Claims Commission, finally established in 1964, was authorized to hear Native American claims against the government, if brought forward from a tribe, band, or clearly identifiable group.

(13) The non-commented collection of objective data was the declared aim of anthropologists, since they did not want to interfere with or alter the interests of the investigated group.

---

(14) Overemphasized by the author, does not reflect the opinion expressed in the text cited

views of social reality. He criticized the social organization theory in traditional anthropology and provided an alternative paradigm, following the premise that the older models are dysfunctional in the land claim process. His main criticism was directed towards the ideologically derived unilineal model of society that does not consider the actual complexity of the underlying socio-economic reality (Gumbert 1984:91). Two factors have to be considered if establishing land ownership, the ideological and the economic right. Both might not separately reflect a specific group, but their active interaction with each other could. This should be considered, when newly assigning land to claimants. Bell (1985/86), who was mainly concerned with the woman's role in Aboriginal society, noted that there are no purely female courts that could preside over women's matters, and which reflect the traditional way of decisionmaking in Aboriginal society. Analyzing the land claims so far, she argued that anthropologists were not able to assist the court as fully as they might have in informal discussions, when creative ideas are not excluded and which do not lead to court decisions that might not be reversible. Bell questioned what would happen if the anthropologist's view is different from those of the claimants he/she represents ? (Bell 1986b:8) Under these conditions, she envisioned empty consultant seats in court, since no one likes to make potentially wrong decisions or give advice that might prove to be misguided (Bell 1986a:28). Finally, in 1989, Neate summed up the problems that arise if dealing with Aboriginal claims in court, particularly where concepts related to land have no parallel in European law.

-Differences between anthropologists as to the composition of key Aboriginal groups and the nature of the relationship between those groups and the land

-Apparent inconsistencies between the evidence of anthropologists and the testimony of Aboriginal witnesses

-The lack of reliable information about the situation before contact with Europeans

(Neate 1989:35)

1.4 EVALUATION OF SOURCES AND TECHNIQUES USED

a) The prepared and continuously developed or altered question catalogue

As early as three months before the intended fieldwork in Australia an interview plan as well as a questionnaire was set up. Knowing little about the investigated culture, this project could never suit the needs of the actual interview situation. Even though a scientist would have not only in-depth knowledge about the small sample of people being questioned but also in-depth knowledge about the population in general, the questions would still be subject to negotiations and alterations. The intensive consultation of literature concerning this theme revealed the different kinds of questions that should be avoided. [e.g. Gorden 1969, Bradburn 1979, Labaw 1980, Bailey 1987:104-146, Schnell 1989:291-384, Browne 1992:394-422] The author learned about leading and loaded questions which indicate or suggest to informants how the interviewer wants them to respond. This, for the proposed research outcome obviously, supportive approach is highly manipulative and should be rejected by every responsible researcher. Also double-barreled questions, those that ask two or more questions at once, are not advisable for scientists who intend to receive clear, unambiguous answers. Usually, the informant will answer the part of the question most important to him/her and will neglect the other part, which might be more important to the researcher. It seems impossible now to interpret the results of the question accurately. A recommendable endeavor, on the other hand, is the rephrasing of questions obviously not understood by the informant or the addition of clarifying points. Questions, presuming prior knowledge of the informant and hypothetical questions, aiming to create fictitious situations, are not desirable in the question catalogue. Questions of a presuming nature tend to eventually create invented answers, since the informant does not like to admit ignorance of the topic. Hypothetical questions may result in a "lie" too, if the informant has a lack of imagination, but tries to give an answer that he/she feels might please the researcher. Those questions that ask for the personal opinion of the informant are called personalized or judgmental questions. They might lead to mistrust and suspicion and end an interview sooner than wished, but, they might also make the informant feel important by asking for his/her personal opinion and raise the standard of the interview. While interviewing, the author had to learn about another type of question that should be avoided, as they can spoil a whole interview if not all subsequent ones in the same tribal community. Those could be described as "embarrassing questions". The canceled question No. 12 (see section Va) could have been asked directly or indirectly, using the word "someone" instead of "you", but it still would have embarrassed the interview partners since they thought it called them liars. Even though Ms. Buchanan and the author stressed the absolute confidentiality with which the answer would be handled, the interview took a negative turn (interview No.4). Sure, if the investigator had negotiated the question with several Aboriginal people of different tribal communities he would have found other words or phrases to ask this question in a less embarrassing manner. This should have been done for the English language as well as for those Aboriginal languages where a translator was used. The impossibility of this undertaking is obvious, if one considers time and money restrictions along with the attempt to investigate a broad cross-section of the Aboriginal public. A question catalogue seems too static to adjust to different author can not speak for other scientists, except for those to whom he talked (see below), but he figured that a continuously developed, in some cases altered, question catalogue, based on a prepared one, appears to be the best solution. So, an attempt to develop an ideal sequence of continuously progressing and improving questions followed (Fig 1). This

IDEAL SITUATION OF CONTINUOUSLY DEVELOPED QUESTION CATALOGUE

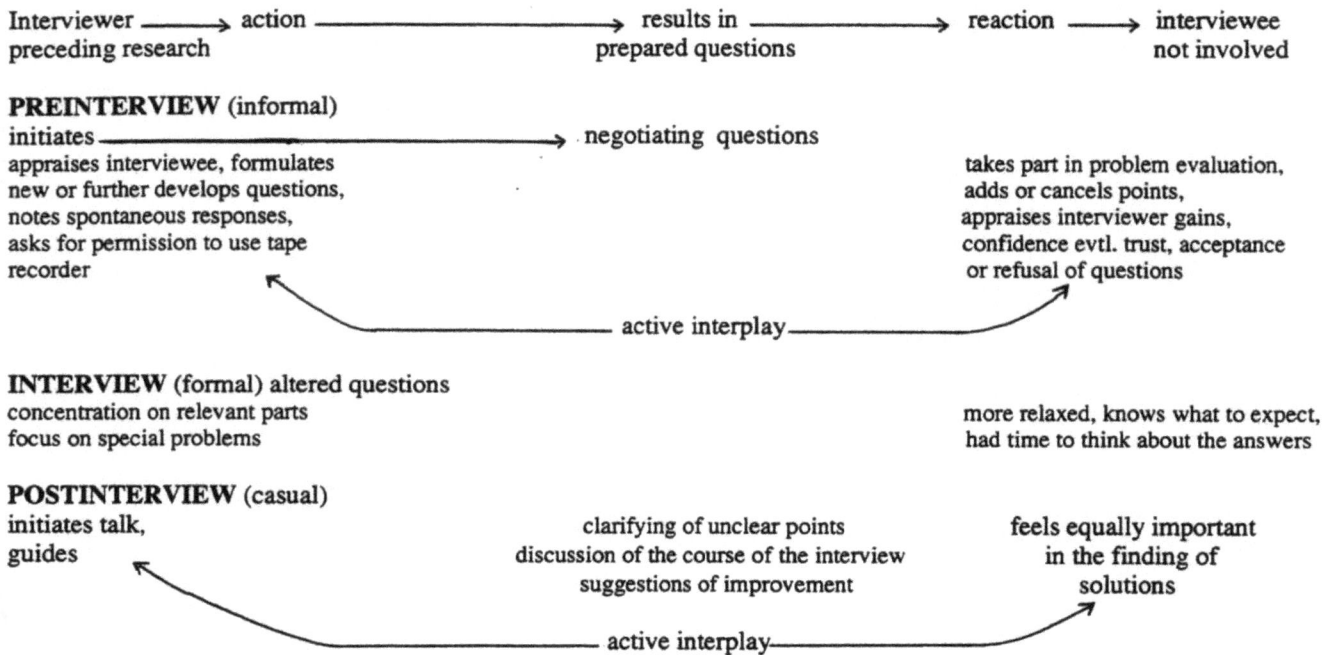

Interviewer ⟶ action ⟶ results in ⟶ reaction ⟶ interviewee
preceding research   prepared questions   not involved

PREINTERVIEW (informal)
initiates ⟶ negotiating questions
appraises interviewee, formulates
new or further develops questions,   takes part in problem evaluation,
notes spontaneous responses,   adds or cancels points,
asks for permission to use tape   appraises interviewer gains,
recorder   confidence evtl. trust, acceptance
                                                         or refusal of questions
                             active interplay

INTERVIEW (formal) altered questions
concentration on relevant parts   more relaxed, knows what to expect,
focus on special problems   had time to think about the answers

POSTINTERVIEW (casual)
initiates talk,   clarifying of unclear points   feels equally important
guides   discussion of the course of the interview   in the finding of
                           suggestions of improvement   solutions
                               active interplay

Fig. 1 The ideal interview (concept of the author)

situations faced in every interview, especially if dealing with diverse tribal communities and people of disparate social and educational background. Nevertheless, a special set of questions, which are thought to be non-judgmental, non-leading, non-double-barreled, etc. had to be previously written down, aiming to structure the researcher's thoughts as well as to give a general guidance to the informants. These questions had to be meaningful in order to obtain meaningful answers. Since little was known about the interviewees before the interview, the questions were written in the way the author would have asked them to an academically selected audience. It was known that many, perhaps most, of the questions the author would bring to the field from the personal study at home would be unsuitable for presentation to the informants. An informant had to be appraised for his/her educational background, social role, etc., and the question had to be adjusted to the respective situation. In the actual interview the questions were phrased in straightforward everyday language.

The question now is if a prepared, or a continuously developed and altered question catalogue, or a mixture of these possibilities would suit the intended research most. The ideal interview scheme was developed because of the apparent lack of continuously developed question catalogs in sociological writings. The only comparable sociological approach is represented in the open-ended questionnaire as well as the unstructured or informal interview, (Browne 1992:406/411) which gives respondents the possibility of expressing their own views, eventually altering subsequent questionnaires because of the obtained response. The basic assumption is that the interviewer's action(s) result in a positive or negative reaction from the interviewee, reflected in the quality and fluency of the responses. The prepared question catalogue developed through preceding research should only be a guide line for negotiations in the informal pre-interview. If presuming, embarrassing, double-barreled and any form of loaded questions are initially avoided, an active interplay between interviewer and interviewee, both being aware of their equal roles, should soon develop.

The main functions of this pre-interview are, aside from the development of questions that suit the interview situation better, the gaining of the interviewee's confidence and trust by the interviewer and the establishment of a comfortable and positive attitude for the upcoming formal interview.

It is extremely important to note the spontaneous reactions and responses of the interview partner to prepared questions and the interview situation in general, as they reveal personality features that might be useful to know for the formal interview and for the subsequent analysis. Permission to use a tape recorder for the formal interview should also be requested. Both the scientist and the informant know what to expect in the formal interview (but be aware of surprises), giving the calmness needed to raise the standard of the interview. Spontaneous statements or other sudden responses are less likely. A casual post-interview is necessary to clarify points that were insufficiently covered. Personal experience shows that it is very important that the interviewer initiates the casual talks and guides the interviewee. It is often the case that major weaknesses are detected that can be solved, either in a second interview with the same informant or in subsequent interviews.

Other scientists the author met in Australia and those recently returned from fieldwork in Africa unanimously stated the rough or tentative nature of a prepared question catalogue developed at home. Only one researcher did not change the catalogue in the sense of adding or canceling points, although a rephrasing of the questions frequently took place. This was especially of interest, since she had visited the respective tribal community the first time. The other scientists explained that their catalogue did not adequately represent the cultural reality faced in the respective ethnic groups. They added, canceled, or rephrased questions in a manner similar to the present approach. The frequency of visits to a tribal community did not proportionally lower the amount of alterations in the prepared question catalogue.

Because the technique of gathering information through interviewing has been borrowed from sociology the two main types of interviews should be mentioned here. These are the structured or formal interview and unstructured or informal interview. Based on a pre-coded questionnaire, the structured interview does not move beyond the answers received. The unstructured interview, on the other hand, may lead to discussions and/or further questions, which can be used in subsequent interviews. These two interview techniques are used in conjunction with either non-participant observation or participant observation. The latter technique involves the sociologist's participation in a group for long periods in order to become an accepted part of that group.

Following the scheme developed by Browne (1992:419/Fig 16,5) the unstructured interview in conjunction with participant observation is most likely to develop more qualitative data. The present approach does not fully fit in that scheme and is therefore further explained in Fig.1.

b) Literature

The attempt to study themes concerning Aboriginal culture is condemned to fail if relying only on literature accessible here in Germany and the rest of Europe. Even though, as mentioned earlier (section 1.3/II), the Australian archaeological/anthropological research is based on the efforts of scientists trained in America and Europe, mainly Great Britain, the refinement of use-wear analysis (Kamminga) and the invention of ethno-archaeology was supported through research conducted in Australia (Gould) and by Australian scientists (Hayden, Jones). Especially typescripts, manuscripts, pamphlets, and bulletins are often only obtainable at the local institute or department which published them. These writings could not even be ordered, since they were not internationally listed or produced with the intention to reach the international public. Preliminary studies in Germany uncovered not even 1/10th of the literature used for this thesis. Striking was the considerable age of the publications found. Writings after 1975 were seldom discovered. Facing these facts, the decision was made to conduct intensive library work in Australia, in addition to the already planned fieldwork. The intensive search was started in Sydney, simply because the cheapest flight from Germany arrived there. Surprisingly, the University of Sydney had no Aboriginal section in contrast to universities in the United States, whose libraries are generally equipped with an American Indian section. The Sydney library seemed to have, according to some kind of inscrutable system, books about Aboriginal culture dispersed all over the numerous floors. Since most of the books found were published either by the Institute of Aboriginal Studies or the Australian National University, the need to do further studies there was realized three weeks later. The easy accessibility of almost every book, pamphlet, typescript, etc., the friendliness of the staff, and their willingness to help, as well as the ability to reserve a studydesk shortened the research time immensely. There was no limit as to the number of books that could be taken the desk at one time, which is especially valuable if working on comparative analysis. The Institute of Aboriginal Studies is a valuable source for all types of research carried out in the field of Aboriginal culture and should be the starting point for every researcher. At this point, the importance of making the finished research (manuscript, thesis) available to the institute (15) shall be explicitly stated. Only then it is guaranteed that the institute keeps up with the latest research and avoids duplications. The Institute of Aboriginal Studies located in Darwin is not recommended, since only a few publications are at hand. This institute might only be of interest if one is aiming to obtain the latest publications about Torres Strait, Arnhem Land or Kakadu National Park, since the Darwin institute will generally be supplied with them first.

As in other countries, the researcher's prestige (authority) in Australia rises proportionally to the number of his/her publications. In this concern, it does not matter if he/she is the

----
(15) Especially for foreign scientists

author or editor. Even though the development in archaeological/anthropological methodology has been rapid and the number of detected sites has increased, the amount of publications has increased twice as fast. Still, the quality of a researcher is thoughtlessly measured by the amount of his/her publications rather than by their quality. The present study attempted to neglect publications that were rewritings of already published research or those that did not develop new ideas or research concepts. Most of the literature used and mentioned in this thesis may be seen as more or less pieces in the puzzle of Aboriginal prehistory. The dominant feature of the conducted archaeological research is its carefulness and application of the newest methods. This research can stand as an example for excellent archaeology/anthropology, which in the end, still does not justify its present performance in terms of the Aborigines' want or need for it.

Part II of this thesis concerning stone tool technology was mainly based on research already conducted in 1989/90 (Masters thesis Deunert 1990), but modified to the specific Australian conditions. Theme related literature was sufficiently available.

c) The use of a middleperson

As soon as it became clear that fieldwork had to be conducted in Australia, the decision was made to use a middleperson of skin color similar to the Aborigines. Personal experiences in a color-mixed relationship showed that more than white people, black people have a strong, color-based solidarity. It is idle to speculate about the reasons for this phenomenon, but the worldwide historical oppression of black people seems to be a main factor. Wherever the author went with his partner, she was approached by other black people, mostly in the author's absence. Knowing that, it seemed to be worth discovering if a similar reaction would be observable in Australia among the indigenous people. Ms. Buchanan immediately agreed to do this thankless job, which required the personal strength to balance the possible betrayal of the people who gave her confidential information with a constant effort to relate (rationally) the state of black/white relations.

Though the author deeply believes that the Australian Aborigines are the least color prejudice people he has ever met, there seems to be a discrepancy between the fluency and willingness to release information to Ms. Buchanan as compared to "white" researchers. It often happened that interviews and even insignificant chats between informants and Ms. Buchanan stopped upon the authors arrival, and they never reached the same intimate state as before. Even if the author just passed by, voices were lowered or the subject changed. Contact with people was rendered more difficult if the author was standing together with Ms. Buchanan, since fewer people came up to talk to us. There were only few situations where the author had the feeling that people were more responsive to him because they accepted him as an authority (16). With these people, even the reluctantly applied direct approach, that is asking for an interview without being introduced by others or without knowing the people for a considerable amount of time, worked, though the information obtained should be biased (Informants No. 34, 67 and 81).

In some tribal communities, gender specific problems arose, though this research does not investigate gender specific roles. The simple fact that Ms. Buchanan was female did not allow her to interview some male members of the community, at least not without the author's personal appearance. And vice versa, the author was strictly not allowed to talk to female members of certain tribal communities, unless approved by the women's council. At this point, the necessity of data being collected by both sexes shall be stated. If studying a culture, one's subsequent interpretation is dependent on one's sex and on one's culturally defined sexual identity. It was not without reason that Whitehead and Conaway defined certain differences in fieldwork experience as sex-specific. They argued that: "female fieldworkers are more sensitive to the field situation than male fieldworkers, and are therefore

---

(16) Mostly on former missions where it was explicitly stated that Jesus Christ and God are white.

more likely to attempt to understand the systematic relationship between the fieldwork process and the fieldworker's sense of self."(Whitehead/Connaway 1986:289, points 1 to 5)

Apart from these gender considerations, a decision had to be made as to what characteristics and behavior the middleperson should display. Since more than 50% of the films and television programs seen in Australia are produced in and imported from the United States, the image of an American woman was also created by the media. Today, even the remotest community has at least a communal TV room, which is often frequented more than the local school. The Aboriginal TV station Impala gladly broadcasts documentations about the American Indians, which stand as an example for the state that the Aborigines try to reach in Australian society. Should Ms. Buchanan, who is partially Cherokee, represent this typical view of American Indians shown on TV, or should she resemble the image that the informants hold of an ideal American woman, or should she modify her behavior to accommodate the standards of the Aborigines and try to mimic the informant's clothing exactly ? Sometimes, as Prof.Dr.Jensen (17), lecturer at the University of Hamburg in the Department of Ethnology expressed it, more information can be obtained without a middleperson by behaving and dressing in the habitual way of the investigated group, as he experienced in Mauritius. The research in Australia showed that a middleperson of similar skin color is absolutely necessary, so that shall be recommended at this point for future researchers. Even though the author is of the opinion that the Aborigines themselves should ideally conduct this kind of research, at this point there are only a few trained Aboriginal archaeologists and anthropologists. Ms. Buchanan was asked to be herself and not to mimic any behavior nor to dress in a specific way. There was only one exceptional situation, when the women of a community asked Ms. Buchanan not to wear shorts or dresses that would expose her knees and thighs. The number of excellent interviews achieved and the hospitality Ms. Buchanan experienced proved this approach to be right.

d) The truthfulness of answers and the credibility of informants

Some anthropologists might be confused by the authors relatively flabby (undistinguished) use of the word informant. Since it was the aim of this research to obtain a variety of answers from Aborigines in different educational, social and developmental states (18) no key informants or co-researchers were selected. Some people, with whom Ms. Buchanan or the author established close, somehow intimate contact, might be seen as consultants, although they were seldom asked to relate to ambiguous answers given by other interview partners.

The author believes that the selection of key informants or, even worse, co-researchers would have adversely affected the outcome of the research. Key informants are defined as those who have been interviewed intensively or over an extensive period of time for the purpose of providing a relatively complete ethnographical description of the social and cultural patterns of their group. A co-researcher or research collaborator on the other hand, "resembles a consultant but has become a member of the research team" (Werner/Schoepfle 1986:248). The focused use of key informants or co-researchers would have artificially changed the social structure of the respective community. The selected person would have become, or simply claimed to have become, of a higher social status, since it was him/her, whom the researcher selected, and not the others. He/She would have introduced the researcher to people that accept his/her position, thus showing uniformity in their answers. This process would not have been advantageous to the present research.

Trembley (1957), who applied the key informant technique in his Stirling County Study, remarks that this technique might be useful if surveying a large number of communities in an extensive area. If doing so, he prefers the careful selection of key informants to a purely statistically drawn respondent. The selection criteria were six fold. The role within the community, knowledge, willingness, communicability, impartiality and reliability, should be considered when choosing a key informant. If the selected person reflects all these attitudes, he/she will be helpful and supportive in the ongoing research (Trembley 1957:691-93).

As nice as this approach sounds, it hardly seems to be applicable to any kind of research where informants are needed. One of the main problems is the time factor. In order to ensure the above-mentioned attitudes that an ideal informant should display, several months, if not years, would be needed to gain his/her trust and to be sure that he/she is not lying or playing a role. To mention only one example, in this case from Australia, Stanner describes one of his Aboriginal in

---

(17) personal communication, February 1992

---

(18) More or less influenced by the western living style. See also note   (depraved versus developed, notes 5,6)

formants Tjimari as follows:" He was the first Aborigine I ever met and, over a quarter of a century, I found him to be a fascinating mixture - a liar, a thief, an inveterate trickster, a tireless intriguer, an artist of high ability and a man of much if inaccurate knowledge.... He was adept in playing white against both white and black.... I thought him an archmanipulator with wit and charm but no principles, and ready for any villainy that paid" (Stanner 1960:68). This assessment of Tjimari was gained after an acquaintance of almost 25 years, and Stanner still admits that some of his other informants surprise him with hitherto unknown reactions. Similar writings about informants as "unknown mysteries" are found in almost every ethnographical report dealing with cross-cultural, as well as inter-cultural, fieldwork.

Another problem of the key informant technique is the somehow naive notion that the anthropologist can carefully select a key informant and then conduct uninfluenced fieldwork as a participant observer. Since the researcher comes as an

biased, considering his/her influential role within the community.

A considerable factor, commonly summed up with the saying "there is nothing such as truth in anthropology", comes from the investigating object as well as from the investigated subject, the tendencies of human beings in general. If reflecting upon one's own behavior, one soon realizes that, how we rig up a story to fit our special purposes depends strongly on the situations and the persons we face, since it is important to impress the respective person we talk to. Are we uncomfortable with the situation, are we afraid to tell the truth, etc ? All these are factors we consciously or unconsciously consider when responding to a question or narrating a story. Recently (March 1992), the author randomly asked people he met if they would always tell the truth if asked questions about their life and if they lie in the daily social intercourse with acquaintances and close friends. They were asked to estimate their truthfulness on a scale from 0 - 100 % in

Release information about towards	The author as scientist	With dcb	Acquaintances	With dcb	Friends
Questions					
-scientific	100%	95%	75%	70%	100%
-general	90%	90%	90%	85%	90%
-personal	85%	80%	X	X	90%
-about others					
a)friends	70%	70%	X	X	90%
b)acquaintances	90%	85%	75%	70%	95%
Reports/Stories					
-scientific	100%	95%	70%	70%	100%
-general	85%	80%	80%	80%	90%
-personal	80%	75%	65%	55%	90%
-about others					
a)friends	70%	65%	65%	60%	90%
b)acquaintances	90%	80%	80%	80%	90%

dcb = different cultural background
X = would not release any information (20)

Fig. 2 Truthfulness of answers within the own culture.

outsider to the community he/she intends to study, he/she is immediately exposed to curiosity, observation, gossip, and even manipulation. The anthropologist as an active agent trying to obtain information inevitably becomes a part of the social life of the people with whom he/she interacts. This is especially true for the key informant, who might gain considerable advantages out of his/her ascribed role. Goldkind concludes in his paper "Anthropologists, informants and the achievement of power in Chan Kom" that "there is some ethical obligation for the anthropologist to attempt to minimize being manipulated or otherwise used by informants who thereby might gain some significant advantage at the expense of others being studied" (Goldkind 1970:39). Even though the researcher tries to hide his/her activity by the means of a "covert" or "secret" participant observer (19) (In: Bulmer ed. 1982), his/her research outcome still has to be

steps of 5 %.

After a few interviews only it became obvious that some kind of a previously prepared answering sheet was needed, since no one was able or willing to answer without any restricting conditions. The following list Fig. 2 (without percentages) was prepared and handed out during the interview.

----
(19) Term employed in professional writing at least as early as 1939 by Nadel (Bartlett 1939:317-27)
(20) Remark: this option was not given, but mentioned by every interview partner.

All together 42 people were interviewed. The mean value of every single answer was established and can be seen in the list.

There is a definite trend to release information about acquaintances rather than friends, at least to people that are not a close relation of the person asked. The slightly lower percentage for people of a different cultural background mainly resulted from the answers from one person who obviously did not like foreigners and had never been out of his country either. Unfortunately, the author has the feeling that the percentage of the people reached from different cultural background does not reflect reality. Many interview partners revealed slight to strong prejudices about one culture or another. The grade of prejudice was directly proportional to the remoteness of the respective culture.

The author honestly believes that almost all of the percentages given are far too high at least by 10%. The simple fact of the conformity of the answers and the promptness with which they were given makes the author doubt their truthfulness. Obviously, no one likes to admit to being a liar or a show off in some situations, especially not in a society like ours with strict rules of behavior.

The author has to admit that he would not be so truthful in certain non-scientific situations. In Australia itself the author experienced interview partners (No. 57 and 58) who had obviously made up stories to justify their Aboriginality to others, but had held on to these "lies" for so long that they started to believe them. These people were unable to distinguish between the true events and the fictitious ones (see also section IV). In other cases where these fictitious stories were not so obvious and easy to disprove, they might have been written or orally handed down and have become history. Other people (No. 14 and 103) were real flatterers, aiming to get a ride in the car (21), or were attracted to Ms. Buchanan.

These people would have given answers that suit the research goals if purposely directed in this way through special questions. Here lies one of the major responsibilities of a researcher, to not use informants that can be manipulated in order to produce the proposed research outcome. Informants commonly pointed out other people that were in their opinion not sound of mind or considered to be babblers. Often these "babblers" would contradict the information obtained from the person that disparaged him/her. The researcher then had to decide who was telling the truth and what could be seen as valuable information for the research project. One way to reduce ambiguities are probability considerations. The more often a story was told in a similar way, the higher is the probability that it contained the truth. Since the present study was thought to establish a possible mutual basis for the work of archaeologists and anthropologists with Aboriginal communities, the willingness to answer the often self

developed questions (see section 1.4a) truthfully can be considered as exceptionally high. The selection of interview partners from all over Australia should have guaranteed a general Aboriginal public opinion rather than just local impressions. The stone tool experiment section on the other hand asked for specific abilities of single persons. The frictionless (smooth) cooperation of the Aborigines, the use of a middleperson, and the public interest in the present thesis made the author believe that the results are accurate, even though absolute truth can not be stated.

1.5 INQUIRY METHOD, CONSTRUCTION OF THE TEXT

The present thesis proceeds from a problem oriented working method. " The precondition for this problem oriented working method is one or several clearly stated problem(s). The clear definition of theproblem(s) enables the researcher to establish criteria for a carefully directed search of information. The division of the problem(s) in several sub-problems is an important step in the problem analysis. Each of the investigations undertaken to solve these sub-problems becomes a separate section in the outline of the final report of the study. With every step (the solution of one sub-problem) the researcher is able to establish a hypothesis that can be tested with the next step. If a solution of a sub-problem can not be obtained, the reason for this must be questioned and a critical review of the research methods is necessary to derive better results. After the solution of every sub-problem and the testing of every hypothesis, the solution of the basic problem(s) can be synthesized." (Deunert 1990:37) Some of the sub-problems (questions in the catalogue) are third party determined, others are established through personal experiences in intercultural relations (see section 1.4 c) and daily exposure to the institutionalized scientific dilemma (see section 1.1). The combination of these sub-problems, their formulation into common demands from modern science, and their exemplary shown solutions shall establish the outer frame of the present thesis.

The Australian archaeological enterprise relies on this method, albeit its performance is less methodical, especially in the introductory part. The clear problem definition, its proposed solution, and the proof of its beneficial purpose are compulsory for every scientific work in Australia, at least for Australian researchers. The immense danger of a proposal of the possible research outcome is the early mental fixation towards this specific solution, so that other possibilities might not be realized. The primary focus on the proposed outcome narrows the mind and makes a critical re-evaluation less feasible than with the step by step solution of previously stated sub-problems, which should derive indubitable results.

Since the present approach did not follow the usual bureaucratic procedure of the land council, the previously described process (regulations) did not have to be observed. At any rate, it would have been impossible to state the research outcome clearly, though the benefits for the Aboriginal people were foreseeable.

---

(21) in order to buy alcohol

2. OUTLINE OF THE ARCHAEOLOGICAL/ANTHROPOLOGICAL INTERPRETATION OF PREHISTORIC AUSTRALIA PRE 1770

2.1 Introductory remarks

Much, probably too much, has been put down in writing about the archaeological and anthropological interpretation of prehistoric Australia, and even my modest contribution (single parts of this outline) can be read a thousand times in various, from simplistic to highly sophisticated, degrees of phrasing. These writings vary in their appearance from colonialistic to "Cambridge scholastic" to nationalistic. Although the author assumes that the colonial writing style is sufficiently known (22) (in Australia it was not much different from research in Africa) the terms "Cambridge scholastic" and nationalistic have to be explained. From 1788 until 1910 the prevailing concern of researchers was the racial distinction of groups and their integration into a quite simplistic hierarchical system ranging from primitive to sophisticated. The years 1911 to 1959 were entirely dominated by amateurs, admittedly eager ones, who mainly dealt with classification and the resulting cultural traditions (23). The "Cambridge scholastic" phase started in the year 1960 and continued up through the seventies. The starting point was the "immigration" of more than a dozen staff and graduate students from Cambridge University to Australian Universities and the subsequent writing of Master and Doctoral theses concerning Aboriginal culture. These people today constitute the core of leading Australian researchers and teachers handing down their knowledge to the upcoming academic generation. In order to enhance the reputation of the Australian Universities, foreign students were bribed through scholarships to continue their graduate studies in Australia. This process stopped around 1980. Most of the students came from Cambridge or other leading universities of the United Kingdom anyway. Du Cros (1983) critically investigated certain direct and indirect environmental influences on fieldworkers in her BA Honors Thesis. She concluded that it is important to know about the influences of the socio-cultural and scholastic environment on the academic or non-academic authorities in order to analyze the fieldwork conducted by the various researchers (Du Cros 1983:67-73). However, this definitely wholesome phase of professionalization for Australian archaeology/anthropology went along with the foundation of the Institute of Aboriginal Studies in 1961. Although the archaeological research level

was not quite proportional to the size of the continent, amazing results were obtained in just the first few years (See below). The development of ethnoarchaeology might be seen as an Australian accomplishment, even though the American Gould was the initiating force in this field. Subsequent research from Hayden (1976) and Meehan/Jones (eds.1988) refined this approach. With the increasing effort put into anthropological and archaeological investigations and the growing demand for the control of land rights for Aboriginal Australians, research in these fields reached the nationalistic state. Facing the fact that there were too few Aboriginal Australian field workers or actively studying prehistorians, the Aboriginal community became aware of the impact that the white man's view of conservation could have on the Aboriginal heritage. The Aboriginal reaction was a total or partial ban on entry to sites concerning their history. This became especially true for burial sites, sacred sites, or areas where Aborigines still live closest to their traditional lifestyle. These recent developments split the researchers into two parties. The first emphasizes the need of archaeology/anthropology for prehistorical/historical sake, or as Murray and White express it:
" Australian archaeology is singular, methodologically and theoretically Australian archaeology, was and is archaeology first and Australian second" (Murray/White 1981:262). The second, not negatively called nationalistic, is still interested in the exploration of Aboriginal culture, but only when complying with Aboriginal interests (24).

2.2) Sunda and Sahul

An interesting factor in the prehistory of Australia is its changing shape, caused by sea level regressions during ice ages. Geological evidence shows that during its last 700 million years of existence the earth has experienced several ice ages, each lasting several 10.000 years. During the Quaternary period the most recent ice age appeared and it is probably still continuing (25). At the height of the last glacial period (26), the sea level was as much as 100 - 150 meters below its present state due to the enormous amounts of water bound in ice (Jennings 1971:4). The ice sheets of the northern hemisphere extended as far south as 40 degrees N in North America and 52 degrees 30'N in Europe. This glacial

---

(22) On the 15th of May 1788, Phillip sent his first dispatch back to England, addressed to Lord Sydney, announcing Australia's first archaeological investigation. (Cited in "Proceedings of the Prehistoric Society XXVII, 1961:56)
(23) Gojak (1982:97-100), influenced by research of Hayden and Kamminga, argues that the terms Core Tool and Scraper Tradition are not correct and that the whole concept of defining traditions should be rethought.

---

(24) The crucial point is the recognition of pure Aboriginal interests. These might vary from tribe to tribe or region to region. It is questionable if these are the interests of the Aborigines living in the traditional way or those influenced by the West, in expressing their needs and demands comply with the European-style legislation. It is especially questionable if these varying needs can be defined in the legal terms commonly used in westernized societies.
(25) Scientists argue that we are already close to the end of the present interglacial and that a glacial period will follow, but this, of course, lies in the time scale of thousands of years.
(26) Wisconsin or Wuerm

began around 120.000 years before the present and supposedly ended about 20.000 years ago. The ice age caused an annual mean temperature decline of 3 to 13 degrees Celsius below present values, depending on the distance from the ice sheets. Chappell (1976:21, see also Barham/Harris 1983:555) discussed the glacio-eustatic sea-level changes especially relevant to the migration of people from South-East Asia towards Australia. He noted that glacial advances (late and middle Wisconsin/Wuerm II/III) occurring around 17.000 B.P. and 53.000 B.P caused the sea level to drop of up to 130 meters. The interstadial period, with its peaks around 28.000 B.P. and 43.000 B.P., would have caused a marine transgression. Bowler et al. (1976:392) derived similar results and referred to geological phenomenons observed in inland sites (See derivation, settlement and subsistence sections). There was never a direct land connection between the Sunda and Sahul shelf, which kept the flora and fauna of this area separated (Fig.3).

Fig. 3 Coastlines of Australia during the ice ages.
After Struwe 1974:30

Knowing that people settled in Australia at least 40.000 years ago (Bowler 1976:64; Bowler/Thorne 1976:134) and having geological evidence that the Australian continental climate at that time was much colder and had higher annual rainfalls (27), we might assume that people had to face different fauna and flora back then.

Indeed, even today the high amount of still living marsupials (138 according to Keast et al. 1959:1963) testifies to the distinctive fauna of prehistoric Australia. Only a few of these species have survived in America, and none in Europe, and the giant marsupials became extinct or reduced in size in Australia as well. Murray (1984) listed the giant marsupials in an illustrative guide based on fossil findings, though his illustrations are only possible reconstructions. Similar work concerning Australia's prehistoric plants was done by Maiden (1889), who gave special consideration to their usefulness to human beings, and by White (1985); however, the listing of them would drift too far from the subject.

How the Pleistocene Aborigines reacted to climatic changes and the subsequently different faunal and floral environment is basic question that researchers still try to answer. When Deacon (1985:5) mentioned south-western Australia and Tasmania as possible refuges during the last glacial maximum, he lacked the knowledge of the inland site Puritjarra shelter, which was only later discovered. It is also questionable if the South African prehistory might be comparable to Australia's, as asserted by several researchers. Further reflections about human adaptation to changing climates will be provided in the settlement and subsistence section.

2.3) Derivation of Aboriginal Australians

The Australian Aboriginal would probably have never "scientifically" reflected upon the derivation or genesis of his/her culture, since all this is an integral part of the so called dreamtime. The dreamtime represents the never-exhausting pool of knowledge about the Great Spirit ancestors handed down in oral traditions, paintings, legends, and myths. From the Aboriginal perspective, it provided a sufficient explanation of their past and composed a vivid part of their harmonizing view of man and nature. Entirely different was the eurocentric point of view, where everything had to be analyzed, tested, and explicitly explained. The first hundred years of European colonization did not show much of that as the Aborigines were thought, or for morals sake declared to be animals rather than human beings and as such were slaughtered instantly or kept as a means of cheap labor. The next 50 years these "creatures" awoke the curiosity of one or the other ludicrous researcher and the following to the most recent years researchers developed scientific explanations without asking the question if they do it for the Abo-

riginals' sake or maybe for their selfish one. Exactly this is the fundamental question that this thesis tries to answer. (See object oriented problem)

a) biologically

Much has been written about the biological origin of the aboriginal Australians based on the careful study of blood types, genes, bones, or simply external physical traits. During the Biennial General Meeting of the Australian Institute of Aboriginal Studies a symposium was held in Canberra on May 21-22, 1974. The biological origin of the Aboriginal Australians was the basis of the symposium that should bring together some of the main results of recent research conducted in this field. Kirk and Thorne (1976) collected and sometimes revised the delivered papers to complete a volume about "The origin of the Australians". The invited researchers were more interested in objective evidence than in a comparison of the physical characteristics of contemporary cultures with prehistoric findings. The latter approach resulted in such derivation theories as Klaatsch's 1922:338 published hypothesis that humankind as a whole originated in or somewhere near Australia and spread thereafter over the whole world. His main marker to this theory was the "apparent similarity" of Australian Aborigines to apes. Schoetensack (1901:129), Sollas (1911:208-9), Basedow (1925:15,23-25), as well as Hrdlicka (1926) suggested through similar studies that the entire population of Australian Aborigines was derived from Neanderthal forms within Australia. Even though the basic arguments of those researchers are untenable, there is some truth to the notion that Aboriginal skulls show slight and sometimes amazing similarities to the ancient skulls found in Java, India and even Africa (Abbie 1966:211). In 1870 - 1885 researchers were already arguing that we have to assume the ancestry of the Australian Aborigines to be outside of the Australian continent (Topinard 1872, Lesson 1880, Turner 1884). This theory was taken up by scientists from the early 1930's to the late 1960's. A hot discussion kindled on the question of a solitary or a multiple origin of the indigenous Australians. Proponents of the former theory were Wood-Jones (1934), Champbell et al. (1936), Howells (1937), and Abbie (1966), those supporting the latter one were Fenner (1939), Birdsell (1967), and Morrison (1967). The "trihybrid theory" of Birdsell was based on research conducted with "Barrineas", a Tasmanoid remnant who was believed to have once lived throughout Australia. During the ice age, when a crossing to continental Australia seemed to have been possible, two waves of people, the "Murrayans" and the "Carpentarians" are supposed to have come over. Interbreeding with each other these three ethnic groups might have established the Australian Aboriginal ethnicity. Abbie and other representatives of the unitary origin of the Aboriginal people point out that "the available evidence does not support any significant degree of multiple ancestry of the Aborigines, nor does there seem any pressing need to seek for a multiple ancestry" (Abbie 1966:216).

Macintosh and Larnach (197:113-26) argue that the Aborigines represent a practically unchanging population over a period of at least 25.000 years and simply exhibit a wide

---

(27) The filling of the Willandra lakes at 44.000 B.P. suggested a substantial change in temperature and hydrologic regimes (Bowler 1976a:136)

range of variability. With this comment they refer to skeletal findings of Kow Swamp, Cohuna, Cossack and those of Keilor and Lake Mungo. When compared with each other, the skulls from the first three sites were found to be robust, rugged, and thick-boned, while the Keilor and Lake Mungo skulls were defined as gracile for their light build and thin-boned appearance (Jones 1979:458). If still thinking in old evolutionary terms and searching for a typological row, one would point out that the robust, rugged, thick-boned type is older than the lightly built one. This would probably still be the prevailing opinion if relative dating through stratigraphy as well as the absolute dating using the radio carbon dating method did not indicate the opposite (Lake Mungo) [Bowler 1976:134].

Knowing that contemporary Aborigines tend to show a light, thin-boned build, whereas the relatively young Kow Swamp skull displays heavy, "archaic-looking" features, contrasting the older, more modern-looking, gracile Keilor and Lake Mungo types, it becomes clear that the Aboriginal population must have already been diversified in the past. Even today the craniometrists, supported by the extensive use of computers and statistical methods, as the multivariate or discriminant function analysis, "still tend to believe that the Aboriginal Australians represent a single population of homogeneous origin" (Birdsell 1979:429).

In 1976 Prokopec and Sedivy presented a paper concerning the dermatoglyphical evidence of the relationship between the Australian Aboriginal series and populations from South East Asia and the Pacific Islands, and the clear separation of those from Africa. The research mainly involved the counting of arches, ridges, and whorls on the individual fingers of different ethnic groups and their statistical comparison (Prokopec/Sedivy 1976:224/25). Parson and White (1976) used both dermatoglyphic material and certain nonmetrical cranial traits. Considering skin coloring variations as well, they concluded that they can not favor one of the prevailing derivation theories, but that "micro-environmental variation may be of considerable significance in the evolution of the Australian Aboriginal both during and after their arrival in Australia" (Parsons and White 1976:242).

Shanghvi's paper (1976:40ff) basically tries to compare the data of an allelic variation analysis from Australia with ten tribal populations from western India. He argues that indeed eight alleles delivered comparative data, but their variability shows a wide range. The variation was lowest for A and Ro and highest for B and M (Shanghvi 1976:409/10). In other words, the mean values of A and Ro have remained closest to each other, while those for B and M drifted apart. He points out that the environmental differences of Australia and India or genetic drift might have caused a disparate development.

Simmons (1976) and Kirk (1976) draw a somewhat dark perspective. After 35 and 15 years respectively of intensive blood testing, they still cannot point out the origin of Australian Aborigines specifically. They do know that there is no obvious conformity between the Australian Aborigines, the Indians, Veddahs, Ainu, Indonesians, and South East Asians in terms of blood groups, serum proteins, and enzymes. Kirk

(1976:344) even argues that the specific serum protein and enzyme markers adenylate kinase AK2, the pe acid phosphatase, and the transferrin B2 alleles commonly found throughout the white population of Europe is not existent in the Australian Aboriginal population.

Even though Curtain et al. (1976:354) seemed to have found a striking similarity in the immoglobulin gene frequency distribution of the Australian Aborigines and adjacent New Guinea people, they have to admit that their research does not lead the question of the origin of the Australian Aborigines to a solution.

Kirk's optimism that the diversification of genetic markers and the intensive use of computer technology might lead to better results seems unfounded, considering Lie-Injo's (1976:277ff) failure with nearly 50 genetic markers combined with the outcome of Vos's et al. and Curtain's et al. research.

In 1979 Birdsell published a critical review of the 1974 symposium. He mainly disagrees with the regional restriction and limited material with which most researchers worked. He also refers to the discrepancy of research done in the Northern Territory with that done in the southern region of the country. Birdsell pleads for fast reinforcement of interdisciplinary work and for regional expansion (Birdsell 1979:425). The last concern might be even more pressing considering the fact that unmixed, full-blooded Australian Aborigines momentarily decline at a rate of 50 percent per generation, which implies a cultural as well as a biological extinction. Despite the critical remarks from other researchers Birdsell still holds on to his trihybrid theory, even though Tasmanian skeletal remains show no differences between prehistoric Tasmanian Aborigines and contemporary mainlanders.

A new approach to genetic affinity has been recently developed at the University at Berkeley by Rebecca Cann (1985). Her study in the field of molecular biology states that the greater the difference in DNA between two ethnic groups, the earlier they separated in their development. These differences are expressed in percentage rates and marked on a scale, so that it would be possible to establish a new evolutionary family tree of humankind (Cann 1985:121). In conclusion one might say that one should not rely solely on genetic and molecular data to determine the origin of Aborigines. There are too many factors other than time that might have caused a variation in genetic material . Even though genetic markers have the highest heritability, they are surely affected by selection processes and environmental impacts (changes). An increase in data and a computerized and statistical revision will not hide the need of new concepts and different approaches (Deunert 1990:23-30). If we do not find striking evidence in some way, there might only be theories in the end.

b) Culturally/Linguistically

Several days of intensive library research and the helpful advice of the staff at the Institute of Aboriginal Studies and Torres Strait Islanders at Canberra did not uncover any profound work in the ethnographic comparison of contemporary tribes in South East Asia and Australia. There are, however, numerous ethnographic reports about tribal groups in specific regions throughout the area in question. To read those and compare them, which would definitely make sense, lies outside the scope of this overview. While pre World War II ethnographers tried to develop race and evolutionary theories in a broader context, today's ethnographers fear that step beyond their investigated ethnic group. This reluctance is somewhat understandable, as subsequent research might contradict their evaluation or reduce it to absurdity, but it is exactly the re-evaluation by other researchers that allows sciences like archaeology or anthropology to live at all. One researcher alone can never find the ultimate solution to a problem, he needs the steady discussion with scientific colleagues to solve another part of the puzzle of the origin of the Australian Aborigines.

Few ethnographical works tried to combine their region of interest with broader questions of affinities and descent. Most of the time they did not solely base their arguments on the comparative analysis of religion, hunting techniques, art, etc., but also on biological and archaeological research. Two, admittedly early writings in this concern are those of Earl (1849/50) and Speiser (1938). Right at the beginning of his paper Earl mentioned the considerably vague arguments one has when working in the field of "ethnographic evidence" among ethnic groups without a written language. Endless speculations will rise that " will ever prove liable to dispute" (Earl 1849:682). He did not believe that "races" could only be established through interbreeding and separation, but also through their mode of life, which causes differences in terms of stature and other physical proportions. In the progress of his paper he pointed out the unique features and customs of the Papuans and searched for similarities among the other ethnic groups of the Austronesian region. The "untamable ferocity" of the Papuans and the custom of raising the skin in cicatrices over various parts of the body, while rubbing clay in the wounds to cause the skin to rise, seems to be an argument for the existence of a unique Papuan culture. This skin raising custom should not be confused with the tattooing or puncturing of skin widely practiced by "Malayu-Polynesian" tribes. The piercing of the nostrils in order to wear bone or wood through it, the grinding down of the front teeth until they become pointed, and the dying of their black hair to a reddish color seems unique to Papua, or at least more closely related to the Pacific Islands than to Australia. Earl, who lived a long time all over Australia, could not find any hint of a cultural relationship between Papuans and Australian Aborigines, even though he admitted that Papuans, similar to the tribes on the northern coast of Australia, find delight in dwelling along the coast. He encountered tribes in northern Australia that were wandering along the coast in family units and crossing the sea to offshore islands in lightly built boats. This observation makes him think that there might have been a crossing between Papua and Australia in one or the other direction (Earl 1849:682-9).

Speiser did not provide any explanation for the earliest settlement of Australia, but tried to show through cultural, biological, and linguistical comparisons the settlement of Papua both from Indonesia and later from Australia. He realized his thesis through a comparison of the cultural inventory of the contemporary cultures. Influence from Indonesia would have left the cultural goods such as the blowpipe, ikat, plangi, wayang, etc., and those from Australia the bullroarer, churinga, and the throwing stick. Speiser saw the earliest settlement of Australia by Paleolithic Palemelanesians as unlikely, but did not bother to show other evidence (Speiser 1938:463-81).

Another ethnographic approach would be the comparison and interpretation of legends and myths told within the Aboriginal tribes. Unfortunately, there are as many (slightly to extremely) different derivation legends and creation myths as there are tribes or tribal communities in Australia. It seems appropriate to select for examination those that intersect each other in general and/or in detail. The chief characteristic of these stories seems to be the belief in an origin in a country to the north or the northwest. The early Australian settlers were either driven by ants or other animals out of their country of origin or were curious about the unknown country to the south. In almost all legends the newcomers had to cross the sea either in canoes or sailing boats, or they were washed ashore on pieces of drifting wood. Shortly thereafter, a leader or leading family was established to reign over the people and to order their lives. Population pressure or disputes split tribes and families and dispersed them throughout the new land.

It is interesting to look at certain creation myths now, especially those mentioning the surrounding environment (In Silver Digest 1970:8). Although it should be noted that several of these myth have been influenced by missionaries, we can not deny the fact that the kangaroo is an endemic species in Australia and is not found in any northern country.

Was, asked Love (1989:1) the dreamtime ever a real time ? If not, that would explain the discrepancies among legends and myths throughout the Australian continent, but if it was a real time, those stories could give valuable clues to the origin and the age of the Australian Aboriginal culture. Love, who studied the Bora initiation ceremony, pointed out that this ceremony, and its accompanying carvings, paintings, etc., could be the link to the events and the environment of the dreamtime (Love 1989:13). Once the ancestors of modern Aborigines had crossed the Wallace Line (28), they faced a different environment that had to be understood and exploited for their subsistence. Archaeological evidence shows that the Aborigines settled the Australian continent at least 40.000 years ago, a time when macro fauna was found. Love believes that this macro fauna might form a major part of the creature component section of the bora ceremony. Although anthropology can never state the absolute truth, a strong argument for the descendancy of Australian Aborigines

---

(28) Arbitrary faunal border that divided the Sunda shelf fauna from those of the Sahul shelf. After the naturalist Alfred Russel Wallace (1823 - 1913). Later redefined by T.A. Huxley and Max Weber.

would be founded, if he could show evidence of that.

The collection of linguistic data in the Austronesian region represents another attempt to find evidence of the migration routes of the Aborigines. Foley (1986) examined links between Australian and Papuan languages using archaeological and linguistic evidence from the analysis of Proto-Australian nonsyllabic verbs and their cognates in the Eastern Highland languages. Since Austronesian languages are relatively slow-changing and the physical separation of Australia and New Guinea dates back about 8000 years, there is a good chance to find linguistic connections. Previous application of comparative linguistics did not establish any connection between Papuan and Australian languages simply because the researchers searched "in the wrong place" (Foley 1986:271). Unfortunately, Foley could assemble fewer than twenty possible cognates, and some of them have problems in their phonetic correspondence. Nevertheless, he notes a genetic relationship between Australian and Eastern Highland languages.

Coberly (personal communication) tries to relate Papua New Guinean languages to North Australian tribal languages. One looks forward to the outcome of her still ongoing research.

Sharpe (1985:122ff) could not trace the migration of the Bundjalung settlement further back than a general splitting of the group and a southern/northern movement. In 1980 Brace demonstrated a gradation of Australian tooth-sizes from a minimum in Cape York Peninsula to a maximum in Murray Basin. He suggested that those changes in tooth-size were due to forced alteration in subsistence strategies and tool technology, as well as to gene flow from outside, where a reduction in tooth-size had begun due to adaptation to earlier Mesolithic developments. Areas where large tooth-sizes persisted were most favorable to human habitation (Brace 1980:162/3). Brace, who had already tried to combine and support his theory through linguistic studies, was supported by Gruhn's (1980:804-6) article about linguistic evidence. Gruhn found a striking parallel in the tooth-size theory and prevailing linguistic assumptions. Consulting Dyen's migration theory, which assumes a greater diversity within a language family (of a certain area) if closer to the geographical center of origin and less divergence as a result of recent language spread, she pointed to a possible linguistical homeland of the Australian language in the Cape York area. Wurm's (1972) work indicated a tremendous diversity of languages in the Cape York area, with 26 - 28 phylic families counted so far. The eastern half of the Australian continent displays exclusively the single phylic family Pama-Nyungan. The expansion and migration of Pama-Nyungan would indicate a recent division and spread over the continent (Wurm 1972:141-45/153-54). Following Gruhn's theory, we would be able to find even earlier habitation sites in the Northern Territories than those already established in the South (Lake Mungo).

The conclusion of the ethnographic and linguistic evidence is simple and at the same time unsatisfying. Up to now these two disciplines could not provide us with real evidence of the origin of the Australian Aborigines, even though researchers tend to assume that the ancestors of the Aborigines came from the north or the northwest of the Australian continent. Linguists once traced back the Indo-European languages to a proto-language. This language is presumably only a few thousand years old and has been reconstructed through the use of written records. The Austronesian languages might be 100000 years old and show no written record. Additionally, the Austronesian languages tend to die or reduce themselves to a few basic groups. Linguists estimate that around 1780 about 200 languages were spoken in Australia, an amount that has massively reduced since then.

If we observe the rapid changes in our own language over the course of time, we become aware of the dilemma linguists have to face in reconstructing ancient languages. A last critical comment might be made concerning the linguistic attempt to physically bind languages to speakers. A language can be seen as an continuously changing pool of knowledge. New impressions might be added, others discarded. If, for example, a pastoral group migrates to the area of an agriculturally established group and decides to stay (By reason of population pressure, protection, etc.), their languages will either mix or one will be abandoned over time. The latter result would leave no linguistic evidence of one group or the other.

c) archaeologically

A great deal of work has been done in archaeology concerning the origin and migration (within Australia) of the Australian Aboriginal people. More than any other branch of science, archaeology proves the early occupation of Australia. It is not quite clear what we should consider as the oldest site yet excavated. In the Willandra lakes system, a series of extinct overflow lakes formed by the Lachlan river, an occupational site dating back to around 31.000 years B.P. was uncovered. This site, commonly referred to as Lake Mungo, in southwestern New South Wales was excavated under the leadership of the geomorphologist Jim Bowler in 1974 (Bowler 1976). Mungo is noteworthy in that no older human skeletal remains have been found elsewhere in Australia. The Mungo 1 skeleton was burnt, so a cremation site was concluded. The radiocarbon date reaches back to a minimum age of 26.250+- 1200 years B.P. (Bowler/Thorne 1976:134). The adjacent burial was dated considerably older due to its stratigraphical position. Another site within the same age range as Lake Mungo is at Keilor, on Maribyrnong Creek near Melbourne (Joyce, Anderson 1976:47ff). The three sediment layers that are found there contain remains dated in chronological order as follows. The lowest, artifact bearing level of the D clay dated from a minimum of 36.000 years B.P. to a maximum of 45.000 years B.P.. The second occupational horizon dated to between 19.000 - 36.000 B.P. (Bowler 1976:64) and contained stone artifacts, animal bones, ochre and hearth remains. The youngest horizon was occupied until about 4.500 years before present, and its sediments embedded the "Keilor cranium", stone artifacts, hearth remains and animal bones. The skull was recently dated to an age of about 13.000 years. The last, supposedly oldest, site is found in Western Australia. The cave site Devils Lair shows thick deposits accumulated by humans whose radiocarbon dates stretch back to about 33.000 years B.P.

(Balme 1978:63/4). Occupational debris, including a cooking hearth, dates to between 28.000 and 6.000 years ago. Among other things the limestone cave yielded the oldest bone tools yet to be excavated in Australia.

Since the early years of archaeological investigation were restricted to geomorphological studies and digging, the prevailing migration theories were derived from geological rather than stratigraphical or material cultural evidence. In 1937 Tindale's approach, the collection of the Kartan implements on Kangaroo Island and on the mainland of South Australia were compared with the "Sumatra" types and Tasmanian collections. The collections were comprised of surface findings as well as stone implements specific to geological layers, which were not datable. The exact number of stone tools studied was not given by the author, but it seems to have included several hundred so called "Sumatra", "Pirri", hammerstones and several "small flake types". Tindale tentatively speculated about possible correlations with predefined cultural industries, i.e. the Fulham and Tasmanian cultures with the Upper Paleolithic of Malaya. The extinct Kangaroo Island culture may have represented the culture that visited and settled in Australia first. The close relation to industries in Malaya may indicate, according to Tindale (1937:56/57), the earliest migrational route of Aboriginal Australians towards "Greater Australia". The carriers of the culture, so Tindale (1937:57) suggests, might have been of Tasmanian type. He derived this theory due to the simple fact that scientists found stone implements in mainland Australia similar to those of the Tasmanian industry. The Tasmanian culture might have developed its distinctive features after its isolation on the island. Tindale lacked the basic ability of abstraction that his theory might be revertible, since he did not provide data. Another attempt in this concern was made by McCarthy, who compared the Australian prehistory with that of Indo-China and Malaya. McCarthy obtained his study material mainly from excavated deposits, however in the geological sense, and from already established typologies and distributions of previous work. This study also involved the investigation of several hundred specimens of points, axes, mortars and pestles, as well as millstones. One of McCarthy's main statements is that the obvious diffusion of traits in stone and bone industries is due to the frequent contact of Australian cultures (especially those of the Cape York region and the New Guinean ones) with those industries of the Hoabinhien complex (McCarthy 1944a:265). The Hoabinhien complex is mainly found in South East Asia, Malaya and Australia, although the microlithic industry of this complex is lacking in Australia. The study of the stone industries of Java and Australia could not state a relationship unambiguously. The closest affiliation was found in the stone industries of Australia and New Guinea, albeit there were some differences.

The comparison of cylindro-conical stones from New South Wales and Java by the same author did show a possible relationship of the two industries (McCarthy 1944:Plate XV). It would be prudent to critically state that these findings were surface findings given to the author by people of little integrity.

Golson (1971:124ff,1972:375ff) correspondingly tried to relate the prehistory of Asia and New Guinea to those of Australia. Unlike the previously mentioned researchers he based his studies on archaeological excavations supported through radio-carbon dating. His conclusions are mainly made through the consultation of well-dated archaeological sequences published by Mulvaney and Joyce (1965), White (1969) and Bulmer (1964). Golson directed his attention mainly to ground and hafted stone implements, since they clearly constitute tools and hoped to show an early relationship between Asia, New Guinea and Australia. Especially the original appearance of new technologies or new technical attributes of stone tools could outline migrational routes and cultural exchange through trade or immigrating groups. An example would be the appearance of points on small flakes in northern Australia in 7.000 B.P., while they appear by 5.500 B.P. in south-eastern Australia. The possibility of migrational routes other then through New Guinea to northern Australia is implied by the fact that leaf-shaped points and backed blades, which probably originated in Indonesia, are not present in New Guinea, but are in Australia. This, so Golson (1972:393/94) admitted, only holds for the late industries in New Guinea and Australia, since no comparative work has yet been done on early industries. Concerning the Hoabinhien cultural complex mentioned by McCarthy (1944a:265), a backdating seems to be appropriate, considering the discovery of some 20.000 year old edge-ground axes in the Australian region and the relatively late dates in South East Asia. Grinding did not appear in New Guinea before 6.000 years B.P., further evidence for a migrational route over the islands "adjacent" to Arnhem Land.

In her doctoral thesis titled the " Inquiries into the older periods of the prehistory of Australia " Struwe (1974) noted that a comparative analysis of the early stone and bone inventory of Australia, New Guinea and South East Asia is inappropriate and misleading since there is an obvious research gap (Struwe 1974:Appendix 2). Especially the ongoing attempt to use archaeological sites as indicators for migrational routes is invalid as long as sites in New Guinea, Australia and the island chain to Timor are abundant or present only in insufficient numbers to be interpreted. Struwe explained the obvious lack of diversified stone artifacts, in the sense of Feustel's "Upper Paleolithic Revolution", throughout the west asiatic region with the relative unimportance of stone artifacts in comparison to those of other material (i.e. bamboo) [Struwe 1974:162ff]. She also referred to the unconditional need to compare the material culture of the Niah and Tobon cave, or other subsequent discoveries in this region, with Australian material (Struwe 1974:171). Her own research, which mainly involved the measurement and frequent analysis of material from Sangiran and Tjabenge, as well as Australian material did not lead to a pioneering discovery. Nevertheless, Struwe stated an older age for these stone industries, possibly similar to the oldest horizons of Tobon, than for the Australian material (Struwe 1974:171/172). Only this last theory would make migration from South East Asia towards Australia possible, considering the age of Australian sites. If she had not implied an older age for the South East Asian sites, a reverse migration would have been a possibility. Subsequent research proved her statements to be true, as we will further see.

Also in 1974, White demanded researchers to abandon their eurocentric view of prehistory. This would be especially useful in dealing with South East Asian, New Guinean and Australian prehistory, as it culturally developed "quite different to that in other parts of the world" (White 1974:112). In the following years a real flood of data and new archaeological discoveries enriched the study of Australian prehistory (Cambridge school, see introductory remarks). Unfortunately, little work was done in Indonesia and a large part of New Guinea. Archaeological projects in New Guinea have been restricted to the coastal areas of south-eastern Papua and the Highlands. No extensive archaeological work has been done in West Irian, the Coastal Lowlands and the islands, which would be so important to verify or falsify migrational theories. The earliest site in New Guinea at Kosipe does not date further back then 26.000 years B.P. and lies in the Highlands in the south-eastern corner of New Guinea. Under a two meter thick layer of volcanic ash, a hafted stone axe was found among other tools. Without considering the possible influences of the volcanic ash layer, which might have caused an early dating, the axe was dated between 37.000 and 45.000 years B.P. (White 1974:109ff; White/O'Connell 1979:21ff)

In the following years a convulsive attempt to obtain earlier dates in Australia can be noted, even though real evidence for sites older than 35.000 years B.P. could not be found in the past 10 years. Earlier dates resulted either from the subjective interpretation of particular geomorphological phenomena, where a natural explanation might be as possible as the human influence, or from the dating of stone tools found in alluvial river deposits, which might be associated with the present sediments only through accumulation. A recent example of the latter type of interpretation would be the thermoluminiscent dating of gravel associated with seven stone tools in the Cranebrook Terrace near Sydney at 43.000 - 47.000 years B.P. (Nanson et al. 1987:72). Singh et al. (1981) and Goede (1989) explained phenomena in sedimentary profiles as human activity, even though there is no clear evidence for it. Singh suggested a human occupation of Australia between 128.000 - 75.000 years due to the presence of a charcoal layer in the geological profile from Lake George near Canberra, which was interpreted as the earliest evidence of human fires (firestick farming ?) [Singh et al. 1981:52/3]. Shell deposits of an eroded cliff line near Warrambool in Victoria have been claimed by Goede to be of human origin, although this could not be conclusively shown. Goede dated these deposits to about 80.000 years (Goede 1989:28).

It should be mentioned that a backdating of Aboriginal history was done through the newest thermoluninescence dates from Malakunanja 2 in Arnhem Land, adjusting the age of stone tools to 50.000 years and the minimum age of a bifacially flaked core and a modified flake from Puritjarra rockshelter, Central Desert to 38.000 years (Flood 1990:83/154). These dates have not yet been confirmed. The author also heard about a new method to date the desert varnish covering rock engravings, which gave amazingly early dates (up to 30.000 years B.P., see Dorn et al. 1988:681-9). Still, the validity of this method has yet to be proven.

Despite these vague facts, Jones (1979) recently tried to conclude the date of Australian settlement and the origin of the Australian Aborigines. Enumerating all the facts and speculations already known for several years and combining them with new archaeological facts and theories, Jones suggested two migrational waves towards Greater Australia. The first colonial wave, by people closely related to the "archaic sapiens" of the Javanese erectus forebearers, occurred around 50.000 years ago. Emphasizing that the early stone tools consisted of "roughly retouched flakes and possibly flaked choppers" (Jones 1979:460), Jones concluded the limited technological capabilities of the early settlers as compared to modern hunters and gatherers. The second wave of homo sapiens of the gracile form arrived in Australia about 30.000 years ago. The interbreeding of the two groups, as Jones inferred, and the quick spread of these "advanced and sophisticated" people through the continent resulted in the ancestral population of the contemporary Australian Aborigines. The technological complex of the Australian Core Tool and Scraper Tradition, including wasted blades, would have been the single achievement of the gracile people. The different physical appearance of Aboriginal Tasmanians to those of mainland Australia might be explained through the separation of the islands after the rise of the sea level. Originally colonized by the gracile people, who settled Greater Australia faster than the "archaic sapiens", the Tasmanians were already genetically locked away when the archaic people reached southern Australia and interbred with the gracile people. The Tasmanian Aborigines may have maintained a genetic pool more similar to the biological heritage of the gracile people than their relatives on the mainland (Jones 1979:460-62). Even though Jones' arguments seem to be conclusive, it is still uncertain that we can conclude all this out of the few real facts that have been collected. For instance the earliest evidence for human occupation in Tasmania dates back to about 30.000 years B.P. (Allen 1989:153). The same author tried to construct a broader, continental history out of excavation projects currently being done in the South and East Alligator river valleys. One of the main results, others will be mentioned later, was the estimation of the earliest, datable human occupation at about 30.000 B.P.. This date would eliminate the discrepancy between relatively old dates in the southern region of Australia and the younger dates in the northern region, since the original colonization of Australia was suggested to be from the North to the South. Here we see the truth of Struwe's (1974:Appendix 2) prediction of a research gap causing discrepancies in migrational theories. It should be mentioned that Groube et al. (1986:453) could date a series of uplifted coral reefs containing evidence of human occupation to about 40.000 - 45.000 years B.P.. This site at the Huon Peninsular in eastern Papua New Guinea was partly mantled by volcanic ash. The date seems uncertain and is doubted by Foley (1986:275). Recent excavations and analysis of deposits in four limestone caves in New Ireland, Papua New Guinea, have indicated that this island was occupied at least 32.000 years ago (Allen et al. 1988:707-9). Again, all these sites are in eastern Papua New Guinea and no evidence was obtained for early occupation in the western regions.

Another, unfortunately even more interpretative approach determining the migration and migrational routes towards Australia was an anthropological-geographical one favored by several archaeologists and physical anthropologists. This approach incorporated the geological knowledge of dropping sea levels (through the binding of huge amounts of water in glaciers covering enormous landmasses in the northern hemisphere during the last ice age) and the simple measurements of distances between islands existing within the Sunda and Sahul shelf interregion. The most advanced attempt in this regard was done by Birdsell in 1977 (Fig. 4). He covered all possible routes early mariners and explorers might have taken. Birdsell implied that one of the main factors in plotting the course, was the visibility of the islands to the voyagers. This visibility was not always present, and in all cases at

able to carry people over these distances. Unfortunately, no archaeological evidence of Pleistocene watercraft has been found or is likely to be found in Australia. Most of the Pleistocene coastal sites have now been submerged by present sea levels and any other wooden material would have perished by now or been eaten up by termites in the northern regions of Australia. All the later prehistoric or historic watercrafts are not likely to have been used for Pleistocene voyages, as they become waterlogged after a few hours and seem not buoyant and sturdy enough to have carried the estimated number of people that initially settled Australia.

For the successful settlement of the continent fertile members of both sexes must have landed. Computer statistics or simple mathematical accounts considering all relevant variables, such as monogamy, polygamy, age group, death, birth rate, diet, number of women, environmental impact, etc., give only a slight chance of survival for a group of three young

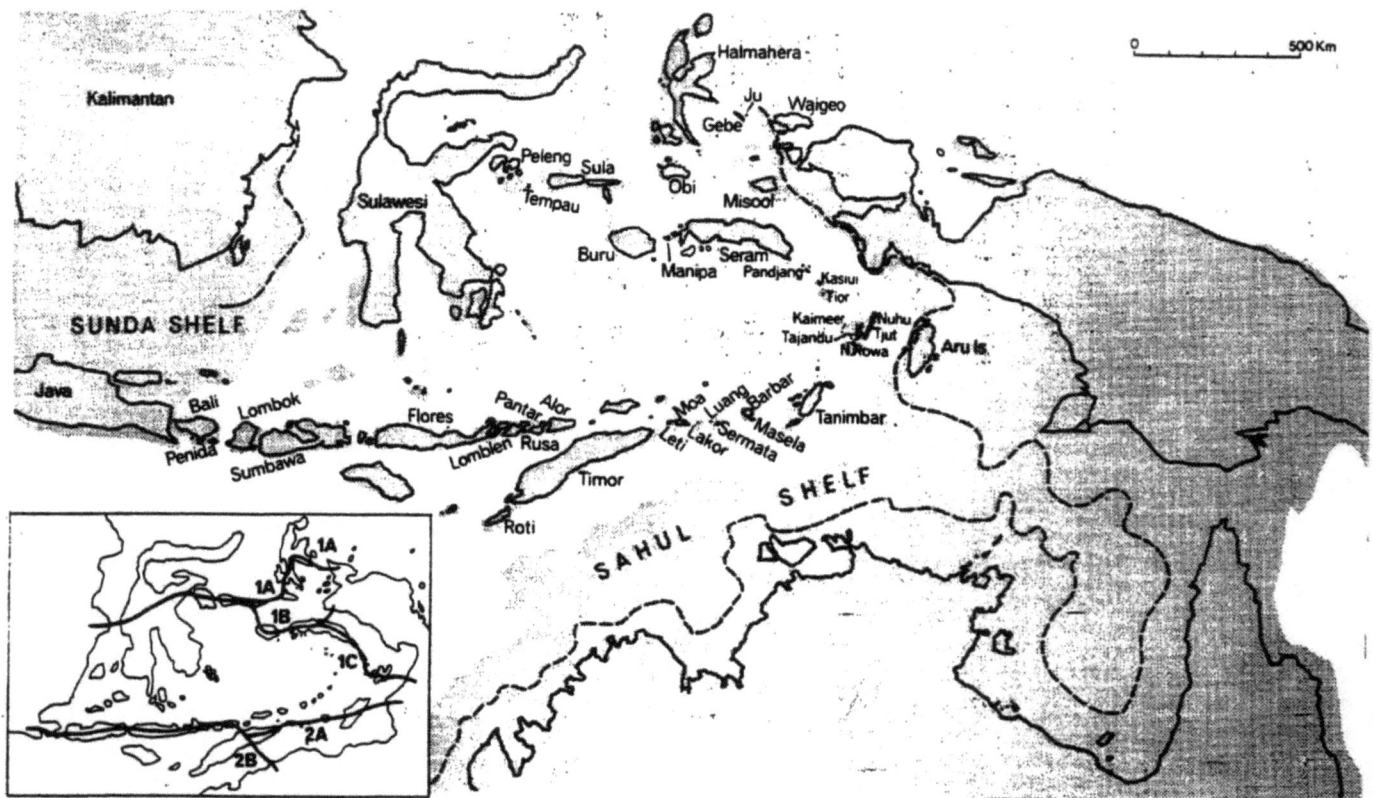

Fig.4 Routes from Sunda to Sahul (Birdsell 1977:122)

least one distance from 68 to 103 km had to be crossed. Birdsell argued that a crossing of 100 km would require approximately 30 hours, considering that a watercraft that floats, sails or is hulled moves at an average speed of only two knots, which would have been a voyage to the unknown (Birdsell 1977:113ff). Dortch and Muir (1980:194-8) offered a quite simplistic solution to the visibility problem. Personal experience showed that bushfires were visible over long distances and may have aroused the curiosity of Pleistocene voyagers to explore unknown land. Birdsell noted that all five routes he offered in his paper were hazardous, so that only sturdy and sophisticated watercraft might have been

healthy couples. Even if we double or triple the amount, a successful peopling of the continent is unlikely. The highest degree of possibility for the initial settlement of Australia might be given if we assume a steady exchange and trade with those groups that stood behind or a mass settlement forced by the expulsion of a group from their home country by a hostile group, population pressure or disease. Problematic would be the need of sturdy, seaworthy watercraft that could take up all the people and bring them over to the new region. Flood suggested that, if "it is possible that the earliest colonists were tide-riders, using rafts like the kalum, a light, triangular, mangrove-wood raft of double construction, used until recently by four tribal groups on the north-western coast of Australia" (Flood 1989:36). It is technically possible to use the north-west monsoon winds to go eastwards across the island chain of South East Asia. If these rafts were built of bamboo and the shafts were coated with silica, which would make them impervious to water, a longer seavoyage, admittably dangerous, would be possible. This last suggestion (Birdsell 1977:164/65) would have required a high level of technology, which can not yet be unequivocally stated.

In 1905 Thomas did a detailed enumeration of contemporary and ethnographically mentioned canoes and rafts. In the introduction he stated that "along a large part of the south and west coasts the natives of Australia seem to have possessed no mean of conveyance by water.....It is recorded that in the western and southern area not only the art of navigation, but even that of swimming was unknown to the natives" (Thomas 1905:56). Indeed, the canoes and rafts he enumer-

that the antiquity of this canoe cannot be accurately indicated. (Fig.5)

Despite the fact that evidence was lacking, Macintosh (1975:15) wondered if the Australians might have been the world's first Mariners, a phrase he used as a headline for his anatomical paper.

Jones and Meehan (1977:16ff) stated the need of Pleistocene watercrafs to exploit marine resources. The experimental reconstruction of a Tasmanian paper bark canoe and the deliberate constructing of a dug-out canoe (lippa-lippa), as well as the skillful operating in aquatic environments by the Aborigines of Arnhem Land, made them believe that a crossing of the sea barrier was possible. The relatively late introduction of these skills through the Macassars, who used to travel to Arnhem Land, does not weaken the argumentation that marine exploitation was of need even in Pleistocene times to enrich the seasonal diet.

Fig.5 Outrigger canoe (after Davidson 1935:16)

ated in the following seem not at all suitable for longer sea voyages. The most promising watercraft is represented by an outrigged canoe of the Cairns District in Queensland, which is now exhibited in the British Museum. Thomas concluded that there was no need of marine technology for the people of south-west Australia (including Tasmania), since it was peopled by a continental and not a coastal route. The lack of contemporary watercrafts in the northern region might be explained through the loss of the art of navigation and of ship building technology, since there was no need for it anymore. Later attempts to bring Australian watercrafts into chronological order or to find the ultimate craft, that might have served the early settlers in crossing the sea barrier between Sunda and Sahul, led to the same solution (i.e. Davidson 1935, Black 1947). Cape York, one of the most likely entry points for migrants between New Guinea and Australia, was mentioned by Davidson (1935:9-10) as one of the few areas where the outrigger and double-outrigger canoes were found. This canoe might have been able to cross the above mentioned distances. Unfortunately, there was a landbridge between New Guinea and Australia in the Pleistocene, so

Also in 1977 Dunn and Dunn unwittingly approached the migration problem from a different perspective. In analyzing prehistoric archaeological sites in order to investigate prehistoric maritime adaptation and marine resource exploitation in the Sundaic sector of South East Asia (Dunn/Dunn 1977;Fig.1:2), they were able to state the continuous use of the aquatic environment throughout the history of the islands. Despite the fact that the archaeological record of coastal cave sites, open coastal sites and even upland sites within the investigated area is still rather meager, these researchers were able to find evidence of the human adaptation to changing sea levels, and its effects on the marine life. Much, so they advise, is still to be done in this field, but only in an interdisciplinary manner. Archaeologists especially are asked to find and explore new sites with Dunn's and Dunn's hypothesis in mind (Dunn/Dunn 1977:16). Since late Pleistocene sites are now submerged by the present sea level, underwater archaeologists find a growing field of activity.

To wrap up this brief outline of scientific derivation theories, it might be said that none of the afore mentioned scientific activity was able to deliver real evidence of a Pleistocene migration from South East Asia towards Australia, even though this seems to be most probable. Archaeology estimates the early occupation of Australia at least 40.000 years ago (Bowler/Thorne 1976:134), but subsequent findings might change this. There is, however, still a discrepancy between early dates in the southern region of the country and the later ones in the northern region. The same might be said about New Guinea, where the eastern part shows significantly earlier dates than the western part. All this gives the impression that these parts would have been settled earlier which is not necessarily the fact. Several factors could have caused this dissimilarity, including the earlier predicted research gap, a dense population in the South of Australia and the East of New Guinea versus a sparse one in the North and the West, or simply the disparate conservational conditions of these regions. Cultural anthropology does not provide us with useful data as it is restricted to ethnic groups living in small parts of the area to be investigated. No broader migrational theory has been developed in the meantime. Physical anthropology and biology/anatomy were among the first sciences that used geological findings (i.e. skeletal remains), as well as the physical comparison of contemporary cultures, to establish kinship and descent. In spite of new techniques like blood serology or dermatoglyphics, as well as the ability to store and retrieve huge amounts of data using the computer, no uniform and evident theory has been derived. Except for Birdsell with his trihybrid theory, archaeologists and many physical anthropologists assume a settlement in two waves. First came the robust people and then the gracile

2.4) Settlement and Subsistence

Meaningful archaeological synthesis in Australia depends either on the analogies of interpretative tools such as the archaeological record itself and the historic or contemporary record of indigenous cultures or solely on the archaeological evidence. The first approach of "actual comparison" of archaeological data with those obtained ethnographically conceals some major weaknesses. The principle uncertain factor is the researcher's choice of culture or cultural appearance for comparison. If constructing an analogy one should stay close to the investigated culture or object. It makes no sense to compare the hunting techniques of North American Indians with those expected in Australia. There would be "no implication of direct genetic relationship nor are any dimensions of space and time implied" (Ascher 1967:320). Since the archaeological finding almost never reflects a momentary state of a living community, ethnographic data may provide interpretations only if technological or traditional sequences are traceable from the prehistory to the very moment of ethnographic recording (29). Modern ethnology and archaeology might complement one another if their common focuses are on the changing or stable customs of communities in transformation over a special period of time. These observations will surely help to interpret manufacturing techniques, tool use-life, discard behavior and as such as they concern the archaeological record. In the following the reader will find the explanation of the settlement and subsistence patterns of prehistoric, aboriginal people generally shared by modern archaeologists working in the above mentioned

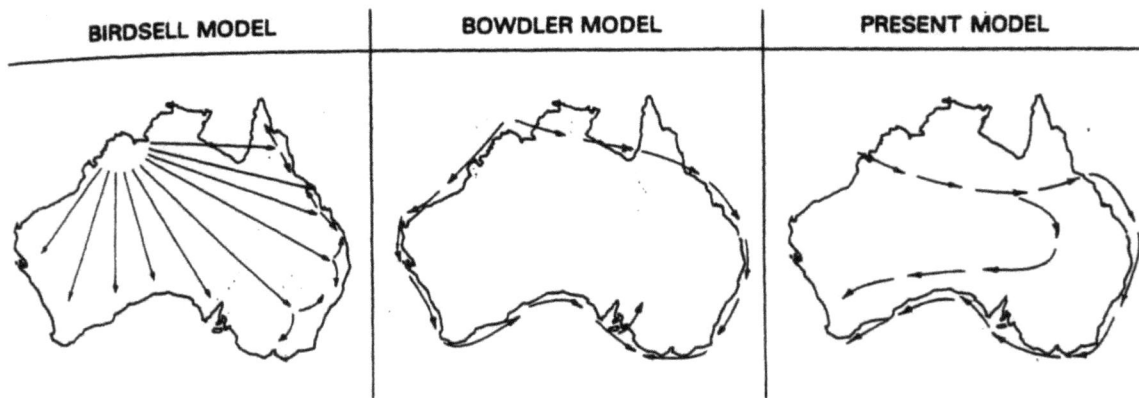

| BIRDSELL MODEL | BOWDLER MODEL | PRESENT MODEL |

Fig.6 Theories of migrational routes. After Flood 1983:78

ones, named after the skeletal findings of Kow Swamp and Lake Mungo, followed by the gradual interbreeding of these groups. Linguistic research seems to be hopeless, considering the tens of thousands of years that linguists would have to trace back and the innumerable factors that have definitely influenced the shaping of the languages. Considering these facts, Dunn's and Dunn's (1977:16) demand for a more careful, interdisciplinary research and study seems to be appropriate and desirable before contriving far reaching speculative theories.

----

(29) Exceptions are circumstances were a community was locked up and sealed in its momentary state through natural catastrophes or the like (i.e. Pompeii). Normally the archaeologists find what was lost, discarded or left behind by the respective group.

manner. If contradictions occur, they will be discussed in the text.

A) Migrational routes in Australia

Knowing that there were definitely people in Australia by at least 40.000 years B.P., the question arises of where, how and with what did they make a living ? The first question could be answered quite simply, since they were everywhere by at least 22.000 years ago. This can be clearly proven by the existence of prehistoric sites ranging from the north (Nawamoyn 21.450+-380) [Flood 1983:251] over the central desert (Puritjarra 21.950+-270) [Smith 1987:710] and to the south (Keilor 31.600+-1300, Kutikina Cave 19.750+-840) [Flood 1983:251]. We can state that the Pleistocene Aboriginal groups were able to cope with the alpine climates occurring in the Australian Alps, the arid interior of the Australian desert and the coastal and fluvial environments in Arnhem Land (Altman 1988:196). Three main models (Fig.6) for the peopling of Australia have been derived over the last 35 years, which might yet be proven to be wrong, but still include conclusive arguments, which combined, might lead to the most probable theory. Already in 1957 (47-50/68) Birdsell argued that the filling up of Australia was a fairly rapid process. Assuming a pioneering group of 25 people, and considering their estimated rate of reproduction and the permanent arrival of newcomers, the critical border of 60 percent of the carrying capacity of the initially occupied area would have quickly been reached. Birdsell tried to assert that these 60 percent would have been reason enough to split into smaller groups, which then dispersed radiationally over the country. The faster the carrying capacity of an area was reached, the sooner the group would have split up and occupied new land. This would be especially true when reaching the desert region that, according to Birdsell, was traversed quickly. Following Birdsell's theory, the occupation of coastal and inland regions was simultaneous, but differed in the pace of the movement. A computer projection resulted in an average occupational rate of 1350 - 2200 years for the settlement of Australia as a whole. Since very little was known about archaeology in Australia at the time Birdsell constructed his model, Bowdler (1977:205ff) sought to contrive a new model based on archaeological evidence. At that time there was an obvious lack of early inland sites, a fact that made Bowdler believe that Australia was colonized by coastally adapted people. She did not believe in the proposition that population growth could be calculated by assuming a certain reproductive rate and generation length, since the size of the original group was unknown. The peripheral distribution of Pleistocene archaeological sites seemed to support Bowdler's model of a gradual, coastal colonization. Bowdler's main argument for the coastal-adapted life style of the early settlers was the carrying-on of a life to which they were used and which would have been a necessity for the initial water crossing. Why should they move directly into the inhospitable interior, when they could instead move along the coast and up the river valleys, where an aquatic economy could be maintained ? When Horton (1981) published his migrational model he tried to combine archaeological evidence, the geomorphological relief of the country and probability assumptions. His theory of an all-purpose economy that moved into Australia and followed well-watered regions throughout the country remains without an explanation as to where this economy came from. This all-purpose economy is surely not found in South East Asia, as the climatic conditions vary. Horton described this economic system as "a system designed to efficiently detect and harvest surplus resources in the environment" (Horton 1981:23) He noted that this all-purpose economy hunted or gathered what was on hand and avoided areas where water supplies or food were rare. Contrary to Bowdler, Horton pointed out that the Pleistocene people did hunt animals of the megafauna. Subsequent archaeological findings supported his ideas.

All of these idealized models are not applicable to the colonization of Australia in detail, but if combined, they might draw a pretty accurate picture of the Pleistocene migration within Australia. The author does not want to imply that Pleistocene human behavior can be measured and stated through a logical enumeration of all possible factors that might have influenced migrational decisions, but today's knowledge leads to the conclusion of a gradual but continuous occupation of all parts of Australia and the perfect adaptation to them.

B) Four Pleistocene sites, their inventory and validity

Decisive criteria for the selection of the sites were their age, location and richness of inventory. At least one coastal site, one inland desert site and one fluvial or lake site had to be selected. A habitation site with a long occupational sequence and a seasonally used campsite, cave, rockshelter or open-air site were desirable. The sites should be located in the North, Center, South and either the West or the East of the continent. These criteria led to the selection of the Puritjarra rockshelter in the Central Desert, Lake Mungo within the Willandra lake system, Malangangerr in the Kakadu National Park and Dry Creek near Keilor.

The Malangangerr site is located in the open woodland to the south-west of the East Alligator River Crossing. [Literature for the following extract: Gallus 1983; Jones 1985; Schrire 1972/82; White 1967b] The shelter is part of a block consisting of massive, sub-horizontally bedded quartzite and quartz sandstone. The shelter opens to the south side, but is partly accessible to the East and West. Remarkable are the 400 m (to the East) and 800 m (to the West) distances to the next permanent watersources. The importance of Malangangerr rockshelter, excavated under the leadership of Schrire (former White) from the 24th of September to the 23rd of October 1964, is two-fold. On the one hand, the earliest evidence for Pleistocene ground-edge axes, mostly ascribed to the Neolithic phase, were found in the lower sands, associated with charcoal and dated to between 23.000 and 18.000 years B.P. The cutting edge of these axes is ground to a sharp chisel-like blade, and the axhead shows signs of grooving, which has been interpreted as resulting from hafting. On the other hand, Malangangerr displays a wide array of hunting and gathering of diverse fauna and flora. The deposits at Malangangerr with a maximum depth of 180 cm consisted of 80 - 120 cm of unstratified sand overlaid by 40 - 100 cm of well-stratified shell midden. Embedded in the lower deposit were chunky scrapers, primary flakes, hammerstones, the above mentioned ground-edge axes but almost no organic material. Schrire suggested the removal of the organic material through weathering, supposedly dripping water. An apparent disparity occurred between the sandy deposit and the midden one. The upper level of the sands was dated to 18.000+-400 B.P. and the base of the midden to 5980+-1400 B.P. Schrire suggested that either the shelter might have been unoccupied for some time or the weathering of the sandy deposit might have caused this time gap. The midden deposit reflects the 6.000 years of permanent occupation until about 300 years when the shelter was abundant. Only for these 6.000 years can we obtain evidence and derive hypotheses that are not unconditionally true for the older occupational phases. The inhabitants of the shelter used a wide variety of implements, such as stone, bone and shell tools, which are now found in the midden deposit. Since a stone tool manufacturing area is absent in or around the shelter, the occupants apparently did not manufacture stone tools at the site. This might have been the case with bone or shell tools however, if the discarded food remnants were made into usable tools. The remains of at least ten individuals buried in the shelter point to primary, as well as secondary burial practices. Broken human bones occur throughout the midden and seem to have been disposed with other midden material. Lumps of ochre are found dispersed in the midden. It must be noted that the inhabitants were artistically creative, since rockpaintings (not dated) are present. The midden zone was composed almost entirely of shellfish remains (up to 93 % of the whole content in a level) obtained from the nearby estuarine and tidal mudflats. The adaptation of the Aborigines to an environmental change was suggested by the increasing number of freshwater mussel remains. Other organic remains such as fish, large kangaroo, emu eggs, bandicoot, dragon lizard, goanna, crabs, birds, possum, wallaby and tortoise, testify to the food diversity of the early economy. Points (30), scrapers, utilized flakes, unifacially and bifacially retouched tools, axes and the like display the manifold tool kit of these hunters and gatherers. The Malangangerr site and others in the Alligator river region were used to construct Pleistocene hunter-gatherer traditions of the so called Kakadu people (31), as they may have existed from the time of arrival to the first contact of Europeans. White (1967b:465; see also Jones 1988:6-9) suggested that the Kakadu people might have lived in a way similar to those outlined by Spencer (1914:31). Spencer, who described and listed ethnographic observations of contemporary tribes and their material culture over a great part of the continent, draws the picture of a hunter-gatherer society that lived in huts instead of caves or rockshelters. Following his recordings, a complex, culturally active community with profound knowledge of the terrestrial and aquatic environment can be imagined. To give more details of the descrip-

tive analysis of the Kakadu people would lead too far from the intention of this outline, but further research might be advisable for the interested reader. Striking, however, is the correspondence between the tool kit of the prehistoric people and the contemporary ones (i.e. Spencer 1914,plate XII 4/Schrire 1982, --Fig.94e). In 1972 Schrire published an article about the subsistence behavior in Arnhem Land, which he inferred through the archaeological record and ethnographic data. Particularly relevant seems to be the maintenance of a specific dietary level, involving the evaluation of the work that has to be invested (input) and the expected yield (output). The settlement pattern would be determined by the environmental variations of the various, settled areas. A nomadic lifestyle can not depend on a repetitive series of stable food sources but has to incorporate a variety of different foods. This implies that campsites were used seasonally rather than permanently. This society could have adapted to new environments easily and might have been the basis for the early settlement of the whole of Australia. Schrire (1972:68/9) argued that rather the introduction of new food in the menu of prehistoric societies, evidently seen through the careful analysis of dietary remains, shows contact and exchange between different groups more than the exotic artifacts found in a site.

The Puritjarra rockshelter in the Central Desert of Australia, 320 km west of Alice Springs, shall be the next site discussed here. [Literature for the following extract: Smith 1983/87/88] Even though early sites up to 500 km inland from the lower ice-age level of the Western Australian coast have been discovered before, the uniqueness of Puritjarra rockshelter lay in its remoteness to any rivers connected to the coast (32). Embedded in layer II at a depth of 66 to 77 cm below the surface, artifacts associated with charcoal were found. The radiocarbon dating established an occupation reaching back to 22.000 years B.P., thus doubling the previously estimated age of human settlement in arid Central Australia. In 1982 Smith carried out limited excavations in Central Australia to determine the existence of possible cultural deposits, their depth, age and contents (Smith 1983:27ff). Despite extensive excavations within four sites Smith had to conclude that it is "possible to built up a reasonably detailed picture of the last 10.000 years, [but] a larger sequence will obviously rely on good luck as much as good management" (Smith 1983:37). It might have been luck or exceptionally good management that made Smith detect Puritjarra rockshelter almost four years later, but it certainly revised early speculations about the migrational routes and settlement of Pleistocene inhabitants (Smith 1987:710/11). The region in which Puritjarra is located, is characterized by low and sporadic rainfall (120-350 mm per annum) and by its ability to store water in its soil. The shelter is situated close to the only permanent water source of this area, but several streams, temporarily filled by the sparse rainfall, contain waterholes and soakages in their beds. The flora mainly consists of spinifex grassland and mulga woodland.

---

(30) In Malangangerr restricted to the upper level, but in other comparable sites such as Nawamoyn and Padypadig also present in lower levels.
(31) Named after the Kakadu region

---

(32) Contradicts Bowdler's migrational theory

The huge rockshelter, providing around 400 m² of level, shaded floor area, revealed a deposit consisting of three well-defined stratigraphic layers. The first layer, 0 -42 cm in depth, displayed loose, gritty, light-brown sand (33), which embedded flaked stone artifacts, grindstones, ochre, charcoal, intact hearth, rockfall and emu egg-shells. Layer I was radiocarbon dated to 5860+-150 years B.P.. A major occupational increase was noted over the last 1000 years due to the number and sequence of artifacts, faunal and floral remains. The second layer consisted of compact, fine, red, clayey sand and seemed to have contained only artifacts associated with charcoal, since nothing else was mentioned in an inadequate report on the nature of the site. The layer extended from the end of layer I (42 cm) to a depth of 101 cm. Layer III [101 - 202 cm (34)] showed no evidence of human occupation and consisted of fine, dark, red sand of a loose matrix along with well-rounded rubble. In 1988 Smith wrote his Ph.D. Thesis about "the pattern and timing of prehistoric settlement in Central Australia", in which he extensively refers to the excavation and further series of excavations (using finer methods) at Puritjarra rockshelter. Unfortunately, the author could not get full access to his thesis in time, so only a short report, published in 1989, will be considered here. Since layer II had a pH of 3.0 - 3.5, no animal bone and/or floral material was preserved. Next to the above mentioned artifacts and charcoal, small pieces of red ochre and fine debitage were noted. The nature of the occupation during the period of 22.000 - 12.000 B.P. was a major problem faced by Smith. The scattered and sparse distribution of stone artifacts in the deposit pointed to a seldom, temporary occupation, whereas the lack of organic remains, due to bad conservational conditions, did not allow such a conclusion. Even though the quantity of stone artifacts increased from 12.000 - 6.000 B.P., a final answer to this problem can not be given. Considering the three factors, "total accessible area", "carrying capacity per unit area" and the "density of watering points" (Smith 1989:103) of the desert regions during the ice age period, Smith concluded intermittent forays into the arid zone from it margins before 12.000 B.P. and permanent occupation of the Central Desert from 12.000 B.P. to 1930, when Aborigines were placed in missions and resorts. Especially important for the subsistence of Pleistocene Aborigines was the exploitation of the most dependable and predictable source of plant foods available, the seeds. This is archaeologically explained through the distinctive seed grinding technology only found in arid zones (see section about stone technology).

The third site that should be mentioned in this report is **Lake Mungo** within the Willandra Lake region. [Literature for the following extract: Bowler 1970/76: Bowler/Thorne 1976; Flood 1990; Mulvaney 1980; Jones 1979] A long time before the discovery of Lake Mungo (Bowler et al. 1970), the

dry sands of the Willandra Lake region had been known to bury diverse evidence of the Pleistocene occupation of humans. The area, today known as semi-arid, with a mean annual rainfall of 250 mm against 164 cm evaporation per year, was once (before 15.000 B.P.) a series of probably overflowing freshwater lakes. In the phase when the lakes were active, high sand and sandy clay aeolian transverse dunes, called lunettes, were developed. This took place between 50.000 (35) - 15.000 years ago. The extensive modern deflation of the dunes, caused by the semi-arid climate, exposed the parts of the high dune ridges commonly referred to as the "Walls of China". Within these erosions geographers/archaeologists found evidence for early human burial practices. Since the upper "Zanci" (Bowler 1970:45) sedimentary unit was eroded, as well as much of the Mungo unit, the carbonate-cemented bones stuck out of the erosion surface. For the purpose of relative dating, the original predeflation sequence had to be reconstructed through leveling and comparing soil and sedimentary units. Recent authors referring to the Lake Mungo cremation (Flood 1990:250, Mulvaney 1980 in Heritage of Australia:182) mention a pit, into which burnt and broken bones were laid, although this conclusion seems unsubstantiated, since the bones were eroded out of the sedimentary context. In order to date this burial relatively, the dug-in horizon (Eintiefungshorizont) of the pit should be known. The dug-in horizon is the actual surface the Pleistocene people stood on, when they dug out the pit. The same critical remark is valid for the second burial, located a few hundred meters from the cremation site and eroded from the sediments several years later. Because the cremated burial could be absolutely dated, this criticism seems to be appropriate only for the second burial, relatively dated after the reconstructed stratigraphy of the first burial. Nevertheless, the two burials indicate the wide array of mortuary practices performed by early Aboriginal Australians. The young woman found in burial one was cremated on the beach and buried without changing the position of the bones from the way they had fallen through the funeral pyre. This was concluded by Thorne (in Bowler et al. 1970:57), in view of their anatomical arrangement. The bones, especially the skull, were smashed afterwards, maybe because of the obvious insufficiency of the pyre to achieve full incineration. The second burial (Bowler 1976:55ff) was that of a tall man who had been laid on his side with slightly flexed knees and his hands clasped. Red staining of the bones and the surrounding soil indicated that the body had been coated with red ochre. As a matter of fact, red ochre is abundant in the surrounding area of the Mungo III burial, so the coloring material had to be especially brought into the burial site. The dating of the burial was, as mentioned earlier, a relative one. An adjacent fireplace, dated 30.780 +- 520 B.P. and the stratigraphic relationship to the first burial led to the suggested age of 30.000 B.P.. In addition to the most remarkable human remains, several other findings have been made that might draw a picture of early settlement and subsistence in this

----
(33) Munsell color scale was used
(34) The full depth of the layer was not established, nor was bedrock reached.

----
(35) Estimated, since beyond range of radiocarbon dating.

area. Knowing that the climate before 15.000 B.P. was cooler and that the annual rainfall was sufficient to fill and overflow the lakes, an absolutely different faunal and floral environment can be concluded. Indeed, at that time mega-faunal creatures were providing enough food, especially over the fall and winter months, for a hunter-gatherer society. In spring and summer, when the rivers and lakes sustained an abundance of life, the prehistoric society (group) gathered around the aquatic environment. Camping along the soft sand dunes bordering the shores, the Aborigines exploited the surrounding food sources successfully. The terrestrial, as well as the lacustrine fauna, found in hearths or middens of the Lake Mungo excavation, provided an excellent variety in diet. At the site evidence was found of birds, bettongs and small marsupials, such as native cat and small macropods, as well as of kangaroo, wallaby and wombat. Seasonality was shown by the presence of emu eggs, which are only available in late winter, and shell fish and perch, commonly caught in the summer or the late spring. The amazing similarity to contemporary Aboriginal groups, ethnographically observed in the last century (Lawrence 1968), may lead to the hypothesis that net fishing was also practiced, considering the fact that the golden perch is an open water fish and seldom found next to the shore. Observations on other sites of the Willandra lake system pointed to the collection of vegetable food, mussels, frogs, yabbies and Murray cod.

Keilor is the last exemplary site introduced to the reader. The site is located near the junction of the Dry Creek and Maribyrnong River, about 16 km north of Melbourne. The accidental finding of a human skull in 1940 led to a still ongoing series of excavations. The primary scientists that worked at the site were Bowler (1969,1970) for the geological part and Gallus (1967,1971, 1972 1974,1976,1983) in the archaeological sphere. A summary of the investigations so far was given by Joyce and Anderson (1976:47-74; see also Jones 1979). The Keilor site is situated in an alluvial terrace formed by the Maribyrnong and Dry Creek Rivers, which have incised their valleys with the rising of the sea levels. Three different terraces have been established by geologists. The two lower ones, Arundel and Keilor, were formed by deposits laid down during a period of low quaternary sea levels. The dating of the lowest deposit is still ambiguous, but estimated to be between 30.000 - 47.000 B.P., while the Keilor terrace was assigned to the late Wurm about 30.000 to 18.000 B.P.. The Maribyrnong terrace is the younger phenomenon. Problematic is the establishment of erosional and depositional phases in order to relatively date the terraces. Since terraces erode and accumulate irregularly, it is not certain that tools found in the same layer are of the same age or even related to the same event in time. Some of the tools might have been eroded from upper, younger layers, or have been transported through the river and deposited there, while others might be in situ and have been covered by or mixed with sediments of a later accumulation phase. The main aim of the excavations had to be to find definite in situ terraces or parts thereof in order to establish a stratigraphy, which is indispensable for relative and absolute dating. These in situ terraces were found by Gallus, who primarily focused on the oldest terrace, the Arundel formation, to find evidence of the earliest human occupation. In the D clay, named by Gallus after his D excavation, stone tools, com-

prised of a variety of scrapers, even of the thumbnail type, were recovered. Remains of Megafauna not directly associated with the tools were found as well. The obvious lack of organic material other than charcoal led Gallus to define the stone tool industries as Arundel 1 to 5, strongly reminiscent of early typologies in that it showed the most simplistic tool at the beginning and the more refined ones at the end. Even though Gallus' typology remains subject to debate, there is no doubt about the early evidence of human occupation and "sophisticated" tool industry. The axe-quarry near Lancefield is identified as a primary reduction place for larger stone tools (i.e. axes) and several other places in Victoria give evidence for the human working of stone as well. It should also be mentioned that some bone tools were found, mainly spearheads, the so called javelins, burins, borers, a hook, harpoons, arrow heads, sickles or knifes, spatulas and stone implements with bone handles were found as well. Even though a detailed analysis and an environmental reconstruction concerning settlement and subsistence is still lacking, one becomes aware of the manifold exploitation of the terrestrial and aquatic environment by the early humans.

In the 1970's a number of BA Honor theses were written about shell midden analysis as an indicator of cultural behavior and change. The sites chosen for analysis mainly gave evidence for human occupation no earlier than 10.000 years B.P.. As example, Bowdler's work (1970) shall be briefly mentioned. She found a relation between the introduction of the shell fishhook and the relative proportions of fish species caught. She pointed out the sexual division of labor in coastal economies and specifically mentioned the use of fish hooks by women (Bowler1970:24). The enumeration and distribution of food resources rounded off her picture of the human exploitation of the environment as derived from deliberate midden analysis.

C) Human impact on the environment

Two major questions arise if dealing with the peopling of Australia. One has to ask, firstly if there was a Pleistocene overkill that might have caused the extinction of the megafauna and secondly, if human fire caused the preferential growth of "fire environmental" adapted plants ? As outlined in part 2 of this short overview, the Pleistocene hunters lived in an environment dominated by giant marsupials. This megafauna included a number of mammals and a few reptiles. Several species of kangaroo and wallaby, such as Procoptodon or Simosthensusus, as well as giant anteaters like the Zaglossus or the wombat-like Diprotodentids, were among the huntable animals (e.g. Flood 1983:146ff). Major climatic changes between 25.000 and 15.000 B.P., caused by the gradual rising of the world temperatures and the subsequent melting off of the ice caps which covered large parts of the northern hemisphere, definitely caused an environment unsuitable for marsupial species. The drying up of waterholes and lakes, as well as the shortage in vegetational food, might have caused their extinction or their substantial reduction in size over time (e.g. Bowler 1976:57ff). Jones (1969:224-8) and Merriless (1968:23) independently developed the theory that humans played a role in the extinction process. They argued that man's ecological impact was mostly done by hunting and by the selective gathering of plants and fire, although they pointed out that the latter factor was the most effective one. Early ethnographic reports mentioned the extensive use of fire for various purposes, such as cooking, burning dry grassland, disinfecting wounds, for warmth, etc. Archaeological evidence points to a pure hunting and gathering economy at the time the megafauna became extinct, so we face the problem of finding out to what purpose they used the fire outside of agriculture (fire-stick farming/slash and burn). Jones offers six possible solutions (1969:226). The first would be the burning of the bush for the pleasure of the blazing of the flames. Secondly, the lightning of fires for signaling purposes. The third and forth solutions would be burning in order to clear the ground for travel free of harm of snakes or to develop a plant growth that suited the Aboriginal subsistence strategies. Fire hunting with the purpose of either collecting the burnt animals later or chasing them in a special direction would be another possible solution. The last offered possibility would be the extension of man's habitat through the burning of the forest and the replacement of it with sedgeland, which is rich in both animal and plant food. Most of these practices would leave large areas of land previously inhabited by a wide variety of fauna and flora uninhabited for some time (36), followed by the appearance of fire resistant plants and the animals that live off of them. Jones also developed the idea that Pleistocene Aborigines rapidly hunted the megafauna to extinction, suggesting that the human impact through overkill was the main cause for the disappearance of the giant marsupials. Especially White and O'Connell (1979:27) doubt this theory. They pointed out that the implication of a selective hunting pattern of the Aborigines is highly speculative. Even if marsupials were mainly hunted, the Aborigines would have searched for other faunal food sources if the ranks of the megafauna had thinned out. They argued that the climatic changes and human activity were in an active interplay which lead to the extinction in question. The drying-up of water sources and their sparse distribution over the country would have forced animals and hunters to live in the same small area, which implies the hunting to extinction of the least environmentally adapted marsupials.

In the following years several publications appeared (Hallam 1975, Ellis 1976, Jones 1979, Gill et al. 1981) dealing with the human exploitation of the Australian environment through fire. Hallam especially showed with the example of the Southwest of Australia that Aboriginal population did change the vegetational and faunal balance. She pointed out that the lasting impact proportionally rises with the aridity of the land (Hallam 1975:105). In 1979 Jones adjusted his previous theory on the massive extinction phase of the megafauna caused by man. Still, he noted that in the long run these species were effected by humans more or less in every spe-

cific region. Since he only referred to fire as a source of human impact, he might have considered the fact that no kill nor butchering sites were discovered in Australia yet. This might be either a research gap or an indication of timid hunting of the megafauna. Ellis reported that the Adelaide open grassland area was described as being caused by fire-stick farming (Ellis 1976:114) and that the extensive use of those practices might have altered the soil structure and the subsequently adapted vegetation. In 1981 Gill, et al. edited a whole volume about the "fire and the Australian biota". Supported by pollen analysis (Singh et al. 1981:23ff), ethnographic data and archaeological evidence the conclusion of this volume seems to be that the gradual increase in the use of fire is proportional to the change in faunal and floral habitats.

In conclusion it might be stated that the early Aboriginal settlers practiced a hunter-gatherer economy. They lived in short term, open air encampments or under rockshelters and exploited the faunal and floral environment. The terrestrial and the aquatic surroundings were successfully used, and no food seemed to be preferred or specially neglected (McArthur 1960:134) The Pleistocene Aborigines were capable of settling in a coastal, fluvial, an alpine, a well tempered, an arid or a semi-arid climate, though it seems that the first one was preferably selected. The remains of this society as found in the archaeological record display a culturally diversified behavior, seen in the mortuary practices as well as in the material culture. Next to the "traditional" hunting and gathering techniques, fire seemed to have played an increasing role in the exploitation of the environment.

2.5) Stone Technology

If dealing with the early prehistory of Australia, one soon recognizes that a number of stone and bone implements are the only valid sources for understanding Pleistocene behavior and technological standards. Early sites are seldom found that include more then bits and pieces of the whole repertoire of "early humankind" in Australia. This obvious lack of diversified sites led to a huge number of publications about tools and their possible classification and interpretation. In general Australian archaeology ran through the same historical phases of research, as the United States of America, which has already been outlined in the author's masters thesis (Deunert 1990:6-21). Since stone tool technology is not the main interest of this thesis, the reader should be forgiving if the following overview is incomplete and some major works are not mentioned. Kenyon and Stirling (1901:191ff) can be taken as an example of the early scientific investigation of Aboriginal material culture. The implements classified by them were surface collections and tools still in use by contemporary groups. The two authors pointed out that little attention has been paid towards stone tools by members of all science branches, so it seemed to be necessary to classify them. This tentative classification, divided into seven main groups and several subdivisions, had aimed more at ascribing findings to special attribute classes than at establishing a typology (Fig.7). The 1914 published guide to Australian Aboriginal stone implements used this classification as a framework (In: Kenyon/Mahoney 1914). In the following

---

(36) Danger of reinforced erosion causing aeolian movement of sand often found in prehistoric sites and explained through humanly induced changes in the fire regime (Jones 1988:10/11)

Fig.7 Classification of Australian stone implements — diagram

GROUPS.	DIVISIONS (A.)	Subdivisions (L.)	Sections (a.)	Classes (I.)	Sub-Classes (a.)

C. Cutting Implements

- **A. Cutting edge produced by flaking or chipping**
  - I. Axes
    - a. chipped
      - 1. chipped one side only — α. acute bevel / β. obtuse „
      - 2. chipped both sides — α. hafted / β. not hafted
    - b. flaked
  - II. Rasps
  - III. Knives
    - a. hafted
      - 1. single flake — α. chipped / β. flaked
      - 2. multiple flake
    - b. not hafted
      - 1. chipped
      - 2. flaked
  - IV. Adzes
  - V. Scrapers
  - VI. Spearheads
    - a. single flake
      - 1. chipped
      - 2. flaked
      - 3. serrated
    - b. multiple flake
  - (VII. Nuclei or Cores)

- **B. Cutting edge produced by grinding and polishing**
  - I. Axes
    - a. grooved for hafting
    - b. not grooved for hafting
      - 1. oblong ovate
        - α. straight cutting edge
        - β. circular cutting edge
        - γ. parabolic cutting edge
        - δ. cutting edge inclined to plane of major axis
      - 2. ovate
      - 3. deltoid
      - 4. gad shaped — α. cylindrical body / β. flattened body
      - 5. adze shaped
      - 6. cone shaped
  - II. Wedges
    - a. single transverse groove
    - b. double transverse groove
    - c. transverse and semi-longitudinal groove
    - d. not grooved
  - III. Knives or Scrapers
  - IV. (Blanks)

Gr. Grinding Implements

- A. Kerns or Mills
  - I. Nether stones with husking hole, spherical hollow
  - II. „ „ without „ „ „ „
  - III. „ „ „ „ „ plane surface
  - IV. „ „ „ „ „ oval hollow
  - V. „ (and upper) stones, circular, also used for pounding fibre
  - VI. Upper stones
    - a. spheroidal
    - b. pestle shaped
    - c. muller shaped
- B. Grinding Stones
  - I. Grind Stones
  - II. Whet Stones
  - III. Rasps

P. Pounding Implements
- A. Hammers
- B. Chipping Hammers
- C. Fibre Pounders
- D. Anvil Stones

F. Fishing Stones

T. Throwing Stones

Ga. Game Stones

B. Basket Stones

Fig.7 Classification of Australian stone implements
(Keaton/Sterling:1901:Appendix)

30

years a growing effort was made in the archaeological investigation. The first excavation in 1929 was pioneering and delivered relatively datable stone implements. In spite of the growing concern over validity of archaeological data derived from typologies and geological strata, Tindale published his theories about the "Karta" industry, which he drew from surface findings on Kangaroo Island (Tindale 1937,1957). His approach culminated in a typology for South Australian stone tools, which has since been proven to be wrong (Lampert 1981). The main classificational types were the horsehoof tool (Fig. 8), the Charta tool and the Sumatralith. The latter is supposed to show a close affiliation with the "Sumatra" culture. The ethnologist Cooper, who accompanied Tindale in his research on the Kangaroo Island, published an introductory survey of 2000 specimens of stone implements, then collected and divided them into three regions of occurrence (Cooper 1943:350-54/368). That the Kartan industry was obviously not restricted to the Kangaroo Island but is also found in south Australian mainland sites, made Cooper suggest and Lampert state that this industry was brought to the island at least 50.000 years ago, when there was a land connection. Similar to Tindale's attempt to define a culture through the stone relics, McCarthy (1940) found another cultural complex, later known as Gambier culture, named after Mt.Gambier. This culture is supposed to have been even older than the Kartan culture and mainly consisted of bifacial cores, commonly referred to as Buandik tools. Even modern archaeological reports are still haunted by these cultural terms, even though they were defined through surface findings and untenable in view of modern archaeological research. The fishhook underwent a similar procedure with its original classification (Massola 1956) to the later seriation. The typological model as a "reliable" means of dating, like Tindale's kodja typology, which mentioned primitive, sophisticated and degenerated tools (Tindale 1950:257ff), seemed to have found its end around 1957, when Davidson and McCarthy published "The distribution and chronology of some important types of stone implements in Western Australia". They clearly stated that a dating must await archaeological investigation and cannot rely on ethnographic reports and surface collections (Davidson/McCarthy 1957:456-57). Although their comparative analysis considering visible use-wear tried to establish the origin of some tools, they did not move beyond archaeological evidence when concluding a chronology. Despite this article, White 1969 and McCarthy himself (1946 and more tentative 1967) derived typologies for a variety of attribute classes. The comparative analysis of these attributes, like the edge angle, degree of utilization, thickness, etc., led to the definition of types that could be related to a special time or "industry". In his Ph.D. thesis in 1971 (19-21) Rys Jones condemned typological studies as useless, since they rely heavily on attribute definitions, and the outcome is strongly influenced by the number of attributes chosen. It seems that this fundamental critique caused an upswing in the archaeological research in Australia, but since Australia was, and still is, only a satellite state of the United Kingdom (37), the real cause might have been the worldwide refinement of archaeological methods. The discovery of Lake Mungo led to one of the first intensive stone tool studies based on the archaeological record. Kamminga (1971) probably realized the need for new concepts and methods

when exploring the Australian past by means of stone tools. Guided by the writings of Semenov and other researchers working in the field of use-wear analysis, Kamminga had already written his B A Honors thesis on the "microscopic and experimental study of Australian Aboriginal stone tools". Kamminga conducted replicative experiments on a variety of stone types, investigated them under the microscope and compared them with the microwear patterns on a wide range of stone artifacts from collections throughout Australia. He discussed the use-wear in the context of morphological and functional typologies. Ethnographic data provided him with analogies for tool functions, which led to his hypothesis of possible tool uses. Around this time forms of multivariate analysis and statistical-mathematical comparisons of frequencies appeared in the Australian archaeological research (i.e. Pearce 1973), but they never quite got of the ground as in other countries. The ethnoarchaeologist Gould, who published major works about Australia with a special consideration of Western Australia, combined excavational and ethnographical evidence for the interpretation of archaeological remains. He especially tried to interpret the Australian small tool tradition (Gould 1973). Between 1974 and 1979 a real flood of Ph.D. theses were written about lithic technology. This started with Struwe (1974), who gave a detailed analysis of Australian stone tools from archaeological sites within Australia, New Guinea and Indonesia in order to state migrational routes. Hayden (1976) chose the ethnoarchaeological approach in the region of the Western Desert. His thesis was thought to equip future researchers with a reliable source for detecting traits of trade, activity groups and ethnic differences within the archaeological material. Although this was not quite achieved, his work nonetheless advanced the investigation of stone tools and led to a new avenue of research. Similar to Kamminga's studies, he also conducted stone tool manufacturing experiments and analyzed them functionally without using microscopic investigations. An interesting idea was his attempt to find special sequences in archaeological excavations of prehistorical and historical sites in Western Australia and to compare these results with prehistoric remains in New England. Finally, in 1990, Kamminga wrote his Ph.D. as a continuous study of his BA and master's work over the microscopic functional analysis of use-wear patterns in a range of Australian flaked stone industries. His main research tools were again ethnographic data, replicative tool-use experiments and use-wear analysis, with which he hoped to establish the mode of tool use. This time he incorporated a comparison of material fracturing from different sources to provide data on the nature and suitability of artifact material. These three major works represented the framework for almost all modern archaeological research conducted in this field. A conference over the validity of different approaches to studying Austra-

----

(37) This more or less political statement is definitely not valid for modern archaeological research, starting in 1970-76 with the refinement of the use-wear analysis by Kamminga and Hayden and with the awareness of Aboriginal rights in archaeology/anthropology.

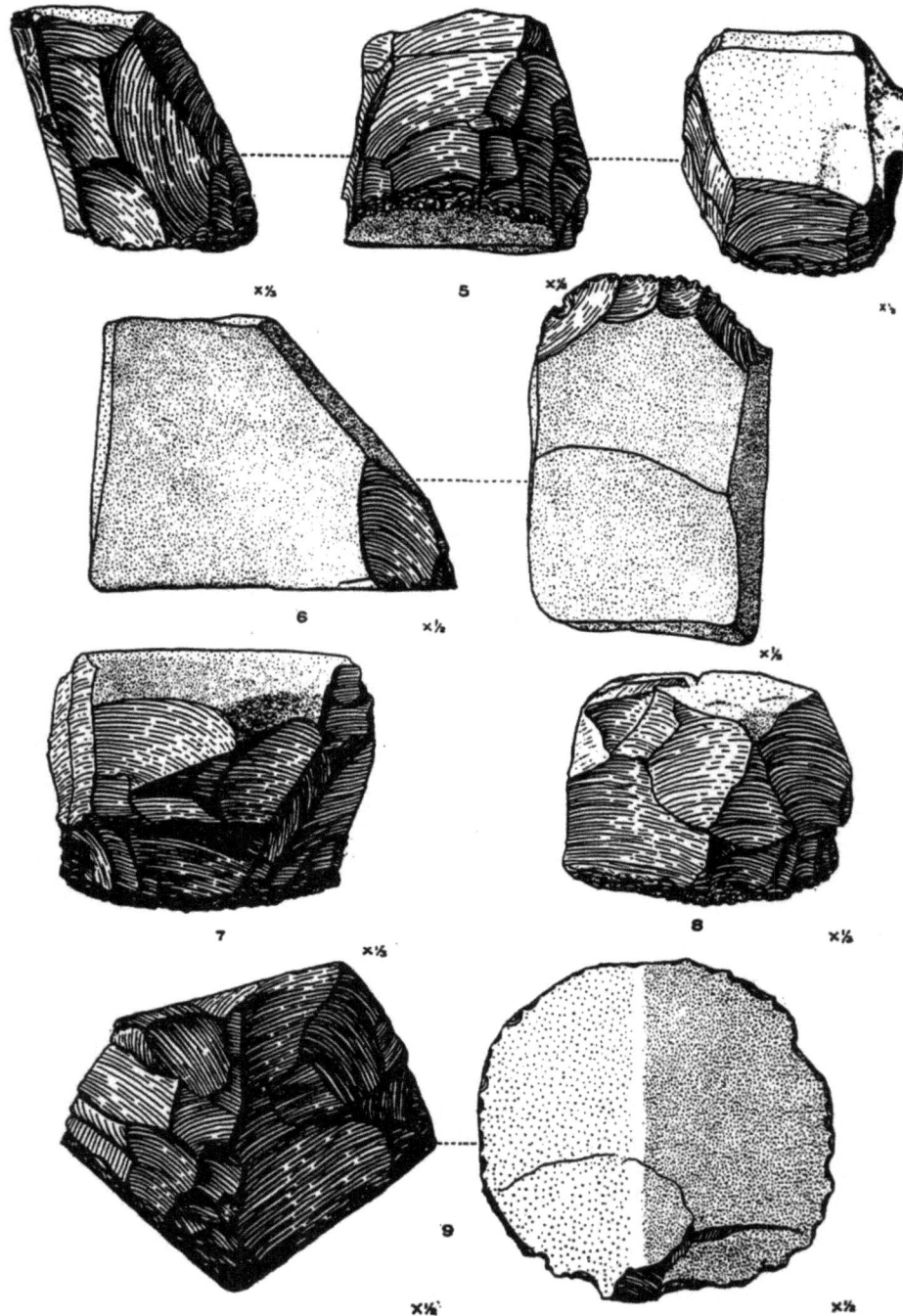

Fig.8 Horsehoof scrapers (Cooper 1943:352)

lian stone tools allowed Wright to edit the papers submitted (Wright 1977). This book covered all major, recently developed approaches for interpreting stone tool assemblages from the Australian prehistory. It includes regional distributions of special tool types and frequency analysis (i.e. Dortch 1977), as well as ethno-archaeological variability considerations (O'Connell 1977). In more recent publications the archaeological view tended to be focused on the "flintknappers" perspective. Several productional sequences and the possible working techniques for such diverse artifacts as adzes, backed artifacts, burins, points, scrapers and utilized flakes were established (i.e. Flenniken/White 1985:131ff). The interpretation of archaeological findings such as a stone tool assemblage of partially worked or unworked stones displaying reduction sequences, commonly referred to as a quarry, was supported through the careful observation of contemporary Aboriginal stone workers (Jones/White 1988:51ff). Jones and White were able to assign special occurrences on the chipping floor, such as the distribution of core, waste flakes, debris and finished flakes, to different areas of activity. They pointed out that this could be done either by one person, changing places with progressing reduction, or by several people, specialized to specific reduction phases. Smith (1988) conducted ethno-archaeological studies with Central Australian seed grinding implements and Pleistocene grindstones. His study showed the uniqueness of the Central Australian seed grinding implements as use-wear analysis of other "grindstones" from different areas of the Australian continent refuted the hypothesis that they represent seed grinding implements (Smith 1988:110). In 1989 Florek investigated the possibility of stone splitting through the use of fire. When he surveyed the Old Woman Quarry at Finnis Springs in 1986 he observed deliberately split stones, which had been altered in color and weight. Replicative experiments revealed that these alterations were caused by the directed use of fire. Several hammerstones and the number of ten stone artifacts per square meter displaying archaeological evidence of knapping made him believe that fire was primarily used to reduce boulders at this quarry. He concluded that there is admittably "circumstantial evidence to suggest that the splitting was caused by human action aided by the use of fire" (Florek 1989:23). In July 1990 Webb and Allen analyzed bone tools microscopically, a task never before done in Australia (except for Webb's unpublished B A Honors thesis in 1987). From the 19 investigated tools, 11 could clearly be assigned to scraping, piercing and, in one case, spearing of soft to medium strength materials, such as skin or bark.

In the following the author would like to give a schematic enumeration of the stone tools found in Australia, without assigning them to time periods, since it seems that most of the tools used in Pleistocene times are still used by contemporary Aboriginal groups. Photographic examples of the tools mentioned in the questionnaire are given in appendix A. No regional distinctions were made (i.e. Tula-adze), and no explanatory terms were used (i.e. magic stone). Only technological aspects were considered. The results of the use-wear analysis were noted as far as they are known and established (Fig.9)

2.6) Art

Some might wonder why art is included in this overview, since the author seems to be the last person who could give a qualified statement about Aboriginal artistic expression. This judgment definitely bears some truth in terms of the interpretation of art styles, and the motivation to produce art. It might even be true that the untrained eye of the author as an observer of Aboriginal art would not be able to detect symbols significant to the explanation of dreamtime phenomena. An admittedly crude, but perhaps justified reply would be to raise the doubt that any non-aboriginal person would be able to judge Aboriginal art. Considering this, the study of Aboriginal art might be an example relevant to the questions raised in the introduction of this thesis.

The mentioning of Aboriginal art in the reports of the earliest encounters between Aborigines and Westeners is stunning. Art, however characterized as primitive concerning the Aborigines, was one of the foundations of the so called civilized countries. How could these "creatures", not even seen as human beings, have expressed themselves artistically. That would imply at least some kind of fantasy and aesthetic or cultural awareness. Since animals do not practice art at least not for art's sake, this was stunning. Perhaps this kind of art was condemned because the age of expressionism and surrealism had not yet arrived, and Aboriginal art could not be economically evaluated. Since it is idle to speculate about the early explorers' and the later settlers' perception of art, the author decided to skip the art history. But the recognition of Aboriginal art as aesthetically important by the wider artistic community no earlier then the 1970's is worth mentioning. This went along with the general resurgence of Aboriginal culture, which had been declared dead for so long.

If talking about rock art, we have to distinguish between paintings and engravings. Petroglyphs seem to be the older representatives of early art expressions, even though some researchers argue that the dynamic style paintings in Arnhem Land belong to the Pleistocene period and might even represent one of the oldest styles. As we undoubtedly see, there is one major problem in dealing with rock art. How can we date it ? One way is the counting of the paint layers, if the paintings were diligently preserved through the centuries by tribesmen. Climatic and erosional factors, such as frost, wetness of the rock or air moisture, have to be considered when establishing the age of every layer. This relative dating does not hold for periods farther back than a few hundred years. A sound basis for the dating of early rock paintings is the fact that a coloring such as ochre has been known for at least 30.000 years, since it was used in the burial ceremonies at Lake Mungo. If one observes contemporary Aboriginal artists, he becomes aware that much of the art produced was never meant to last, since it was only used for short term ceremonies. Engraved images have a much better chance of surviving. This is especially true if engraved in stable rock. However, there will be still a dating problem. Modern dating methods, pioneered by Dragovich (1986:149-51) and successfully applied by Dorn, Nobbs and Cahill (Nobbs/Dorn 1988:108-124; Dorn/Nobbs/Cahill 1988:681-9), could establish a minimum age of rock engravings from the Olary region at 31.500 years ago. No one knows if this method is directly applicable to the rock varnish on the petroglyphs, since it needs a bigger sample for reliable dating that far back. This is especially important when considering that the Accelerator Mass Spectrometry (AMS) is a relative young method and that the capability of achieving exact radio carbon dates has to be proven. Conventional dating methods rely on lucky circumstances, such as the burying of engravings by archaeological deposits (38) or the growing of stalactites directly on the engraving or painting (39). Another method would be the analysis of drawn fauna and flora that became extinct. If one knows the approximate date when these specimens became extinct, one can state that these paintings or engravings must be at least as old as the extinction date of the drawn fauna or flora. (Hunting scenes)

---

(38) Early Man Shelter/Queensland
(39) Cave in Cracroft valley/Tasmania

Tools		Skin	Bone	Worked Material Wood	Stone	Seed	Material not established
Scrapers	Large steep edged	X		X			
	Small steep edged	X		X			
	Micro-retouch scraper	X		X			
Microliths	Thumbnail			X			
	Micro-Burin						
Points	Uni Facial						
	Bi Facial						
	Backed/Bondi	X	X				
	Plain edge bifacial						
Blades	Retouched						
	Utilized						
	Backed/Elouera			X			
Knifes		X	X	X			
Burins							
Chissels							X
Flakes	Uni						X
	Bi						X
Awls		X					
Adzes				X			
Hatchets							X
Grindstones					X	X	
Cores						X	
Anvils						X	

Fig.9 Results of use-wear analysis

Page 34

Artists distinguish between three Aboriginal art styles. The panramittee, figurative and finger markings . The three basic methods used for engraving were friction (using a harder stone tool to be pushed across the stone surface), drilling, and hammering (probably with a chisel) [After Burnum Burnum 1988:26, no further reference provided]. The paintings consisted of drawings and stencils, although the latter seemed to be the more popular technique. Using the bare hands, a boomerang or other utensils as stencils on the rock, a powdered or liquid pigment was blown or spilled against it, leaving a lasting impression of the respective object on the rock surface. The colors were mainly obtained from the diverse varieties of ochre, which was either pulverized to keep the original color or burnt to obtain variations. But Aboriginal art is not only found in caves and on other stone walls or objects. Every weapon and tool, even the domestic utensils, could have been decorated. Most impressive are the richly painted shields and the carefully painted barks. The most perishable art is represented in the regionally diversified body paintings.

3. STATUS OF ABORIGINAL PEOPLE IN A CHANGING SOCIETY A BRIEF HISTORY

3.1 Introductory remarks

The reader of this thesis might wonder how in taking a closer look at the status of the Aboriginal people in a changing society will lead to a solution of the present problem. The author will try to show how the social pressure and the influential Western philosophy of life changed and will change the Aborigines´ view of their own heritage and as such their reflection upon archaeology as a primary investigational discipline. The clarification of the Aboriginal status might derive from a justification or neglect of the archaeological enterprise in the Aboriginal's as well as Western society's perspective. This brief historical overview covers especially those years of white occupation and dominance from about 1770 up to the present day. The traditional life-style of the Aborigines is being based on archaeological remains as well as ethnographic reports and at the same time will represent the basis for any comparative analysis to later times.

Factually, this overview will be restricted to the most salient changes in Aboriginal life within three self determined time periods. It is appropriate when writing such an overview to clarify three terms used in the headline.

The term society is defined as the total number of human beings locally restricted to the continent of Australia with their prevailing values, morals, opinions, and the subsequent laws and political systems already established. Since the number of Aboriginal people has been steadily reduced, in recent years at least percentage wise, the term society became more and more foreign determined.

The status, more restricted to the social status, is a term borrowed from sociology showing the grade of social esteem and position within a social system (society). Indications of social status today are the so called status symbols like education, titles, and possession. Social outsiders do not attain many of these status symbols nor do they share the interest in them.

Aboriginality represents a term, which has not been commonly defined, and is even considered by full blooded Aborigines to be a point of controversy. When should a person be considered as Aboriginal ? Is the color of the skin an indication, the tribal membership or the family tree showing the purity of blood and outside genetic influences ? The author dares, at this point to introduce his own definition since it is important for the subsequent conclusions based on statistical data obtained through the interviews of "Aboriginal people". The author dissociates himself from the official and legal Australian definition of Aboriginal people, even though all interviewed Aborigines were also recognized as such by the Australian legal system. An Aboriginal is one who feels as such, has some genetic tie to Aboriginal ancestors, and cares about Aboriginal interests. He/she might be initiated or not, mixed or unmixed, and living close to the traditional life-style or in a Westernized way.

3.2 Traditional Life-Style

When trying to outline the traditional life-style of Aboriginal groups, one has to rely upon the data obtained through archaeological and anthropological investigations. Commonly, in non-scientific writings, traditional Aboriginal culture is noted as being stable and unchanging throughout time and space. However, we can not assume that behavioral patterns have not considerably changed over time. The land in Australia was changing and so the people changed, in an attempt to adapt to the new environment. Traditional Aboriginal society was dynamic and considerable changes did occur, especially within the last few thousand years. The cultural identification of Aboriginal people is seldom considered in their society as having been in transition. Old sites and dates are used to show proof of their antiquity and justification for their traditional life-style, though archaeologists know little about the earliest settlement and especially, the behavior of the ancient Australians. The reason why archaeologists know little about the first 30,000 - 35,000 years of Aboriginal prehistory might be explainable by their semi-nomadic life-style (Tindale 1974:75). Comparisons to contemporary hunter-gatherer economies and ethnographic records of Aboriginal groups show that often only shelters rather than stable huts were built at campsites, features that do not show up in the archaeological record (Tindale 1981:1863).

Aborigines did not tend to collect objects or have any sense of private property (Berndt 1964:430) so that no hoards are found, further more, objects were just discarded along the seasonally determined hunting route, with few objects being enclosed in the grave. Most of the organic material deteriorates if special circumstances do not apply.

The Aboriginal burial practice seems to be a major handicap for archaeological investigations. The disposal of the corpses varied between burials, exposure on a platform or tree, and desiccation or mummification to cremation and burial in a hollow tree. " These categories are not mutually exclusive. For instance, some time after burial the bones may be collected, and later reburied or carried about as relics. Or the body may be left on the platform until it has decomposed, and the bones finally placed in a hollow log or in a cave." (Berndt 1964:392) Most of these burial practices do not leave archaeologically detectable traces.

The few things that might be securely stated about the early Aboriginal hunter-gatherer economy are summed up in section 2.4 of this volume. The author of the present thesis, however, is of the opinion that the developmental state of Aboriginal culture should be considered when talking about traditional Aboriginal life-style. The traditional Aboriginal life-style would be represented in that state, which was encountered with the arrival of the European people.

Although it seems to be easier to reconstruct those comparatively late prehistoric times there are some difficulties in interpreting them. As described earlier, the eurocentric view also in archaeological investigations was predominant until recently (see section 2.1), leading to misinterpretations and a distorted views of Aboriginal history and life. Since the

Europeans who conquered Australia had their own ideas about how human beings should behave and function, they judged the Aborigines' by these same standards. Heaps of valuable information, probably only obtainable at the time of the early encounters have been lost forever. Some, more useable ethnographic reports of that time consider the Aborigines to be an homogenous group without, referring to local variations. Nevertheless, some basic, commonly applicable information about the "traditional Aboriginal society" shall be given in the following documentation.

It can be stated that the Aborigines, in general, seemed to have had strong ties to their land, which has often been wrongly interpreted as them living in harmony with nature (See settlement and subsistence). Many places and objects in their nearby environment are declared sacred either because of legends or events that might have taken place at the respective location. Each single Aboriginal group has a complex social system comprising several different controlling factors (Tindale 1974:16ff/30ff). Most important is the social role of a person within the tribes, skin, or language groups, which is traditionally determined. In Aboriginal Australia kinship was the main measure for all social interaction (Tindale 1974:14-15). The kinship system established a network of interpersonal relations within a unit. In Aboriginal society kinship was not a pure accidental phenomenon, rather it was determined by complicated marriage practices. The elders or respective parents decided on future marriages that were set up long before the actual offspring reached a marriageable age. Self-determined marriages lowered the status of the respective persons and were often accompanied by severe sanctions. (See below about birth control) Each marriage has to be seen in terms of reciprocity between two groups and not just as an exchange between men and women. A marriage represents the exchange of gifts, rights and privileges, obligations and responsibilities (Tindale 1974:16ff;Keen 1988:82ff).

Also gender and age are considerable factors in the network of behavioral patterns. In order to avoid incest there are several avoidance taboos between siblings of the opposite sex. Furthermore there are other sex-related restrictions to avoid rivalries. In general the status and authority of a person rises proportionally to the age he/she reaches, even though some exceptions apply (Merlan 1988:15ff).

Especially interesting are the mechanisms of maintaining law and order within Aboriginal groups. Though the governing of Aboriginal Australia at large was unknown, a deliberate self-governing system was established for every Aboriginal group or tribe. There is, however, no law court with judiciary functions, which meets regularly. The jurisdiction is exercised for small delicts, by the family or the elders, for more severe delicts, by the tribal council and for inter-tribal issues, by the participants of the more or less formal discussions preceding or following inter-tribal ceremonies. Even though the existence of tribal councils as an overall feature is still under scientific discussion there have been several slight references to them in various ethnographic reports. These councils seem to have specifically handled those offenses that might have caused continued hostilities between tribal members of different groups seeking retaliation. Issues that arose in the

tribal council would be " murder, abduction of women, adultery, or raids on, or by, other tribes. " (Howitt 1904:351) Other issues handled by the tribal council include sorcery, incest, offenses against sacred rituals, or breaches of the moral code. One has to know, that all these examples represent breaches of Aboriginal law and might be punishable if found guilty, by death. Since the essence of Aboriginal maintenance of law and order is the prevention of uncontrolled retaliation often other reciprocal settlements are found. Some offenses including even death and injury might be compensated for through the exchange of women or goods. The judging council, in every single case has to decide if the compensation is adequate enough to equal the loss of the offended party. The leading positions in the council are held by the headman and the elders. Often ethnographic reports speak of the council of elders as being the de facto decision maker within a local group, but handling similar issues as mentioned above (After Howitt 1904:295-354).

Another important factor to be considered in Aboriginal custom and behavior was the carrying capacity of the respective area each group or tribe settled in. Except for the tropical north of Australia, where an abundance of wild food was at hand, most other regions were extremely arid and drought was a common occurrence (Kershaw 1981:81ff). Naturally, the Aboriginal population was controlled by the food recourses available, including storage practices, which in turn were related to water sources. This natural population control would imply a high number of deaths caused by famine in times of drought and a population increase in good years (See also Gray 1988:136). In order to break this deadly circle the Aborigines developed (regionally), very different techniques to control the number of their population. The most common and ideally practicable technique was the use of the already established system of marriage practices (Tindale 1974:16-17). When uniting older, already sterile female members of the group in marriage to young men, no offsprings could be expected. On the other hand preventive measures such as, the cutting of the urethra close to the root of the penis were known, so that the semen would spill out there instead of being introduced in the female vagina.

Though there are no exact demographic data of the Aboriginal population of Australia at the time of European arrival there are several estimated numbers. Elkin (1954:10-11) suggested that by 1788 the Aborigines would have numbered 300,000. Birdsell (1957:47ff) considering the maximum carrying capacity of Australia confirmed this estimate. In 1988 Graetz and McAllister (page 109) published a total number of 251,000 Aborigines, a number uncritically overtaken from Middleton (1987). Moreover, the last "estimate" is separated into the different Australian states and territories.

The health and life expectancy of Aborigines before the coming of the Europeans and Asians might also be of considerable interest. Furthermore, we move on the ground of speculations, albeit there were possibly no venereal diseases on the continent. Trachoma, leprosy as well as yaws, and boomerang legs may have been present. Since several European introduced diseases had decimated the Aboriginal population immensely, (See section 3.3;also Smith

1982:117ff) it can be stated that these diseases were unknown before, as no antibodies were inherent in the Aborigines' blood. The infant mortality rate in traditional Aboriginal population seemed to have been high. Also, a considerable amount of young men might have died through warfare. Nothing, on the other hand, contradicts the idea or belief that Aborigines reached the age of 60 or older, though this might have been seldom the case (Kirk 1981:1804-09;Tindale 1981:1863).

A final remark may be devoted to the educational system in traditional Aboriginal society. Imitation of adult activities in childplay may have been the main learning pattern. An early division of gender related activities was made in pairing the girls with the women and the boys with the men. In some tribes no formal teaching by adults was practiced at all, while others learned through narrations of older men and women. The initiation ceremony was then the final educational step where last secrets were uncovered and the person was treated as an adult (Refer also to Willmot 1988:244ff).

3.3 Changes within the first 100 years of occupation

Although it is well known that Captain James Cook did not "discover" Australia, no one is absolutely sure who actually did. There is still an ongoing, historical dispute between Portugal, Spain, France, and the Netherlands. However, in 1625 (40) and 1688 (41) the first Europeans arrived on Australian soil. It is assumed, however, that these dates did not have a strong impact on the Australian Aboriginal culture. It should not be omitted though, that, from at least 1650, onwards fisherman from the islands of Indonesia made annual visits to the northern coast of Australia. Most of them were Marcassars from the southern part of the Island Sulawesi. The influence of the Marcassars can be seen in the work of contemporary Aboriginal tribes in the northern part of Australia (pottery, glass, harpoons, dugout canoes, metal knives).

It was not until 1770 that Capt. Cook claimed Australia as a property of the King and Great Britain (Wharton 1968:300ff). The settlement of Australia in the following years never would have taken place so rapidly if North America had not declared its independence from the British Commonwealth in 1776. Since North America was lost as an outpost for the deportation of the numerous British criminals, King George III announced the removal of prisoners to the newly claimed country of Australia (Shaw 1974:1). In this way, Australia started out as a penal colony. Already in 1788 a convict settlement was established. Capt. Arthur Phillip was in command of the first fleet of English ships that sailed for Botany Bay in May of 1787 (Stone 1974:19). His order was to establish a self-supporting prison farm. Capt. Phillip

had 717 convicts plus soldiers to help keep order at the initial settlement. Only few free settlers came with the first fleet, albeit Capt. Phillip continuously asked for more convicts and free settlers to cultivate the Australian soil. When Phillip left Australia in 1792 he left 4322 people in the settlement he governed (Shaw 1974:6).

After the settling of the East Coast had "successfully" proceeded along, a second separate settlement was established in Western Australia in 1829, probably in order to forestall an eventual French settlement. Initially, the first settlers were asked by King George III to treat the indigenous people with fairness and respect due to all British subjects (Stone 1974:19). Maybe it was because the Aborigines were not literate and had no obvious social organization, that they were looked upon as less than human (See also Rose 1988:10). As a result of this composed declaration, the land of Australia was classified as desert and unoccupied, Terra Nullius (Definition Cook), the land belonging to no one. What proceeded to happen in the conflict between the Europeans and the indigenous Australians, happened to almost every nation that had the dubious opportunity of being discovered by the Europeans. The Aborigines were slaughtered whenever they were spotted, and the tensions between both parties increased in direct proportion to the settlers' greed for more land. But there was also another reason, why the settlers felt they had the right to murder the Aborigines. In traditional Aboriginal culture every Aborigine had the right to hunt on his own tribal land. The settlers had brought with them sheep and cattle and the Aborigines hunted and killed the stock as they had the kangaroos. In retaliation whole massacres began, in excess wiping out all Tasmanian Aborigines (Reynolds 1982:159-69).

Was the primary interest of the first European colonists to establish a prison camp in order to get rid of the numerous, often political, British prisoners, changes occurred in the years to follow. Starting in 1808 the number of convicts sent to Australia was constantly being reduced also in 1838 and in 1848 respectively in Tasmania, the deportation ceased altogether (Nicholas, Shergold 1988:25). The settlement within Australia's interior between 1830 and 1875 through free settlers culminated in the most radical expulsion and extermination policy of the Europeans (Stone 1974:27). A decisive factor, which helped jump-start the rapid immigration to Australia, was the gold rush in California (1848) and Alaska which made many people think they could also find gold in Australia (Irving 1974:188). Within 10 year gold rush period the population of the State of Victoria, for example, increased from 77000 to 540000 (Census data). Though gold finds were soon exhausted most of the people stayed farmers (Knott 1988:48).

By 1875 80% of continental Australia was opened for settlement, leaving only a few parts in North and Central Australia for the indigenous Australian population to habitate. Most preferred to settle in the regions today known as Victoria, Tasmania, New South Wales, Queensland and parts of South Australia (Knott 1988:49). The main strategy of this radical phase of European settlement can be initially described as "eliminating the elite and enslave the guideless rest" (See also Bayne 1988:214). Since Aborigines were of

---

(40) 4th of June 1626 the Dutch merchant ship "Batcura" under the command of Captain Francis Pelgagert
(41) 1688/1691 Wiliam Dampier at the West Coast of Australia

no use as slaves (See next part) the elimination of all Aborigines was decided upon (Stone 1974:36-38). Alongside, the beneficial characteristics of Australia for the Commonwealth became obvious. On the one hand Australia was seen as a trading outpost and resource provider for the aristocratic class in Great Britain, while on the other hand the British citizens, who had little or no rights sought to own property in Australia. Conveniently, European law in Australia did not recognize any legal rights of the Aboriginal people to their tribal land (Bayne 1988:213ff). There seems to have been little evidence of European knowledge or concern about the relationship of the Aborigines to their tribal lands and sacred places.

Even today it is widely believed by many people in Australia that there was little or no resistance to the European occupation of Aboriginal, tribal land (Bayne 1988:212;Reynolds 1982:61-127). Although the Europeans fired upon the Aborigines at the slightest hint of hostility justifying their deeds through the term "pacification by force" the first official recording of Aboriginal resistance was in 1841 (Reynolds 1982:78/79). This attack was supposed to avenge the constant shooting of Aborigines by "cedar getters". Today several scientists agree that the Aboriginal resistance was vigorous and of guerrilla-type since their traditional weapons were no match for the settlers' armament (Reynolds 1982:61-127). Additionally, Aboriginal social organization did not include organized warfare and alliances with other tribes (See also Gumbert 1984). Officially, Aboriginal shootings did not take place, not other than for the Aboriginals pacification, and resistance was not offered at all. Between 1850 and 1860 the Native Police Force was established, comprised solely of young Aborigines bribed with money, food, clothes, and eventual education. The Aboriginal Fighting Force was used against officially non-existing Aboriginal resistance (Reynolds 1990:41-84,esp.48).

At this point in history the world did not seem to care much about the events in Australia at all, although the Aborigines were dying out so that often only small detribalized remnants were left (Middleton 1987:Table 9.1;Graetz/McAllister 1988:109). However not only did war reduce the Aboriginal population, also European introduced diseases like syphilis, pulmonary disease, tuberculosis, small pox, influenza, measles, and whooping cough (Basedow 1925:210, Berndt 1964:18). Estimated, though sometimes amazingly securely stated (Middleton 1987:Table 9.1), demographic data are available. At the time of settlement in 1788 between 250,000 - 300,000 Aborigines were present on the Australian continent with about 500 tribes ranging in size from 100 - 1500 members (Stevens 1970:364). By 1900, only 67,000 were left (Graetz/McAllister 1988:108;Radcliffe Brown 1930:696;see also Encel 1970:137).

3.4 Later changes

In the middle of the 19th century the colonies of Australia were independently governed. It was not until 1901 that the Commonwealth of Australia was established (Crowley 1974:260). It took another 66 years to install a common Aboriginal politics. Up to 1967 every single colony and later state used to handle "native politics" differently. It is beyond the scope of this thesis to show these differences, instead commonly applied criteria will be mentioned.

Aboriginal protection acts were founded between 1860 (South Australia) and 1910 (Northern Territory) on the one hand, stating the Aborigine's existence and trying to improve their living conditions adversely affected by the Europeans, but on the other hand to segregate them and when placed on missions to religiously re-educate (brain-wash) them (Graetz/McAllister 1988:108). Since so called fringe dwellers were a thorn in the urban European people's side, reserves and missions occurred to be a fast solution to this problem (Reynolds 1990:131/135). These reserves would probably have never been established if the Australian Aborigine would have been of any use as a slave. But slavery and any kind of imprisonment (See section 3.5) of Aboriginal people lead to a rapid decline in their health conditions and often to death (Aboriginal death in custody report 1988;see also Reynolds 1982:140-43). Not having the legal authorization to kill the Aborigines, but urgently needing cheap labor for the flourishing Australian economy, the Aborigines were put away on reserves and missions. More than 60,000 South Sea Islanders, used as slaves (only in Queensland), helped to establish the Australian sugar industry (Australian South Sea Islanders Report Feb.1991:6 - Price 1988:124 contradicts these numbers). It is interesting to note that the South Sea Islanders received citizenship earlier and still have a more respectable status than do Aboriginal people in Australian society today (See also section 3.6). This is proof that the denial of the Aboriginal people is not solely color related. The author should mention though, that "the South Sea Islanders are politically discriminated against because they are not eligible for benefits available to Australian Aboriginals" (Australian South Sea Islanders Report Feb. 1991:10). The establishment of missions and reserves started a new, dark chapter of forced Aboriginal assimilation into westernized culture. The encouragement of Aborigines to adopt the western way of life and its beliefs rather than holding onto their own cultural values was enforced through absolute control of individual life from birth to death (Reynolds 1982:141). Control was reached and confirmed daily through Employers/Protectors Rights, marriage laws, as well as detailed instructions on how to behave on the reserves or missions (See also Broom et al. 1980:180). This so called "act", refers to the Aboriginal Protection and Restriction of the Sale of Opium Act of 1867, updated in 1901 with subsequent amendments in 1927, 1928, and 1934. Specifically of interest are the act of 1901, section 12, 12(2), and 33, the acts of 1939 section 19(1b), and the act of 1934 section 24 restricting the present, commonly accepted right of the free choice of occupation, equal employment, standardized salaries, and unrestrained marriages. These rights, if you consider colonial history as quite lenient measures of force were obviously never thought to improve the living conditions of Aboriginal people.

The actual outcome of the reserve and mission strategy was characterized by low level education, poor health standards, housing and hygiene, unemployment, loss of religion, lack of any incentive, break-down of families, despair and the constant denial of any right to take part in decision making. The

Aborigines listlessly drifting through life were most susceptible to vices like alcohol, glue sniffing, and other drugs (Graetz/McAllister 1988:108). Unfortunately, for the colonial settlers, the birth rates initially inclined, then declined, and inclined again (Graetz/McAllister 1988:109). Other ways had to be found to reduce this constant nuisance. Stating, that the Aborigines were unfit to take care of their children, they were taken away and put in other reserves or in homes. Part Aboriginal children, in particularly were taken in the hope of "breeding-out" characteristic Aboriginal features (See also Reynolds 1990:174-83). Many of these children were taken only a few month after birth (Koori News July 17, 1991:23) and did not have the chance to get to know their original families (Reynolds 1982:149; Bayne 1988:215), nor were they allowed to have contact to full blooded Aborigines. These children were taught to feel ashamed of their traditional culture and heritage. Being illtreated over so many years it is not astonishing that even after the abolishment of the "act" many of the "half-casts" (Refer to Reynolds 1990:119-127), as they were called, denied their Aboriginality and called themselves Indian or Greek Refer to interview section, question 2).

Also Aborigines were made to feel inferior to European Australians, many of them imitated a westernized life-style, wearing western clothes, fixing their hair in similar ways, as well as developing a desire for things that were absolutely useless to them before (See also Reynolds 1982:209). They worked as stockmen or domestics on the farms of European landowners, and they continued to do so after their legal rights were confirmed (Reynolds 1982:159ff/1990:85-127,esp.105). Davis and Encel remarked in 1965 on this phenomenon:" It is apparent that in many parts of Australia the Aborigines earliest contacts were with men interested in them as source of cheap labor and sexual services and that, in general, the natives fulfilled the demands in order to obtain European commodities." (Davis, Encel 1965:281)

Though one might think that the Aborigines were put in those areas, which were absolutely useless to the Australian economy, later industrial developments rejected this idea. Had the gold rush already interfered with established Aboriginal territories ? The diamond, opal, bauxite, and uranium findings drove Aborigines from once lawfully provided areas also (e.g. Tatz 1982;Baldock 1974:80).

Having historically reached the end of the colonial epoch, which still has its implications in modern Australian society it might be appropriate to explicitly state the economical and social changes in the Aboriginal life-style. The economical existence as hunters and gatherers was forcefully hindered since it did not correspond to the stationary subsistence of the European settlers. Even occasional hunting trips were soon abandoned. The women stopped the gathering of local food and began to rely rather, on the distributed rations of the newly introduced food (Stone 1974:103). The traditional social organization broke apart since old tribal communities were decimated and resettled often in areas of former rival tribes. Also, the traditional marriage system was forbidden and clergically supervised. Robbed of their traditional culture, the Aborigines did not have another alternative other

than to submit to the westernized way of life, since they were also forced with political and economic dependency.

3.5 Recent changes - todays conditions

In the mid nineteen thirties the notion of a "treaty" relationship with the Aborigines was clearly a contrast to the actual law and what the common practice was, which previously had been applied to the Australian colonies. Even today, the legacies of these 19th century attributes and the law, which grew around them, can provide complexities, which may come as close to seeming as insolvable as they were a century or more ago.

In a 1951 meeting between the Commonwealth and State Minister of Australia, it was decided that the future policy should be directed towards making Aborigines Australian citizens, since Australias image was suffering as a protector of overseas minority rights (Stone 1974:193-200;Bell 1983:1-19). In 1969 the Aborigines received the non-compulsory right to vote. If full-blooded Aborigines thought they could manage their own affairs they could apply for citizenship, though the procedures of this application were protracted and difficult. People who were part Aboriginal received citizenship automatically (Graetz/McAllister 1988:110).

An admittably abstractive view of the problems that arose in the interplay of the Aboriginal and westernized culture might be entitled "suction effect" (Fig. 9). Envisioning the westernized culture as strong and the Aboriginal one as weak, which does not imply any judgment about quality, only considers the obvious direction of assimilation, a clear process is perceptible. The strong culture, now basically in full possession of the country [42] including governing and legislation, as well as, judicial (law enforcement), influences the weak culture immensely. Since the weak culture did not produce any in the strong culture's perspective measurable goods, it was even morally and esthetically classified as weak (See also Reynolds 1982:140-44). The moral and legislative turn-around for the salvation of this weak culture seems to be only an auxiliary construct to keep a culture alive, which will definitely be engulfed by the stronger one somewhere along the line. The strong culture willingly or unwillingly exerts power over the minds and behavior of the weak culture through their cultural achievements (43),vices (like alcohol), diseases, advice, their products, etc., and gradually closes the gap between them. The money support by the government

----

(42) Except the areas that were set aside especially in the Northern Territory, these areas have no economic value and this includes tourism.
(43) Also important is the evaluation of those achievements. To be proud of the material or intellectual items produced might adversely effect the evaluation and understanding of items produced by other cultures.

Suction Effect

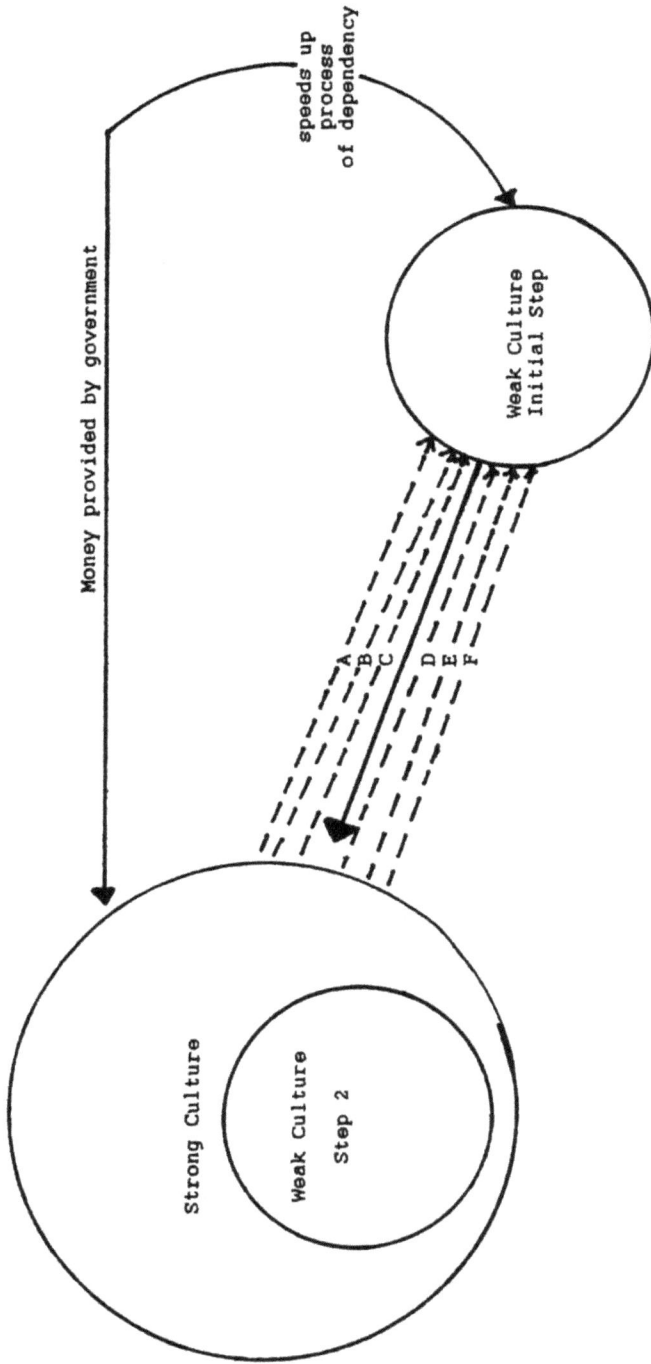

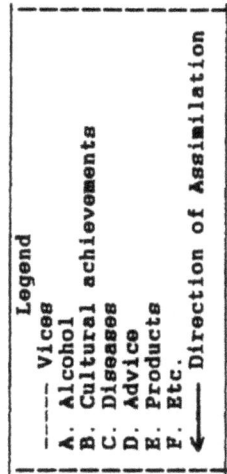

Fig.10 Suction effect

Page 41

Legend
----- Vices
A. Alcohol
B. Cultural achievements
C. Diseases
D. Advice
E. Products
F. Etc.
——— Direction of Assimilation

Money provided by government

speeds up
process
of dependency

Weak Culture
Initial Step

A
B
C
D
E
F

Strong Culture

Weak Culture
Step 2

and the equal opportunity policy (44) speeds up the process of dependency of the weak culture towards the stronger one. The initially self- sufficient culture is now on its way to becoming a part of the strong culture. This way has no return. The weak culture might maintain its special status, but only within the system of the stronger culture. All efforts to strengthen the weak culture, as for example through rectifying writings of westerners by Aboriginal people or institutions acknowledging and working towards the Aboriginal rights act within a system that the stronger culture established. A return to the original state of Aboriginal culture seems neither possible nor wanted. Aborigines were not only brought economically into absolute dependency. Having had taste of westernized vices, many Aborigines spent their whole paychecks or unemployment benefits on desirable goods, often carelessly neglecting essential needs for food and other necessities.

In order to end this "unpleasant state" of drunk Aboriginal people hanging around liquor places and other parts of villages and towns the "two kilometer law" was established in the Northern Territory (O'Connor 1983/84:201-7). This amendment to the Summary Offenses Act made it an offense for any person to consume alcohol in a public place within a two-kilometer radius of licensed premises.

Though the intention of this law was addressed to anyone who stood in the Northern Territory, it primarily affected the Aboriginal people. Another negative side effect of alcohol dependency, as well as, the high unemployment rate (Graetz/McAllister 1988:111)) was the steady rising rate of crime among the Aboriginal population. The imprisonment rate of Aboriginal people is 16 times higher than that of white Australians and about 775 out of 100,000 Aboriginal people will be imprisoned. Though mostly minor offenses like the inability to pay for fines caused the imprisonment, the Aboriginal people are the world's most jailed people. Maybe its because of the alcoholic drying-out effect or the direct effects of imprisonment, that the death rate of Aborigines in prison is 50 % higher than for white Australians, so Aboriginal imprisonment for minor offenses seems to be ambiguous (Aboriginal death in custody report 1988).

Also in the 20th century, employment strategies seem to have had little in common with equal opportunity employment (Altman 1988:203/Census data). Although Aborigines amount to only 1.4 % of the total Australian population (Price 1988:124) they comprise 4.2 % of the unemployed (Graetz/McAllister 1988:111). The total unemployment rate is officially stated as 30 - 40 % albeit the number of undetected cases might be a lot higher. If employed, the Aboriginal person has to face low salaries (Graetz/McAllister 1988:110) and seven day-week jobs often with 12 - 13 hours of work. Little reason is needed to fire an Aboriginal person (Personal communication with Aboriginal stockmen, Santa Teresa).

In more recent years, Aboriginal people have increasingly gotten a lobby within the European Australian population (Graetz/McAllister 1988:113). There has to be a clear distinction made between those people, who honestly try to help and others, who are more interested in the Aboriginal culture because of their own monetary benefit. In times of deep recession, the backbone of the Australian economy seems to be tourism. Most European Australians are well aware that most of the wealth obtained through tourism is because of the Aborigines. As long as the tourists were attracted to the Aboriginal image of Australia, ways had to be found to economically exploit the tourists' desire most efficiently.

Two main Aboriginal goods are touristically of interest, their art and their land. Expectedly, one neither finds an Aborigine selling his/her own art in the local galleries in Central Australia, nor working as a tour guide, not to mention lecturing at the university. Although Aboriginal paintings, bush tucker, and artifacts are the life-line (bread-line) of Alice Springs, the indigenous Australians are usually seen sitting outside of the air-conditioned shops that sell their culture. Since Ayers Rock in the Uluru National Park as well as other natural phenomena (Simpson Gap, Katharina Gorge, Devils Marbles) were tourist attractions, reserves were either planned around them or a return of these areas was bound by a lease to the government for at least 99 years. The annual rental fee of A$ 75,000 as well as 20 % of the gross park entrance fee might seem like a lot of money for the Aborigines, but no one has ever shown them how to use this money most efficiently so consequently, a lot of people rip them off or the money is spent for unnecessary goods (alcohol, sweets)[Altman 1988:207].

Health and education are other major issues that arise when talking about Aboriginal culture today. The life expectancy of an Aboriginal male is 48 -61 years compared to 72 years for white Australian men. For Aboriginal women it is 57 - 65 years compared to 79 years for white Australian females (Census data 1988;see also Thomson 1988:249). "Even though official statistics were unavailable until 1971, it was evident that Aborigines were substantially disadvantaged in a variety of ways relative to whites. In the area of health they experienced levels of infant mortality more akin to the underdeveloped world than an advanced industrial society." (Graetz/McAllister 1988:108) In fact the infant mortality rate represented one of the worst in the world. The infants especially were the greatest sufferers. Growth retardation, hearing loss, vitamin and mineral deficiencies, gastroenteritis, respiratory tract infection, leprosy, influenza, measles, and significant levels of malnutrition were directly related to poor housing, inadequate sanitation, poverty, insufficient water supplies, hygiene, as well as discrimination and social pressure. (Aboriginal Health Bulletin, Feb. 1988/The Medical Journal of Australia 1986, 144:55-8) The Henderson Report from 1975 stated that 50 % of the Australian Aborigines were living below the poverty line and under 20 % above it and that the health standards of the Australian Aborigines were among the worst in the world (See also Graetz/McAllister 1988:108).

Though medical services have improved, i.e. World Flying Doctors Services, limited education about health and nutri-

---

(44) Equal opportunity if judged by western standards

tion (Graetz/McAllister 1988:111), restricted food choices, unsatisfactory living conditions (Smith/Biddle 1975:61-67) as well as high rates of alcohol abuse are still limiting factors in Aboriginal health standards. In contrast to traditional (See section 3.2), education in colonial times was mostly the duty of the church. The missionaries attempted to educate the Aborigines in the way of the British Empire and Christianity. Though the education was limited and the world view taught, extremely distorted, the Aborigines acquired at least some formal education. The positive side effect has been, that the older Aboriginal generation often speaks sufficient English, a language desperately needed to deal with the modern Australian society. They also have quite a reasonable knowledge of geography and basic mathematics. The younger generation, especially in rural areas, on the other hand does not seem to have the desire and motivation to go to school (Personal experience. Refer to interviews, see also Thomson 1988:248).

Among other things, the Whitlam government provided money for teachers, who were willing to teach Aboriginal children in the communities often in remote areas (Gayle 1988:243). The motivation for those teachers to go to such communities was often the high salary rather than an ideological perspective. The author of this thesis does not want to judge the qualification of these teachers, but after talking to several, it is obvious that most of them would gladly leave if they found employment in the cities. In the end it suffices to state that Australia has been reprimanded twice for their treatment of the Aborigines (United States. House of Representatives. Committee on Foreign Affairs; Senate Committee on Foreign Relations. Country Reports on Human Rights Practices for 1979;96th Congress, 2d Session, February 4, 1980:427-29. Country Reports on Human Rights Practices, 97th Congress, 1st Session, February 2, 1981:561-564. Country Reports on Human Rights Practices for 1981, 97th congress, 2d Session, February 1982:533-56).

3.6 Own experiences/common view

Since the Aboriginal status was and is created by white Australians it was of special interest to investigate their attitude towards Aboriginal people. This investigation has to be seen in the broader complex of a changing Aboriginal society and proportionally, the Aborigines view of an archaeological enterprise. The white Australian's attitudes towards Aborigines are a direct indicator of the main trend in the Aborigine's assimilation process. The following questions were thought to investigate the white Australians general point of view in :

1. Do you like Aborigines ?
   a) How many Aboriginal friends do you have ?

2. Would you marry an Aborigine ?
   a) Other people considered as "black" (i.e. African, Caribbean ,etc.)

3. Would your friends or family support you ?

4. Where did you obtain your knowledge about Aborigines ?
   a) School -- teaching method

b) TV, friends, books
c) Studies -- discipline

5. Do you think that the traditional way of Aboriginal life is desirable (for them/for you) or is it a relic of the past ?

6. Do you think there is a black movement/awareness (reinforcing) ?

7. What is your opinion about the monetary support for Aborigines, i.e. grants, alcohol programs ?

8. Do you think that your way of thinking might be different from the Aboriginal one ?

The interview situation experienced here was not quite comparable to the one observed while interviewing Aboriginal people especially those living in the communities. The main body of interviews took place on the interviewees premises, where electricity was provided and where little background noise disturbed the recordings. Forty interview partners were easily found and they all gladly answered the questions since the "Aboriginal problem" (Informant No.4) was constantly on their mind. Before the author presents the main results of the interviews, the author will acquaint the reader with some other survey results concerning the attitudes of white Australians towards Australian Aborigines.

In 1964 Fay Gale noted that the " attributes prevalent amongst members of the white community were found to vary considerably with individuals, their place of abode, their age and their personal experiences " (Gale 1964:332) Prejudices worsened amongst residents of smaller towns, older and less educated people, and those, whose economic status had been depressed. Philip, who did a study in 1958 found the most biased people to be the employers, rather then the working people of a community. J.S.Western pointed out that "the attitudes of Australian whites to Aboriginal Australians could be probably most accurately be described, until very recent times, as one of indifference. The Aborigines were no economic threat. It would be hard to conceive of one's daughter as likely to marry one and one would be unlikely to find an Aboriginal taking up residence next door. Indeed, for the majority of Australians the Aborigines were not as visible as their counterpart, the American Indians. Their fate was of no greater concern." (J.S.Western 1983:53)

In contrast to the present study Graetz and McAllister stated that almost 50% of the Australian population "would not be uneasy if a close relative married an Aboriginal" (Graetz/McAllister 1988:112, also Table 4.19). The present investigation confirmed most of the previous results, but noted a general worsening in the negative opinions expressed. The most positive reply to question No.1 was: "we like those, we have met" (No.78), while several others expressed that they would have a slight prejudice against Aborigines (No. 1, 27, 31), few interviewees answered strictly with "no" (No.7, 28). Over 50 % of the interview partners have no Aboriginal friends or even acquaintances, while only 6 % of the interviewees have 3 or more Aboriginal friends. The differences in culture, as well as the physical appearance, would hinder at least 92 % of the white Australians asked at least to marry a full-blooded Aborigine. None of the interviewees would find support from their families if they did so. Forty-one % of the informants, on the other hand, could imagine a possible marriage with other people considered to be black, but still would find little support from their families (Contradiction to Graetz/McAllister 1988:113, Table 4.20). Knowledge about Aborigines and Aboriginal culture seems to have been majorly obtained through TV, the school, and personal experience. As expected no white Australian informant would be willing to cope with the traditional way of Aboriginal life. Although most of the informants pointed out that the traditional life-style is a relic of the past and Aborigines should proceed in adapting to the "commonly accepted" (No.9) Australian society, some interviewees saw the importance of Aboriginal cultural values. Informant No. 8 expressed it as follows: "It is a very relative part to them, but the only way it is relative for the white Australians is for tourism. People take photos of them or buy their art, but they are not interested in the culture, especially not in the traditional because it is not genuinely promoted by the tourist bureau. You can't take it away from the Aborigines, it's like taking my Christian belief, but I couldn't live like them." It is widely believed that the Aborigines today adapt far easier to society than a few years ago, where there "have been some nasty eruptions". (No.11) Most anger and negative feelings were expressed in the answers of question No. 6. The following two answers can be seen as representative of the other 38 interviews: "I think it is good if it goes to a positive source. I think it should go towards education programs, housing, and so on, not just giving them money, a check or something like that, because a lot of them spend it on things that are not socially desirable. Some came in a state of disrepair, I would like to see them as people to respect and admire, but they haven't shown much success in going the white man's way. You put them in alcohol programs, they come out and drink again. I wouldn't really mind them if they would wash every now and then, and maybe wear some shoes." (No.35) " You give them property, 5 - 6 month it is nothing productive coming out. If this goes on, it can just get worse for Australia. You give them money, they buy alcohol. Every station that has been handed over to them has been a disaster. We would like to see them economically compete with other stations." (No.21)

It was quite interesting at the end of the interview that most white Australians acknowledged that the Aborigines are not very materialistic or ambitious (No.35), while they on the other hand, would need to obtain things, to grow, and produce (No.17).

In order to sum up the outcome of the interviews it has to be mentioned that many Australians are poorly educated and out of work, the whole country is in a very depressed state and, maybe, because of that, a large number of people focus their anger and frustration on the Aborigines, who receive governmental help even though they seldomly pay taxes. The large amount of money given to non-Aborigines finds no consideration. Though most European Australians seem to have a feeling of guilt about the way Aborigines have been historically treated, they think all possible means of help have been given to the Aborigines, and all have failed. Since other black people in Australia are accepted in all social activities and enjoy a very high status, it can be assumed that the prejudices shown are not color related, but are a cultural problem. The following prejudices were common through the whole of Australia.
Aborigines :

- are dirty, drunk, illiterate, ignorant
- get money from the government and spend it on alcohol
- are given land from the government and don't develop it
- are not biologically fit to handle alcohol

3.7 Summary, conclusions

The status of Aboriginal people has changed considerably throughout time. They were unable to traditionally determine their status themselves, and so in the end it became increasingly foreign determined. The western colonization of Australia was a process of cultural change which mainly had negative effects on the indigenous people. The only possible and offered way of survival was the total abandonment of their traditional culture for the benefit of the forcefully imposed westernized one.

Not only did the Aboriginal people increasingly lose their cultural identity, they also partially ended a process of successful knowledge conservation, the oral tradition. An ever shrinking number of mainly old people handed down their knowledge of traditional Aboriginal culture and values to a younger generation that was taught to feel ashamed of their Aboriginality. The motivation to keep up with this more than a hundred years old tradition reached its lowest point with the beginning of the 20th century and was only partially restored in the most recent years (See section IV).

Robbed of their traditional way to pass on information about their cultural heritage, the westernized culture did not offer an alternative, since ideologically undermined educational programs were prevailing and modern education is admittably positive, but might come too late to support the conservation of an already lost traditional, cultural knowledge. An important step towards such a conservational process would be the absolute recognition of Aborigines as an integral part of modern Australian society, since displacement is a commonly recognized feeling of Aboriginal people.

One of the main problems still is, no matter how successful the majority of the Aborigines will become (successful as judged by western standards) they will be measured by the few, who do not follow suit.

3.8 Futuristic views

It is always difficult to predict the possible advancement or retrogression of a whole culture since a variety of factors are involved, which might reduce any speculation to absolute absurdity. A main trend, however, which is clearly recognizable seems to be the continuation of the historical assimilation process as outlined earlier. Oral tradition, i.e. the dreamtime stories will still be passed on from generation to generation, but start to lack any deeper meaning, since they are seldom understood in their entirety. Path is given to a wide array of interpretations. The same is valid for paintings or, archaeologically interesting, for tool manufacturing of any kind. If paintings had and still have a more artistic value, incorporating events passed on through dreamtime stories, then tools were primarily thought to be functional. Today both of these traditionally valid presumptions lack any basis. Paintings are touristically produced, displaying dreamtime motifs, often only artistically applied or reproduced, without sensing their delicate testimony.

Tools, if boomerangs, digging sticks, or stone tools, have lost their practical use and, as such, will be produced only by those, who see an economic value in them. Today's production often lacks functionally determined productional sequences, but shows deliberate performance for the buyer's eye (see also Reynolds 1988:201). Although the Aborigines seem not to receive the main profit in the art sales, so they know about their economic value. The author personally does not think that the process of an increased loss of cultural identity as well as traditional knowledge and values will come to a standstill or is reversible. The Aborigines will or already have lost the sense for their traditional way of life and with it gave up their inherited dreamtime stories in their original meaning.

The upcoming and reinforcing cultural awareness (See part IV) might try to reestablish a tradition, which has never been existent in the newly promoted way. Only archaeology might be able to set the record right through clearly probative methods (See part IX). Unfortunately, archaeology has no lobby in Australia and is often misinterpreted as a subdiscipline of anthropology, which Aborigines have lost their respect for (Refer to interviews, question 2). One of the main obstacles for providing the Aboriginal movement with a valid historical base is the unjustified animosity by Aboriginal people towards archaeology as well as their inflexibility to modern scientific results.

4. CULTURAL AWARENESS AND ASSERTIVENESS

4.1 Black movement

Since the main problem in Australia is not a color related one (Refer to section 3.4:115), the term Aboriginal movement might seem to be more appropriate for the subtitle of this section. The Aborigines, on the other hand, clearly identify their movement with that of the United States years ago and try to organize it in a similar way (Jennett 1988:230). Concerning this point, it is also interesting to note that the Australian Aborigines as well as few Maoris want to establish a connection between themselves and the American Indians. While some Maoris believe to be descendants of the American Indians some Aborigines believe that the American Indians came from them (Personal communication).

In the 1960s Australia saw a significant increase in political activities by organized Aboriginal groups giving the Aboriginal people more power and thereby introducing many other helpful groups and organizations (Thomson 1988:251-52), which forced a closer look into better education projects for Aborigines (Willmot 1988:247). The 60s, as well as, the 80s, marked the beginning of a new era of Aboriginal community controlled adult education. There was, however, a small amount of government provision in addition to private funds, which helped develop a number of educational projects in Aboriginal communities (Refer to Foley/Flowers 1990).

One of the most spectacular, and probably the movement initiating Aboriginal activity, was the formation of the Aboriginal Tent Embassy on the 22nd of January 1972 (Middleton 1987:359). It was erected directly in front of the House of Parliament. The catalyst for the tent embassy was the fact that the campaign for land rights in federal territories suffered a distinct set back on Australia Day in 1972, when the Prime Minister Mc Mahon confirmed that the government would not legislate to change the present standing of the government (Jennett 1988:230). The reason for the embassy was to form a greater awareness for Aboriginal land rights and the stronger involvement of Aborigines in political institutions dealing with Aboriginal affairs (See also Perkins 1988:237). Although the tent embassy, which remained for 6 month and was then forcefully removed, did not accomplish much at once, it did have positive effects on future Aboriginal politics, as it drew world wide attention and made Gough Witlam promise Aboriginal land rights in the Northern Territory once his party was elected (Jennett 1988:230).

In the late 1980s and early 1990s several positive educational projects both controlled by Aborigines as well as Europeans have been established and most have schools started to offer Aboriginal history and culture courses, but it seems that they still do not do much to counteract all the hate and prejudice that has characterized European/Aboriginal relations. Only recently has the Commonwealth government placed Aboriginal adult education and training high on their agenda (Flowers 1990).

In Darwin, several art galleries are owned by Aboriginal people now, selling Aboriginal handicraft exclusively. Most of the Aboriginal health workers have passed through an intensive training in order to be valuable mediators between Aboriginal communities and local health institutions. More and more community councils are run by Aborigines, who also have the motivation and knowledge to fulfill such tasks. Some Aborigines have made use of the governmental policy to study at colleges and universities on the basis of grants, though some abuses of this system have been encountered (i.e. if a person is only 1/16th Aboriginal).

The main interest of Aboriginal people though is the claiming back of their traditionally owned land (Jennett 1988:231;Perkins 1988:238). As earlier mentioned (3.5) land claim processes are especially successful in economically useless areas. The government will always be reluctant to give up productive, densely populated and/or rich lands. Over 5 years ago Prime Minister Hawk promised to sign a "symbolic" treaty, which would recognize Australian Aborigines as the original owners of Australia. This has never been done since many people argued that future land claims would be harder to turn down (Developmental stages, refer to Perkins 1988:237).

At this point, it is of interest to clarify where and what the main forces of this movement are. Although the author has traveled to all states of Australia, with the exception of Western Australia and Tasmania, it would be impossible to mention all small, active Aboriginal groups in each state. To give an example, the politically, most active region and the least active one were chosen within the Northern Territory as subjectively experienced by the author. While especially middle-aged Aboriginal people and increasingly also younger people in and around Darwin demand and assert their rights, only the older generation in and around Alice Springs does so. Men and women are equally active in Darwin, but in Alice Springs the women especially push for changes. In both regions, generally those Aborigines that produce and sell art of all kinds (paintings, music, etc.) seem to be the main forces behind any Aboriginal movement.

The major question now is, if this movement is creating a new identity or is trying to restore traditional values. It is clearly recognizable that the Aboriginal movement today is trying to improve the living conditions of Aboriginal people within modern Australian society. For active Aboriginal groups it is important to know about legislative and administrative institutions and their most effective use with respect to how the Aborigines can benefit from them. By doing so, one would move beyond the traditionally applied measures of problem solving and decision making. Only in land claim processes does the claimant have to show proof of his/her historical title to the land. If there are no colonial records the claimant has to convince the court through profound knowledge of traditional dances, paintings, genealogies, etc. of the respective area. The claimant's knowledge has to correspond to anthropological, investigational results and has to be confirmed by an anthropologist (Refer to Bell 1986:20-9).

Applying this system, the traditional Aboriginal culture is assumed to be investigated in every area and the results obtained are valid. The author personally thinks that the modern court system needs unbiased and fixed data to base its decisions on and that this is the major reason why anthropologically obtained data have a legal character, though they might not display traditional reality. It is important to note that modern Aboriginal movement does not try to nor is it able to (See section 3.8) restore a traditional Aboriginal way of life, but rather tries to incorporate what is thought to be traditional values in modern Australian society.

4.2 National/International work up

In Australian newspapers or national broadcasting systems little is ever mentioned about Aboriginal interests and activities. It seems that the official policy of the general Australian media is not attempting to improve European Australian/Aboriginal relations (Jennett 1988:252). The considerably growing Australian film industry "uses" Aboriginal people to spice up some never ending soap operas with mysticism or to add some sort of realism to adventure movies moving beyond common imagination (Jennett 1988:252/53). Some Aboriginal music groups, even use these tricks.

The image of Aboriginal people sold to the consumer is only a tiny reflection of the real Aboriginal life-style which includes behavioral patterns and religion. Aboriginality is advertised and reduced to exhibitions and the performing arts as practiced today, as well as, the mystification of the anyhow mythic dreamtime stories. Visually unpleasant or consumer "uninteresting" themes like Aboriginal alcoholism, health and housing standards, etc. as well as their life experience, wisdom, and attempt to cope with modern society are barely considered or are not considered at all.

Publicly less effective than the mass media, since only locally receivable, are Aboriginal newspapers like the Koori Mail or the Aboriginal TV station Imparja. Though mainly Aboriginal people are reached, it has tried to acquaint the well-balanced reader/spectator with Australian politics and its effects on the Aboriginal community, Aboriginal activities and legal procedures. Although the "Aboriginal media" does not include far reaching historical or prehistorical perspectives, they do try to enhance the living conditions of Aboriginal people in modern society mainly through enlightenment (Jennett 1988:255).

Internationally, the Aborigines, their treatment, and their living conditions are a major subject of interest especially in the United States where a similar colonial history was experienced. Often Aboriginal artists are invited to the States; scholarships are given to Aboriginal students, and representatives of American Indian organizations give advice to Aboriginal communities (Koori Mail, Wed. July 17, 1991:23).

In Europe, more specifically in Germany, the main interest in Aboriginal people seems to be a curious one. Although they have been scientifically studied for years, the general public knows little about them, and Australia and its indigenous inhabitants still have a mystic and adventurous stigma. Only recently has the media started to do reports about Aborigines, their history, and future perspectives in modern Australia (e.g. PM 2/1992:16-22, 3/1992:28-34, 4/1992:88-94, 5/1992:90-96).

4.3 Evaluation of this movement

Generally, every movement towards equality and better living conditions can only be positive. What are criticized, are the measures taken to reach this state, as well as, any ideological background. As an archaeologist the author would have wished for a return to the past and would recommend for any future movement, a stronger involvement of archaeology, in establishing a true cultural identity rather than relying on a newly created one.

Though archaeology will never be able to indicate behavioral patterns in detail it is the only science which would develop unbiased data. Modern Aboriginal life-style as practiced in diverse Aboriginal communities should not generally exclude social science and judge researchers upon the mistakes made by colleagues in past years. Modern archaeology especially, has no lobby in Australia and is often mistaken for anthropology. Researchers should be allowed to preserve what is left of traditional knowledge. Excavations could clarify true Aboriginal history, a history, which might be lost otherwise, since older people, who might be able to confirm data, have died.

5. APPROACHING AN ABORIGINAL COMMUNITY

Anthropologists and, in some cases, archaeologists will be required to spend an extended period of time with the people whom they are studying, regardless of their specific interest. Before those scientists are able to impose themselves on the people whom they intend to visit, they have to pass one or more bureaucratic obstacles (offices/laws, etc.). These obstacles, their often sedate handling of applications and the regionally different evaluation criteria, frequently make months of intensive field work preparation null and void.

The important initial contact phase effusively praised by anthropological textbooks takes preference, in many cases, over institutions. The researcher aiming to conduct fieldwork, already has to rely on the previous introduction of workers from these institutions to the respective community. Unfortunately, this contact will not be established by members of the community to be studied, frequently not even by members of the same ethnic group. The community council or the tribal heads make their decision based on the information obtained from the institution. The scientist him/herself has no opportunity to bring forward his/her own vindication. This process either results in half-hearted approvals or rejections because of non-convincing introductions. Some researchers (personal communications) regretted that they had been approved rather than rejected since the community did not have any interest in their study or did not even know about its full extent, even though the institution had pretended great interest (in Australia the land council).

The author himself went to the land council in Darwin to obtain information about requirements, proposals (see also part 1.5), and personal references, in addition to the processing time of 8 to 10 weeks and decided to try it another way.

In New South Wales, a close relationship has already been established with some workers of the Aboriginal Health Department. This is a relationship that was thought to be extremely helpful in maintaining contact with Aboriginal communities in Arnhem Land and the semi-desert regions of Alice Springs. Other avenues in which to establish contacts would have been the Aboriginal Legal Service, the Aboriginal Employment and Training Branch of Commonwealth Employment Service, the churches, and the National Parks and Wildlife Services.

In order to give future researchers an idea of the obstacles to be faced along the way, individual experiences shall be mentioned subsequently giving scientists the opportunity to avoid those mistakes. The health workers in New South Wales recommended the author to health workers in Darwin. Upon arrival there, a very hostile climate was experienced, albeit no one knew the author or Ms. Buchanan personally. There was one health worker especially, who tried to influence the others in a negative way by greeting us extremely frostily. Her attitude (generally positive) was to consider the practical use of a research project - "How does your research benefit my people" -. This turned out to be meaningless since the author personally had the feeling that she made strong generalizations not only about scientists, but also about the wide array of Aboriginal tribes and communities. Her pride in enumerating her educational background and the 15 years of experience in the field of Aboriginal health, seemed particularly to predestine her to judge the scientists, their research purpose and the possible outcome for the Aborigines. To phrase it a little polemically the author would say she feels like a God-mother, who spans her protective arms over the under-aged Aboriginal people.

Unfortunately, this attitude was not a unique one. It was found by at least one person of every even least important institution handling the interests, or what was thought to be the interest, of the Aborigines. Questioning the church to establish contacts one has to face the ridicule of some pseudo-anthropologists, who require the proof of your scientific accreditation but cannot or are not willing to show proof of theirs. Often scientists have to face open verbal attacks and accusations, i.e. the judgment that a researcher might rather be after a nice vacation than a scientific goal.

Facing these hostile conditions one might consider the following approach commonly applied to the present research. At this point the author would like to take this opportunity to thank Ms. Buchanan, who established the necessary contacts by whom the following approach was made possible. With respect to this, it is important to know that anyone who has an invitation from an Aboriginal may visit him/her without any problem as long as an oral (45) or written (46) permission has been given. Ms. Buchanan, who talked to and interviewed Aborigines along the way, often got spontaneous invitations to visit other family members or to participate in community festivities. On one occasion, she even met the sister of the president of a community, dwelling along a dry river bed. The woman talked to her brother, who, in the same fashion happened to be passing by, at that very moment. The result was an official invitation to the community, even an introduction to and the participation in a council meeting.

On several occasions, Aboriginal hitchhikers were picked up, and were so glad to catch a ride (sometimes they stand for hours since no one likes giving them lifts) that an invitation to their community seemed to be an obligation.

----

(45) It is important to be able to state the name of the person in order to pass eventual controls either by the regular police or the Aboriginal police on the reservation

(46) The author personally would advise insisting on a written permission

Often it was hard to decide whether it was gratitude or the selfish interest to be driven home over sometimes, 200 km dirt roads that were off the main highways. Due the welcome received and interest experienced towards the present studies, the decision was made to leave after a few days or in some cases months.

In the following the author has developed a scheme (Fig. 11) comparing the common model and the theoretical (wishful) model to handle a researchers request to visit and investigate an Aboriginal community. The common model did not give the researcher the opportunity to introduce his/her research project to the community council unless the land council and community council decided so.

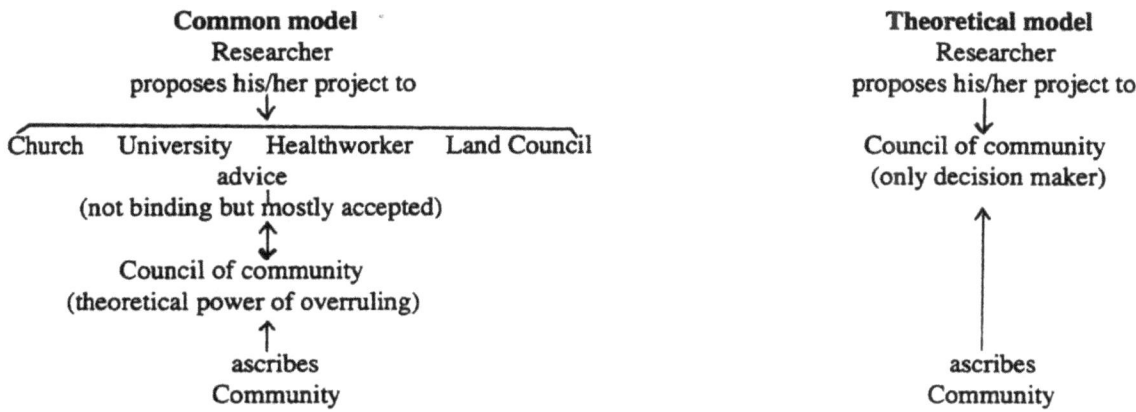

If the scientist finally has the permission to visit an Aboriginal community the following advice might be of interest. Before an approach is made to the community it is advisable to telephone someone or at least to have the name of a contact person to ask for on arrival (47). It makes no sense to try to conceal the actual reason for the researchers visit. As soon as the first interview takes place or pieces of the equipment are uncovered from some curious Aboriginal kids, which can be a real plague, the whole community will definitely know what this "stranger" has come for. It is easier said than done, to approach with sympathy and an open mind though your stay might temporarily be a real drag. Most importantly the researcher should always approach the relevant people (de facto decision-makers) of the commu-

Common model
Researcher
proposes his/her project to
↓

Church   University   Healthworker   Land Council
advice
(not binding but mostly accepted)
↕
Council of community
(theoretical power of overruling)
↑
ascribes
Community

Theoretical model
Researcher
proposes his/her project to
↓

Council of community
(only decision maker)

↑

ascribes
Community

Fig. 11 Common and theoretical model of application treatment

Theoretically the land council is thought to be the main institution that substantiates the scientist's application. Practically everyone, including the church, university, healthworkers, etc. has the same power concerning the communities they look after. The intention of these institutions is to advise the community council. The advice is not binding, but mostly is accepted. Seldom does it happen that the community council makes use of their theoretical power of overruling. The community council itself is ascribed by the community. The author would like to mention that he met few Aboriginal people when dealing with the church or the land council. Also the community council often consisted, next to the Aboriginal people, of one or two white Australians.

The theoretical model on the other hand works without the intermediate stage of the land council or other institutions. The researcher proposes his/her project directly to the community council, which is the only decision maker. By doing so, the Aboriginal people themselves have to decide how this project can benefit their community or the Aboriginal people in general. Unfortunately, such a model will not be workable since the Aboriginal communities are only theoretically self-governed, but practically bound to decisions of the land council or the Australian government due to economic dependency (see section III).

nity first and ask them for other people that might be interested in the research.

After the researcher investigates the "official opinion" it is always recommended that the scientist tries to contact and interview those people that the scientist has not been specifically introduced to. Such contact might be established when asking other informants for the person aiming to be interviewed. This approach might either awake the interest of the person the researcher obtained information from or result in a clear rejection to be involved in the scientific investigation. Personally, the author mostly experienced an increased interest that forced people to come up to Ms. Buchanan and ask why she was trying to obtain information about them.

Since every single Aboriginal community is different and has its unique features no other general advice can be given here, but it shall be referred to the anthropological/archaeological literature available for many communities from which valuable information can be obtained.

----

(47). An increasing number of communities now have a telephone

6. THE QUESTION CATALOGUE

The question catalogue as well as the stone tool experiments represent important tools in measuring the status of archaeological inquiry within Aboriginal thinking. The question catalogue will be the more theoretical evaluation of the main problem to be investigated in this thesis, while the stone tool experimental part will show the practical effects. Some results of the theoretical examination might even be testable through their practical imitation. Following the assumption that the questionnaire should not only incorporate solely archaeological questions (See section 1.1), but also themes of Aboriginal interest in order to raise the standard of the answers obtained, questions investigating the Aboriginal identification problem had to be included. As mentioned earlier (Section 1.4a), the catalogue was prepared once but has been continuously altered throughout the interviews. Though some questions were canceled others have been added. (See section 6b. Alterations)

It might be interesting to note, at this point, that only 11 of the 120 Aboriginal interview partners have allowed their names to be publicly stated in the present thesis. This statement opens a wide array of possible interpretations. Although the author believes that the reason for the requested name disclosure has purely been a practical one, (they did not want to be interviewed by anyone else, especially not a white person and no other than Ms. Buchanan), several other explanations are possible. One explanation model could even question in depth the honesty of the answers since a re-evaluation of the interviews through other researchers seems to be impossible.

The fact is that 120 Aboriginal people were interviewed, 103 by Ms. Buchanan and 17 by the author. A translator was needed 20 times, since an interview in English was not possible. 41 of the interview partners did not want to state their names and addresses at all, even though they were known by the author and the rest, only 11, were content with the normal name disclosure in the thesis. It was decided not to mention any names in the thesis but to number the interviews. The names of the interviewees as well as time and location of the interviews might be released to other researchers upon request. The same procedure will have to be executed with the tape recordings. 11 of the interviews can be obtained immediately and without any restrictions, but the release of the other 59 recordings needs the previous permission of the interviewees.

In the following, the reader will find the actual question catalogue used in most interviews as well as the mentioning of the prepared and added or altered questions. At the end a critical evaluation of the question catalogue will uncover eventual weaknesses in and provide suggestions for improvement.

General Questions

1) Tell me about the derivation and genesis of the Aborigines (or your tribe) as far as you know.

2) Where did your opinion/knowledge mainly derive from ?

> Newspaper___,
> scientific reports___,
> missionaries, traders, etc___,
> anthropologists___,
> (oral)tradition___,
> TV___, popular literature___,
> others (specify)___

3) Name one or two archaeologists/anthropologists that mainly worked on Australian Aborigines!

4) Do you think that prehistorical/historical research is important, even an integral part of your cultural awareness.

5) Do you think that future research might contradic your representation in some points or on principle, and is this research worth knowing or are you content with your point of view ?

Specific Questions

1) Do you know the use and/or meaning of these stone (bone, etc.) tools and do you still use similar ones in traditional or modern appearance ?   (Show photos or copies)

2) Are you able to manufacture some of the stone tools, if yes, would you prefer others with varying
> a) shape
> b) appearance
> c) weight

Produce simple tools to be used as
> 1) scraper,
> 2) hammer,
> 3) awl,
> 4) knife/blade,
> 5) projectile point

3) Do you think that Aborigines were the first people on earth, if yes, tell me why you think so ?

4) Do the people here of European descent have a desirable living style (also with respect to health care) or would you like to live in the traditional way and/or to maintain particular cultural values ? (please name them)

5) What do you expect archaeologists/anthropologists to do when studying your culture ?

6) Is today's archaeology/anthropology carried out in Australia, constructive or destructive concerning your cultural identity ?

7) How could these sciences be more supportive of you ?

8) In the following I would like to tell you how modern scientists (Archaeologists/anthropologists, etc.) explain the traditional form of Aboriginal culture. Please tell me why you think the theory or parts of it are wrong/right.

9) Should anthropologists be considered as expert witnesses in court?

10) Do you feel sufficiently recognized in Australian law, if not where are the major weaknesses ?

a) Prepared

When deriving the question catalogue, the author's main interest was the development of a set of questions fitting to focus on the main problem of the thesis. The questions had to cover archaeological as well as anthropological perspectives hardly separable if investigating the most recent horizon in archaeological stratigraphy. Additionally, the questions had to be determined in themselves and complement each other. It had to be easy to rephrase the scientifically stated questions in a common understandable fashion. The author decided to divide the questions into general and specific ones. The general questions at the beginning of the interview were thought to introduce the problem and as a warm-up, so to speak, for the interview partner. Soon it was established that the initial question, now on position No. 4, was too important to be mentioned at this point. Most people interviewed felt intimidated by the question right at the beginning, since they imagined the other questions to be even more copious so that an enhanced measure of frustration and resignation was noted.

Surely, the interviewees were positively surprised when the relatively easy and relaxing questions No. 1, 2 and 3 (originally on position No. 5) were asked, but the chance of a comprehensive answer of the important question initially asked had passed. The results obtained through question No. 5 (originally on position No. 4) strongly indicated an enhanced willingness and ability to answer meaningful questions after a set of relaxing ones, which may have been answered easily, but represented an important part of the subsequent evaluation. The specific questions 1 to 3 were prepared and had not changed at all.

The stone tool technological questions were thought to address only a small selected group of people with previous experience in knapping. Question No. 3 tried to test a commonly heard statement that the Aborigines were the first people on earth. It also uncovered eventual religious influences of the church, when Adam and Eve were mentioned for example. Questions 4, 5 and the immediately omitted original question No. 6 were prepared, but slightly, or considerably altered. In question 4, health care as an important part of Aboriginal life was added and question No. 5 was rephrased. Why question No. 6 was omitted will be explained in part b) Alterations, but the question itself shall be mentioned here.

6) Would you always give a truthful answer, if asked a question by researchers, even if the foreseeable outcome does not interest or benefit you ?

b) Alterations

The alterations applied to the prepared questions were already mentioned above. The only explanation the author still owes the reader is the question after the omission of the original question No. 6. This question had to be stricken because of the embarrassment and confusion it caused. The interviewees thought they were being called liars and refused to answer any other question, though this one was asked last. By working in a small community these interviewees would have negatively influenced other possible interview partners so that unfavorable preconditions would have been established.

The same can be said for the shortly added question No. 11 which was phrased as follows: Why do the Aborigines not let the people (companies) know where their sacred sites are before a mining, building, excavational, etc. project is coming up ? Although this question was developed by an urban Aboriginal working group, the author initiated in Sydney, the Aborigines still living on their land or the rural areas they were settled on have a strong aversion to anyone even mentioning their sacred sites.

Questions 6 - 10 were specifically added to the catalogue, reflecting the progressed investigational level of the thesis as well as suggestions from Aboriginal people. Question No. 8 was added experiencing surely long, but insufficient answers for question No. 5. The definite cause of this insufficiency was rather the lack of background information than the indignation to answer. In abstract, section 2 of this thesis was used to acquaint the interviewees with the subject.

Question No. 6 and 7 were developed out of the common concern of archaeologists/anthropologists in Australia and Aboriginal groups for the use and abuse of scientific investigation concerning the Aboriginal culture and its remains. Question No. 7 specifically asks for the beneficial characteristics those scientific investigations could have for Aboriginal people. Question No. 9 and 10 were suggested by Aborigines since they express their main struggle in modern Australian society. The answers to the questions are indirectly applicable to the main theme of this thesis and were therefore added to the question catalogue.

c) Weaknesses

Albeit the author tried to develop the question catalogue from his own knowledge, there are some weaknesses to be mentioned here. On the one hand, a more careful preparation of the fieldwork by means of literature and collegial exchange as well as a more complex question catalogue would have been desirable. On the other hand the unconventional methods and sometimes naive notion of fieldwork present in this research caused spontaneous responses that lead to unexpected and surely different results than expected if a more complex study would have preceded.

Often the rephrasing of the scientifically written questions was problematic and lead to misunderstandings and undesired answers. This was especially true if questions were oversimplified, making it impossible for the interviewee to see the full extend of the problem. Additionally, at least a previous explanation of the term archaeology and today's research perspectives should have been given before the actual interviews took place, since most of the Aborigines had never heard this term, though they knew about archaeological working techniques. Anthropology was sufficiently known through land claims in court.

The archaeological/anthropological explanation of the traditional form of Aboriginal culture (Question No. 8) could have been expressed more interestingly. Also important points should have been stated more clearly especially in the first fifteen interviews. Since the expressiveness of some questions was lacking (Question No. 7, basically due to the fact that the term "archaeology" was unknown), a second, more pressing question, aiming for the same answer should have been asked, in order to obtain a sufficient answer. Though today the author would try to avoid the mistakes mentioned he does not believe that these weaknesses are so weighty that they would have a considerable influence on the outcome of the research.

7. THE OUTCOME - EVALUATION OF THE INTERVIEWS

The author of a scientific paper always has to think about the best, most clearly arranged, and most interesting presentation of the main data. When dealing with interviews, the most common approach would be the presentation of the interviews in typescript in the appendix or a second volume. Not assuming that the respective author added or omitted facts, this would probably be the most complete and easily reexaminable method. Considering the number (120) and the length (up to 4 hours) of the interviews, the author of the present thesis chose a different approach.

In the following the reader will find an evaluation of every question in the order that they were asked. Percentagewise the main trend of the answers will be ascertained. In full or partially through extracts, this main trend, as well as possible differences, will be mentioned in typescript. Interpretations will solely be based on the answers shown in typescript. The possible reproach of omissions, especially of those facts that speak against the prevailing idea expressed in this thesis, might be valid, but can be tested if the cassettes or typescripts are requested. Those might be released after the explicit permission of the interviewees. (See also part VI.)

General questions:

Question No.1 (most commonly phrased): Can you tell me about your tribal or common Aboriginal history ?

No.17 " We came from the north."

No.88 " I know I was here all the time, but I don't know where my ancestors came from. We are from Alice Springs and we have a dreaming that is called caterpillar and that's for all the Arunda people in Central Australia and we call it the caterpillar dreaming. "

No.61 " Hmm, there is a bit too much European in it to say to carry on one mile by the other, isn't it ? But when I hear, outside this, and this is very common at the border of existence to hear as an advice, but I will say this, that I noticed that the anthropologists tend to judge Australia along with the, and I wonder whether it is a reflection of the US centricity, that the blacks must have come here because the whites came here too, you see. I see, and on the same line there is a book called "Tribes of the nomads" by J.P.Blainy, and in there, there is a classic example, a source that I'm thinking about, there is a map in the book, which is the top end of Australia and the islands, to the north Indonesia and so and we've got these two continental parts moving together and there is a line drawing across, a big dark, bold line and it says. "The garden in advance", and the garden is the god damn Australia. [Laughter] Jesus, I laugh when I see that because at first the garden is Australia and the Macassars and those other people, which came down from Asia and the fisherman stopped here, particularly the Macassars, for up to six month at one time, actually had gardens planted, and the blacks used to look at them and asked: "What are you doing that for, we got provided for, we don't have to go through all

that stuff.... As time goes by the research tends to push the date further and further back and I can sit back quite comfortably and I know it is quite scientific and say: "You still haven't found the apes yet." Most people say we came from Asia, but there is no way to prove it."

No.57 (See also section 1.4 a)" I believe that we were always here because there have been different times where the old people I have been talking to told me about an old, old story the Aboriginal people maintained and the young people don't know about. There are actual drawings in secret places only the Aborigines know about, and they are very, very old. And they tell a story about the Aborigines long, long ago. Though I haven't really gotten my hand on this stuff, I know that the American Indians have the same initiation rituals then we do. And even in Sumatra, Java up that line their script language has the same symbols we do, also in several different parts in the world and especially in Egypt. Some people say, oh, the Egyptians must have been into Australia, but the old people know that the Egyptians are ancient Aborigines. And the ancient Egyptians were black too. And also, what most people don't know, there is an ancient Aboriginal language, a special language, that was spoken when I was initiated, and that shows traits of all the languages spoken today, and that is why, and I can't prove it, that the Aborigines were the first people on earth..."

No.31 " ....They took me out to the bush for initiation. That's when I learned everything I know now about my own tribe and the Aborigines. But the initiation and what was taught is secret. Yes, I can't talk about it. The people came from all over the place, from all over Australia and they taught me, the elders, you know. "

No.42 " Well, European wise it's been proved that the Aboriginal people are South East Asians. They originally came from South East Asia, I might teach you myself, ehm, but with my skin group it's all from the South of the desert, all my mother's people are from there..."

No.90 " Our history goes far back, long before the European people came to our land. My people came from Alice Springs, but there was another man called Umbana, and before they had another name far up in the north."

No.13 " I don't think I know that, weren't they always here ?"

No.110 " That's a strange one. I'd say we came from Indonesia, but there is a good possibility that some were already here in New Guinea, I don't know, I can't answer that."

No.35 " We were always here, lately just pushed around by the whites, but we were always here and we will always be."

Comments: Although the reader found question No. 1 often quite elaborately answered, so the fact should not be hidden, that several interviews, especially those recorded on tapes, were short and hardly audible because of background noises like birds, dogs, children, and the wind. Various interviewees also played with the microphone. Some interviewees gave essential information only after the actual questioning had ended. Sometimes the tape recorder was still running, or, as done in most other interviews, the essential parts were written down in shorthand. The answers shown here, for example, represent a mixture of tape recordings and shorthand writings. The reader will notice that most of the informants refer to the Aboriginal people as "they" even though they are Aboriginal themselves. A possible explanation might be the changing status of Aboriginal people in society, especially considering the new cultural awareness, a culture, which seems so remote from the traditional one often being asked for in the questionnaire (See section II and III).

Question No.1 primarily was thought to break the ice and give the informant the possibility to talk about his/her or common Aboriginal history from his/her point of view. Foreseeably, this question would and did lead into 120 different stories, which could not possibly be mentioned entirely. Most informants were talking about their personal family history (No.88) and only few did mention parts of the derivation and genesis of the Aboriginal people in prehistoric times. Since Aboriginal prehistory was meant to be uncovered, only the latter was partially presented here. What was interesting was that 7 informants mentioned that those themes were taught at the initiation ceremony and were therefore secret (No.31) Basically, two different answers were given, one stating that the Aboriginal people came from the north, most probable South East Asia or New Guinea (No.17, 42, 90, 110), the other declaring the origin of the Aboriginal people on the Australian continent (No.61, 57, 13, 35). Informant No.61 pointed out the impossibility to trace back eventual migrational routes of prehistoric Aborigines. Such an enterprise, so he stated, could only have been escaped from a European mind, which seems to need an airtight historical evolution. The differences in subsistence of South East Asians and Aboriginal Australians as well as the early archaeological dates make him believe that the Aborigines originated in continental Australia.

A quite angry response was experienced from informant No.35, who thought it rude to even assume that the Aborigines might not have originated in Australia. Informant No.57 developed a fascinating thesis, about which the reader might judge for him/herself. What was kind of tricky was the answer of informant No.42, who cited the official version, so to speak, without mentioning her own opinion. This particular interviewee stated later (General Question No.5) that she would apparently agree about other people's opinion even though she thought differently. 53.3 % of the informants mentioned the north as a possible place of origin, while 32.5 % believed that the Aborigines originated in Australia. 10 % had other opinions or wanted to keep their answers a secret. 4.2 % preferred not to answer at all.

Question No.2 Where did you obtain your knowledge from ?

No.26 " Yeah, hm, certainly not from the past, but I had a little bit of a chat with my mother at the time I was little and talking to Maori people, I figured the differences are pretty elementary, as for example as my grandmother lived in terms of culture and so on. And the knowledge I've got has come from talking to people and comparing the essentials to the books I've read and asking myself: "were the books true", but I tend to believe people first, because I give a shit of academic accreditation [not understandable] The academic work-up of Aboriginal history has interested me, but did not satisfy me, as my people did. "

No.54 " The first contact with Aboriginal people and their culture I had when I was a little girl, because I was born there. Then, taken away, I lived in white men's society and developed over the years a terrible thirst for knowledge about my history. And so I asked a lot of questions, the people I lived with couldn't answer. By the time I met Aboriginal people again I was a grown up woman. I asked them about my mother and my tribe and I constantly was in fear that I might hear something terrible. After I talked to my people I got sick of what I was reading in those books about us. Is that answer enough ? "

No.35 " ... Let me tell you something, even though I did not have a proper education, there is a lot of bullshit what they are writing about relatedness, how do you call it, kinship, I guess. I was out there with one of these anthropologists, as translator you know. We were sitting down in the grass with all the other Aborigines of that tribe and that person tried to figure who was related to whom. He did that in a mathematical-analytical way attempting to sort out a family tree and in the end he got everything messed up. Though it wasn't true, he seemed to be satisfied. He never found out what it meant, when they told him:"This is my brother, but he is also my uncle, this is my sister, but also my mother." That's the reason why I ask my people first before I believe what was written down by some researcher. "

No.95 " Hey, say, I am Aboriginal, I was born as an Aboriginal, and I will always be an Aboriginal, so I know. "

No.32 " From my father, he told me a lot of what has happened in the past and where [the Aboriginal people] they came from.

No.64 " I just know it by the history books , I suppose. "

No.84 " My father told me. He was a young stock man like me, during the war, during the second world war, he was here in Alice Springs. "

No.52 " I met a lot of Aborigines, I went to Aboriginal college. I can't say, you are just Aboriginal inside, it's a little thing in you that says you are Aboriginal, you know. It's a feeling that identifies you as an Aboriginal.... I read a lot from books about Aboriginals, but most things you read in books about Aboriginals are about what they did. I don't think there is a lot of information about Aboriginals, when they came and settled Australia. "

No. 92 " A lot of it came from our grandmothers, the old people. Right now I pick up history books and read a lot about it. The knowledge about Aboriginal people, again European anthropologists have written, but then again how do we know it is true what they have written, because the Aboriginal people will not tell the whole truth about themselves. They ain't not selling themselves. "

Comments: Ms. Buchanan and the author were amazed that no one even mentioned school as a factor in their derival of knowledge about Aboriginal culture. Even those informants, who grew up on a mission or in a westernized way in the city without any contact to Aboriginal groups rather mentioned their own studies through books (No.64) than through school. As a matter of fact, even modern Australian schoolbooks devote only 2 to 5 pages to Aboriginal history in general. Albeit question No.2 was not thought to cause any criticism of anthropology and in some way ethnoarchaeology, brief words of criticism were included in several answers. The main criticism was the inability of the scientist to grasp the Aborigine's way of living and thinking if approaching in a mathematical-analytical way. Every attempt to do so will undoubtedly lead into misinterpretations, which the informants regard as lies (No.54).

Another problem, scientists will face, is mentioned by informant No.92. She tends to believe that most Aboriginal people will never tell the whole truth about the respective themes being investigated. Interviewee No.35 believes that scientists are not interested in writing the truth, since they seem to be satisfied even though they might know that their results are untrue. Interviewee No.26 phrases the problem in such a way, that he does not acknowledge academic accreditation, but people, who lived the part of the Aboriginal history themselves. Some interviewees wanted to know about Aboriginal history, simply because they are Aboriginal, probably referring to an intact Aboriginal community, where knowledge is passed down through the elders and parents (No.52, 95).

In general, knowledge was obtained through talks with the parents and/or grandparents (No.26, 32, 84, 92). Girls learned from their mothers and/or grandmothers and boys from their fathers and/or grandfathers, as stated by 64 % of the interviewees. 11 % learned on their own, whereas TV and books were the main aids. 15 % knew already, since they were Aboriginal, and the rest did not answer at all.

Question No. 3 Name one or two archaeologists/anthropologists who mainly worked on Australian Aborigines.

No.93 " Professor Elkin, Tindale, Bobby Sykes, Burnum Burnum "

No.13 " I only know you "

No.29 " I don't know "

No.76 " I know one bloke, who came around at land rights meeting time [and do you know his name] No. "

No.72 " Marthia Lengthon, there is a couple of others, but I can't remember their name, quite a few are archaeologists some are anthropologists. I guess you've got to believe it. "

No.9 " No only you, you were the first that showed up here. "

No.38 " Yes, I know several [not by name though] "

Comments: The answer to question three shown above depicts no representative sample since over 90 % of the interviewees simply replied with no. Even though informant No.29's answer was a little longer, it expressed the same. Informants No.9 and 13 pointed out that Ms. Buchanan and the author were the only scientists that ever showed up at their place, an answer, which can be assumed more often. Only 3 % of the interviewees knew at least one person, although they could not remember their name. Only informants No. 93 and 72 were able to name some scientists. At this point the reader's attention might be called to something that is quite consistent throughout the interviews.

Most Aborigines only refer to anthropologists, since these scientists are mainly working with them, especially in land right cases. Archaeology is either unknown or so remote from their daily activities that the Aborigines seldom include this science branch in their answers directly. Ethnoarchaeology, albeit unknown by the Aborigines, is indirectly criticized when critically talking about anthropological field methods or better the actual carrying out of them.

Question No.4 Do you think that research of the past is important and do you need it to identify with Aboriginal culture ?

No.93 " I wouldn't say so. The process of identification to me is primarily as an Aboriginal person even though I was raised in a totally different situation, as I said, as a white person. Part of my family did maintain their quite European existence even though they conciously know about their part Aboriginal originality. I am now 47 years old and it has been only the past 5 or 6 years that the question of what Aboriginality meant was an issue to talk about. The different culturally distinct background of Aboriginal people and the social injustice in Australian society began to interest me...., but I really needed to get ready to understand who I were, who those people were and where did I stand. Over the time the whole issue of what an Aboriginal is has changed, quite considerably throughout the last few years. And then I started reading all the stuff written by the Europeans. Some of it was foolish, but some quite perceptive. And probably the most significant thing I have seen, I suppose, would be the map of Australia with the bandages on it, published in 1971 by Tindale, probably the first time that such a map has ever been produced. And knowing that the modern Aboriginal is a European construct, I would like to go back and see what those bandages was like. [So, you say that you did not need this research to identify with Aboriginal culture?] No, I did need to go through it, I went through it, but it was a very critical process for me, a lot of this stuff is already discarded, the most important thing, I said, I remember from the antiquity was this map...."

No.83 " I think the research of the past is very important because it is doing, hmm, to me as a person a lot of different things.... 50 years ago it was very shameful to be black. I am 56 now and I was raised in this believe. Always I had this terrible urge in my body to know about my past that was carefully hidden from me. So I started to learn and do research and it wasn't just my family and I guess I had a feeling of pride that I was one of the wonderful people. I asked the elders and they taught me a lot and I was finally initiated. I learned to produce art and really got into bush medicine. I learned to understand the law and I know all about it. I agree to live by that law.... And it is a shame that you (author/Ms.Buchanan) have these problems down here, but the research that everybody is doing, a lot of Aboriginal people are against and, I am thinking about Boris now as an archaeologist, a lot of Aboriginal people hate archaeologists and they hate what they are doing, but I think it is very important because the archaeologists are the ones, who are actually digging up the past and saying:"hey, these black people were here", I mean, I say that to the white people, you've only had your Lord Jesus 2000 years, we've had ours up to 50.000, 60.000 years. There are footprints coming down and he gave us the law.... So it is important to know about the past and that there are people to show us what happened in these 50.000 years. And we shouldn't be afraid, we should be glad because it is a known truth, that we knew a lot and that will be found out. "

No.40 " I think it is important. "

No.27 " I think it is important because a lot of Australian Aboriginals didn't learn how to write so they don't really understand what happened in the past. It's good to know what went on in the past because I think it is good that Aboriginals understand the future too, can think into the future too, the past now is just the past. A lot of Aboriginals still dream of past times, its not on anymore its just [pause] I think it is good to understand how things were and what people used to do, I don't know, I think so, yeah. "

No.36 " For myself ? Yeah, 'cause I think a lot of what is coming up now is a lot that I've missed and looking at the different tribes that are around here in Australia because some of them have got a different sense of dreaming to other particular parts and it is good to have their dreaming and how long ago they think it started. Is that the answer ? "

No.85 " No, I've heard from my father everything that is to know. "

No.62 " Yeah, if the research would be about the family, sort of a family tree. "

No.91 " It's kind of a hard question because I did not grow up with my own people, I grew up on a mission, I was taken away when I was a little baby. [Do you think that it helps that scientists do research on the past now ?] You certainly could do some on mine, that's on my mind. "

No.111 " Yes "

No.51 " Yes, certainly "

Comments: This question was directly asking for the importance or insignificance of archaeological investigations for Aboriginal people. A second, often hesitatingly or not at all answered part, aimed to find out if the prehistorical research would effect the Aborigine's cultural identity. The only people, who definitely stated that the prehistorical, but also the historical research would effect their identification with Aboriginal culture were those, who were taken away as children or grew up in a solely westernized way. They thought to have missed out on some important issues in Aboriginal life, which would come alive again when studying books concerning these themes (No.36).

Informant No.36 referred to the collecting and preservation function of anthropology/archaeology (See also specific question No. 7), which will be beneficial, especially for future generations. While interviewee No.93 did critically evaluate prehistoric research and appreciated it in some way, he thought that it was little important for his cultural identification.. He also noted a considerable change in the view of Aboriginality over the last few years (See also section IV).

Overall only 5 % of the interviewees referred to prehistorical/historical research as being significant for their own cultural identification. Though it seems that these answers about the importance of prehistorical research were 2-fold, there was actually a third interesting version. About 59 % of the informants answered with yes (No.111, 51, 40), but if asked again, 30 % of them would restrict the research to genealogies mostly of their own family and would show little interest in overall features (No.85, 62). The main obstacle, so informant No.27 declared, is the lack of education, which makes the Aborigines still envision that they could reach a state, that they once had in the past. He thinks that knowledge of the past will help the Aborigines to understand the future, to cope with it, and maybe positively help create it.

Informant No.83, although pointing out the dark sides of archaeological investigations (See specific question No.5), generally agrees on prehistorical investigations since only this science would undoubtedly discover the unique status of Aboriginal people. She also believes in the positive influence of science in the society, which allowed her to be proud to be black. Still, 29 % of the interviewees declared their knowledge about the past to be complete through handed down information of their relatives (No.85).

Question No. 5 If someone in the future comes to you and tells you something different from your dreamtime stories would you believe him or would you believe the dreamtime stories ?

No.42 " I'll believe the dreamtime stories, but I might, if it is a European person, I might make him think that I believe in what he said, you know, I would always believe in the secrets of the dreamtime stories. "

No.116 [Even though his father told him the dreamtime stories} " I want to know more. "

No.118 " 28 years ago I was walking around in the bush and found some relics within an old fireplace and this was along a sand dune, where Aboriginal people used to camp. And just for curiosity or so I took the ashes from the old fireplace, which I found, which was about 36.000 years old, when it was carbon dated, and I picked up three flint heads, which the Adelaide Museum said were arrow heads and I assumed that these people were using drugs, ever thinking that we might have used bow and arrow. We used the spear and most importantly the boomerang to hunt kangaroos. And the old people never mentioned anything else. I believe them. "

No.75 " A lot of dreamtime stories could be related to history. Let me tell you something about dreamtime stories. Some people say they are just stories, they are not real, just stories. No one realizes that some of these dreamtime stories could be [true] history.... that does not need to be interpreted. I suppose you've got to listen of what he [Aboriginal elder] said and you've got the dreamtime stories. It is very difficult, but a lot of white Australians say they live in their dreamtime, look at that person, and that site, take that horizon. That are just stories of my life, they are not written down history, you know. I guess you have to listen carefully, you've got to know that. "

No.43 " I don't know. Honestly, I don't know, probably if I say something to that it'll contradict itself in a few years. "

No.85 " I believe what my father told me. "

No.47 " I believe the dreamtime stories, as told by my family because there is a law, and a very strong law, how the dreamtime stories are handed down, must be absolutely true in every detail. If it is a story and it got a different angle on it, it could be a different interpretation from a different culture or a different skin group, but normally there aren't very much, usually they are the same stories. "

No.111 " I won't believe anyone else. "

No.93 " ... There has always been, as far as I know from the reading that I have done in anthropology, there has always been in these dreamtime stories, what you might call a consistent pattern. You've got these ancestral themes traveling across the continent, I mean from country to country all through. And the story of each country tells you roughly the same, the same thing, but they've got individual variations. Those individual variations I, and European wise, you know, sort of, I can understand that, and anybody should be able to understand that there are individual differences especially if asking various questions occurring in Europe. I guess as far as peoples believes change and so they have a different past and future, why should everything be equal if the needs are being met properly, but the foundation of their believes should not be scattered. The scattering pollutes, but what would you say if someone just woke me up and says: "This was it and I did see", but if you ask again and your guts are hanging out and barely seeing what was between these

wild people and the apes maybe then you start thinking again. But I think that question about the truth of the dreamtime stories being passed from one person to the other you have to see, people have been weird at these old times, that's them. "

No.31 " Well, many people came to me in the past and tried to teach me their religion and they asked me if I believe in god and I say: "Yes." And now you ask me if I believe in the dreamtime stories and I say yes too. How could that be. I believe it has been told by the same people... [In the following the bible is compared to the creation myth of the Aborigines] "

Comments: Looking over the answers given in question No.5 it was quite interesting to note some contradictions compared to the answers given in the previous question. Although the prehistorical research seems to be important to informant No.111 and others, they would not believe the outcome in case it would contradict their dreamtime stories. Informant No. 111 can not even think of the possibility of eventual discrepancies between dreamtime stories and archaeological evidence (See specific question No.8)

All of the interviewees stated that they do believe the dreamtime stories rather than the scientific research. Only few, like informant No.116, would like to broaden their knowledge through future research. Informant No.75 suggested that the dreamtime stories would reflect real events in prehistory. Careful listening to the Aboriginal elders could uncover hitherto unknown facts. There would be a very strong law on how dreamtime stories are handed down, according to interviewee No.47, which insures the accuracy of those stories, although local differences apply.

Informant No. 118 tried to develop a reasonable explanation of why he would rather believe in the dreamtime stories than in any scientific explanation. The frustration expressed about scientific theories mostly resulted from the negative outcome of the comparison of the scientific research with the dreamtime stories. Negative in the sense that the scientific explanation contradicted parts of their handed down knowledge. The only insecure interviewee was No.43, who was aware of possible and valid scientific contradictions in parts of some of the dreamtime stories. Here, and in some other answers, the reader will observe the historic work up of the westernized culture with the Aboriginal one, especially concerning religious themes (No.31).

Specific Questions

Question No. 1/2
Question two was exclusively used for the stone tool experiments and only asked if question No. 1 resulted in a positive answer. Since some of the answers from question number one uncovered some problems dealt with in other questions it shall be mentioned here.

No.74 " Yes I know many people who make stone tools and I make stone tools myself. " This was a quite common answer, but if the author asked them to produce some tools, they either found an excuse or were unable respectively became unable to do so.

No.26 " No I don't " or shortly No.68 " No "

No.96 " No I don't know how to make stone tools, but I do know old people and there in Pitinjarra there was an old man, there was an old Aboriginal Afghan and he used to produce tools of flint or whatever he used to spear the guts because stone was a lot sharper than the other things he had, but that was a long time ago, I don't know anyone at the moment that still do. "

No.99 " No, I can make my own, yes. I can make a boomerang, I can make a shield, an Alla Alla, another boomerang and I can make a flip knife. If you go back you can see an old man, it is my father, he can make almost everything, you can ask him. "

No.43 " I can't even make my bed properly, no kidding, no, there are some people that make some, but they don't really use them. "

No.24 " Well, I have never made a stone tool, but I know one person, no two people, no three people, who make stone tools. As far as I am aware, in the case of the first one, he was sitting down there in the middle of the river bed, grabbing the one or the other rock nearby and beating them with particular hammerstones he got out of a vessel he brought with him. He produced spear heads and stone knives, and I thought by myself how nice it would be to have this skill because if you were in a situation were you need a knife you just pick the nearest rock and make one. I have to admit though that it seemed to be a very laborious process to produce useable tools. So, I don't regard the technology as being in any way sort of antiquated, you know, unless you've got all the baggage that goes with university culture with you, were you define advanced and retarded productional skills. The other two people were doing it too, but more still saw it as a sort of survival skill, you know. "

No.4 " Yes, I can make stone tools. At that time I was still making some we used flint and also chert. I was always interested how my grandfather produced these wonderful tools, which were so nicely useable for various purposes. A stone knife he produced in a few minutes, a useable spear head took several hours.... And then, one day I was collecting bush medicine and actually grabbed a piece of chert and cracked it, then using a hammerstone as my grandfather did, I was actually shaping the stone until I had a handy and sharp tool. Over the time I learned more and more so that I can produce now a whole set of tools, and I try to teach this to our young generation. I also made digging sticks...."

Comments: Only two of the 120 people interviewed were able and willing to produce some stone tools (No.99, 4). Several referred to another person they would know, who still produces stone tools, while that person again referred to another one and so on (No.4, 96). Often the name or place

of residence of these people was unknown, so that the actual number of stone tool workers was small. Informant No. 96 noted that stone tools were preferred to iron tools because of their extraordinary sharpness.

Interviewee No. 24 reported on the laborious process of stone tool production, which had to be meticulously conducted. Some Aborigines, who still live in the bush would need this skill for their survival. Along with several other informants, interviewee No.24 admires those skills, which seem to be a major characteristic for them in defining traditional Aboriginal culture. Only little effort seemed to have been put into the handing down of stone tool manufacturing skills. Without any known exception, the youngest Aboriginal generation obviously was not taught this discipline. An honorable attempt was made by informant No.4, though she admitted that little interest was shown.

Question No. 3 Do you think that Aborigines were the first people on earth, if yes, tell me why you think so ?

No.2 " No, I don't think they were, I think they probably came from somewhere else, but we were among the first people on earth. "

No.100 " That I knew, Yes. "

No.50 " No "

No.42 " Yes, it's been proved, people found bones that date back 40.000 years ago and there have been studies in that and they found that have been Aboriginal bones through the shape of the skull and the teeth, because Aboriginal people, there's another thing that has been proved, Aboriginal people's teeth are really hard to decay, and if you see a dentist, if you go to a dentist, you can ask a dentist about an Aboriginal person pulling out their teeth it is very hard, I reckon, what did this dentist say, it is stronger than, it has something to do with concrete, you know, when you drill there.... and you know they found a lot of skulls and teeth are still preserved. And you can see it they were adult 'cause the teeth have been worn down to a certain shape in the mouth so that is how they know they were Aboriginal people. "

No. 32" No, Adam and Eve was. [And Adam and Eve, did they live in Australia or where did they come from ?] You know we Aboriginals believe in our own god. [And he derived from Adam and Eve ?] No, that are different cultures. "

No.43 " 40.000 years, they must have come pretty close to the first people in existence. "

No.114 " They maybe were the first in the stock use. I don't think so, I think pretty close they were the first one, pretty close, they weren't the first that started making things, yeah, making objects, but paintings are the first that were made here. You've got 27.000 - 20.000 years, but the Aboriginals got 70.000 maybe 60.000 year old paintings and here, so there is a 40.000 year gap, that make Aboriginals the oldest, the first people to think about art, and they weren't amateurs. "

No.31 " Yes, I can't tell you one of the old stories, which was told at initiation, it's a secret, but yes we were first. "

No.86 " It is possible that there were a number of Russians hiding in Siberia, no kidding, I'm quite happy for the Aboriginal people that they were first. "

Comments: The majority of Aborigines answered spontaneously with yes or no as if their thoughts had been occupied with that question before. Insecurity in answering the question was only observed by interviewee No.43. 58 % of the interviewees answered with yes, 39 % with no or "amongst the first" (No.2), while 3 % did not comment on this subject at all. Again informant No. 31 referred back to the dreamtime stories, which can not be told to an outsider, but would clearly indicate the primary settlement of the earth by Aboriginal people. Informant No.114 disagreed with archaeological/anthropological knowledge that the Aborigines might have been the first people to domesticate animals. Additionally pointed out was the unique and ancient appearance of Aboriginal paintings. Since art is practiced in leisure time and demands abstract thinking, he emphasized professional performance.

Scientific proof of the antiquity of Aboriginal culture has been witnessed by informant No.42 who mentioned skeletal remains, especially stressing the importance of tooth decay. The careful reader will undoubtedly have realized that informant No.42, especially (See also general questions No.1 and 5) seems to use modern scientific results to verify the truth of the dreamtime stories and indirectly to raise the Aborigines' status. Disproving scientific results are not considered. The influence of the Christian church will soon be understood when considering the answer of interviewee No.32. Although the missionaries introduced the bible, the original belief seems to run parallel to the modern belief.

Question No. 4 Would you rather live in a modern way, where people have houses and color TV; would you rather live in the traditional way, in the bush, or would you like to have a mixture of both ?

No.54 " I think, I have a problem there. I have been brought up with all the modern things, but having them, I actually lived in the bush as a child and I knew people who still lived in a cave and I have been with them several days a month and to me it has always been a party. Because everything was there. Though there was no water as I was used to get it from the tab, there were several other ways to drink. And there was no knowledge, which we had, which I loved on the other hand, but we had bush races and they gave me sweets too from the bush like the honey. And I remember that specifically when we wanted to eat, we had to hunt or collect it, there was a totally different relation to food and it did not need to be prepared all fancy. And I felt quite comfortable in the bush after a while and I didn't miss much of the modern life. [But what would you prefer ?] I would prefer both, see how we are living right now, we have no electricity, the water comes from the dam, I have my work in the health

department and I love to go out in the bush. I tell you what, if all this comes to an end, I could survive in the bush. "

No.94 " .... This is a question that never came to my mind before. I was living in the way my parents showed me. I always thought it was the way to live. Then getting older, I went to Alice Springs and experienced another way, though I already knew a lot from TV. Now I attend Aboriginal College and I am aware of the problems Aboriginal people have here with modern society. As much as I love to go back to my home, friends, and family, I'd like to continue living as I do now and don't ask me whether it is modern or traditional. This is the way I chose and everyone has to decide for himself. "

No.23 " This is a strange one. Look at our language, most of the terms for modern products we overtook, we mostly live in houses, with TV and electricity, we hunt with bullets, we drink tab water. Only the old people still know how to make a living in the bush. It is sad, I would like to have both. "

No.27 " I like to have a car and I like to have a TV, I also like the living, I like the old ways, only because I am Aboriginal, I have to understand some aspect of the old way. I don't think going back fully would be right, especially not in a world that is changing so rapidly. [So you would like to have both ?] I would like to have both, lets say with a color TV and a car, though I walked a lot, I'd like to go back, do something in the old ways sometimes, but I couldn't do it all the time. "

No.7 " I like the way I live now, I have everything I need. " [Interviewee lives on a reserve in a small village, but inside a stone house with water, electricity, and all modern electric appliances]

No.78 " Oh, I can live in two ways, in Arunda, [Pause] White people also have to learn and respect Aboriginal culture, so that Aboriginal people would always, would respect and, hmm, would respect the white people's way too. So it's both, two ways of learning and, hmm, we always got to go forward on the time, so I like living in a house and also we can't stop in hunting all our life, and we have to step forward and we can't feel sorry for what has happened in the past, we always got to look forward, but we also have to respect our tribal laws. "

No.35 " I rather live in the bush without the modern things, but unfortunately the modern ways force you to live in a certain way. "
No.112 " Well, I suppose if I only grew up with one culture and I didn't have the taste of the other culture, I suppose I have to go for the bush. If you mean if I have to start all over again, yeah, I would go for the bush, 'cause I love the bush, I feel at home when I am out there. That would be nice, more then here because you have all the problems that you haven't had before. "

No.43 " I never lived in the traditional way, this is the life-style I lived here. If you put me out there I would be completely lost. And this is all for all and this is all I want. I mean if we would live in the bush and have everything there and would live in a nice place without stress, you know and have everything easy, I would sure go there. Of course I would take my car and TV, the freezer, air conditioning...."

Comments: The purpose of this question was to try and investigate whether the Aboriginal people are determined to return to their traditional life-style (if possible), prefer the westernized way, or see their future life-style by incorporating both attributes. While informant No.94 grew up quite close to the traditional way in a small community without houses or electricity, he prefers the newly experienced way as integral part in a westernized culture. Interviewee No.54 on the other hand would not mind living in the bush, although she grew up in a westernized way. Childhood experiences and the intensive study of Aboriginal culture made her choose a life-style that incorporates both, the traditional and westernized way of living. Within other things the house, TV as well as the car seems to have become an integral part in modern Aboriginal life-style. A possible return to the traditional way would only be conceivable if they were able to hold on to those status symbols (No.43, 27).

The bush is thought to be a stress free environment, which would not cause those problems, that are often found disturbing in modern/westernized culture (No.43, 112). Informant No.35 remarked on the impossibility to return to traditional life-style since westernized culture would hinder it's free development (See suction effect). Most answers show that the majority of the Aborigines is deeply rooted in the bush though its nurturing function seems to have diminished (No.112).

Insightful ideas were developed by informant No.23 and 78. Already modern Aboriginal languages have shown a dependency on westernized products since no Aboriginal words have been found for them (No.23). The mutual respect of both cultures, the Aboriginal and westernized one would clearly enhance the living qualities of both cultures. Every step back to old, traditional values, which can not be kept in modern society, would adversely effect Aboriginal life (No.78), although any future development should incorporate Aboriginal values.

Informant No.27 commented on the unconditional obligation to understand at least some aspects of traditional Aboriginal life since it could enhance every other life-style. The results are summarized as follows: Traditional life-style 7 %, Westernized life-style 5 %, Both 87 %

Question No. 5 What do you expect from archaeologists and anthropologists when they are studying about your culture ?

No.104 " What do I expect ? Well, the truth I guess, write the truth, listen to the people and understand them. "

No.20 " It's a difficult question, What I expect is to obtain knowledge to give an answer to the either studies or to answer to other reasons whatever they are studying it for. And to obtain that, that at least needs to have probably about 6 to 10 years living with the race of Aboriginal people. The

first three years will be required to get the trust of the people and the second three years and there on will be needed to interpret the means of what the people say because people can say something, particularly Aboriginal people, and they maybe guarding a secret and they may use different words and so therefore they can throw the anthropologists right off track, dreaming of a totally different concept of what they actually talking about. It is like the bible with all the different religions everyone interprets differently. And I think they need a lot of experience and I get a bit disappointed with anthropologists because they are so young and they don't have the necessary foresight or the necessary background to go out into the world and interpret people having been around for thousands of years. I know anthropologists that are only 24, 25 some are only 20 years old interpreting greens and green stories, but people who are 60 years old telling them soon their own interpretation themselves. I find that a bit inferior. "

No.107 " I just want them to find out the, em, maybe the truth, where Aboriginal people really came from, yes. "

No.120 " I'd like to know my family tree, you know, I'd love to have known my mother, she passed away. [So your main interest is your own family tree and not about all the Aboriginal people ?] It all depends on the Aborigines you are talking about, there is a lot of difference. "

No.45 " I suppose a clear view on, you know, I suppose on how the Aborigines existed, I suppose I could understand how the Aboriginals [lived] 'cause there is not [pause] There have been a lot of people around in Australia for years and years and years and never have really taken into account Aboriginals, you know, and they are important. I think that, what anthropologists do, they all show that the Aboriginals are today and they are important and have their qualities. "

No.77 " They should write the truth and stop their constant lies. Anthropologists tell me, how I feel, how I live, and how my forefathers lived, I know better. I don't know much about archaeology, but what they dig up is there, I mean existent, anthropologists just write lies. "

No.83 " I expect them not to make any quick decisions. The most important thing is to respect the people. Definitely respect the traditional people and respect the people, that is very important because they know everything and tell those people [scientists] about their culture and they get nothing back. I always wanted to be an archaeologist and I would love being an anthropologist, but you have to have very, very wide [broad] knowledge. I guess that's it, I would love to respect those people [scientists] and not to make any hate figures and make people to have a very open mind about anthropologists. And when they do finally respect the people because in the past they didn't, they dug up the bones of people and put them in jars and took them away and the people are still looking for them to try to get them back. And most archaeologists take things from this country and take it to their country and never take it back, and that is very, very wrong. No things should be taken from the land it belongs. They can study it there, they don't need to take it. There are probably more skulls and bones of Aboriginal people throughout the world than there are of any other people studied. ...[Talks about anthropologists, who go to communities and immediately ask their questions and wonder why they don't receive sufficient or true answers] If you go to a traditional community you go in and sit down and say hello and you greet everybody the first day. And the second day they start greeting you and they start being nice to you and sitting down and on the third day you talk about family and what you are doing and on the forth day they might ask you why are you there and then on the fifth day you tell them on the six and seventh and eighth day they go on distance and by the 10th day or two weeks they may put a few points out, but that is hard work and it depends if you are a man or a woman. "

No.35 " I don't know. I don't like the superiority they handle things with and their attitude, but I think this is because of the European situation, there is only one solution, there is never a whether...or. Everything is analytical and with their results they are walking to Parliament House and say:"That's it",and we've got our stamp for life. They should be more careful in their statements. "

Comments: A major demand towards science from an Aborigine's perspective is the investigation and publication of the truth (No.104, 107, 77). Unfortunately, the truth is a double-edged sword. On the one hand, especially with respect to archaeological research, since probative (No.77), might have found the truth, which will eventually be unacceptable by the wider Aboriginal community when contradicting their dreamtime stories and on the other hand anthropological investigations might develop a truth, which cannot be tested and still might be accepted or rejected by the Aborigines.

Although informant No.77 described anthropologists as constant liars, other Aborigines saw that the main problem was in the anthropologists' training and life experience. The minimum time spent in a community should be 10 days to two weeks, in order to get at least some useable responses to the questions asked. Within these two weeks, certain guidelines, as to how the Aboriginal people are approached, should be followed as outlined by informant No.83. No anthropologist, so interviewee No.20, would have the necessary foresight and background to judge people, when the researcher is not older than 20 or 25. In his and the majority of the other informants opinion, 6 to 10 years of living with Aboriginal people would be needed to understand the Aborigine's way of thinking and to interpret it appropriately. If those necessary preconditions are not given, the outcome of the research becomes extremely dubious.

Several Aborigines that were interviewed did not show any interest in archaeological/anthropological research at all, unless it was about their own families or at least about people they were better acquaintance with (No.120). Informant No. 45 had a different perspective about the main task of anthropology. Albeit she did not comment on the quality and honesty of the anthropological investigations, she thought that all research would raise the status of Aboriginal people since it would show their importance.

Informant No.35 on the other hand saw an immense danger in anthropological investigations, especially if carried out by non-Aboriginal people. Their analytically obtained results would effect the Aborigine's public viewing for a lifetime if carried into The House of Parliament. More careful statements would be desirable (No.83, 35). A common criticism of archaeology, and this seems to be a worldwide issue, has been the collection and analysis of human remains, their being scattered throughout the world without ever being returned.

Question No. 6 Is today's archaeology or anthropology carried out in Australia constructive or destructive in the way that you identify it as an Aboriginal person ?

No.6 " I have to say I haven't really had contact to archaeology or anthropology. The only contact I really had, would have been personally in contact with that woman from the land council and the other archaeologists and anthropologists that work there, but this are not archaeologists that are only anthropologists and they maintain the cultural identity as they think it was or should be. But still I couldn't judge their work, I don't know enough about it. See, if you look around you see a bunch of Aboriginal people starting to behave like country people, our whole society is changing. I think anthropology/archaeology rather preserves a state, which isn't there anymore. "

No. 111 " I think the sword cuts both ways. These sciences can be constructive if they work towards my ideal of Aboriginality as well as they could be destructive if working against it, but every Aboriginal person thinks different, you know. Tribes in the north identify themselves other than we do. It's hard to say whether anthropology is constructive or destructive. Can archaeology be destructive ? [What, if they find evidence for something that contradicts your dreamtime stories ?] They won't. "

No.51 " I don't know. I have never met anyone, who has done research here. I don't read no books. "

No.20 " I think there is room for improvement. I do say that there are some people around here extremely skillful doing that type of work, I don't know, I haven't met many, I have been unfortunate and haven't met those people yet. I personally got a little disappointed in the people I have met because they seem to have a one track vision of what they want to hear and if they don't hear it they seem to alter everything in what they want to hear and then they confirm it themselves and they go and write it into their books. "

No.13 " Well, like I said you are the only first two that came to Central Aus... I meant to Aboriginal community and stop here for a while and if you got to study Aboriginal culture you got to be here to understand and to feel it so you can't just get a book from the library and just say: "bang, bang, bang", write everything down and you don't even know and that's not fair you have to come to Aboriginal community and feel how Aboriginal people live and to see how Aboriginal people live today. Not just read a book about Aboriginal people and it's not true because they only see bad side of Aboriginal people, they don't see good side of what

Aboriginal people are doing, no, they just want to write down bad things. And they think all Aboriginal people are bad, but they are not. "

No.116 " That is really a hard one 'cause, em, I don't really get into books and read a lot what people have written about Aboriginal people except from the Aboriginal people themselves. People like Sally Morgan and Lisa Clarence, Pat Swamp [two other names not understandable] and, em I don't know because it is coming from the heart, but what other people do you don't really know. Is it that how you wanted me to answer that? [if it is the way you feel.] Yeah, that's a bit of a question, but what I said I don't really get involved in what comes out of it. I just think sometimes people that study Aboriginal people they get more recognition than the people who were actually talking about the culture. There have been a couple of times were I have known Aboriginals, also local ones, who had a lot of input into things about bush medicine or whatever they should have gotten recognition for, but the person actually produces the book and that sort of thing, they get the recognition and not the Aboriginal person. It's nice to have it, yeah. "

No.62 " It can be constructive and it can be destructive. I mean, what is destructive, it depends on the information, if the information is correct and the source of information is legitimate. But it is good to understand what went on with the Aboriginals, I mean you've got a culture that went on a 100.000 years, there is nothing been similar. You have one culture being on one spot at one particular time for so long, you have to understand what happened to them. I don't think it is destructive it's just a matter of, um, making a few mistakes. "

No.76 " Well, whatever you want to put there, I think it is all right. "

No.43 " Let's be true, I don't honestly know, I suppose there is a bit coming out of that, a lot maybe. People of different ways are doing things. It doesn't change anything for me, and if I wouldn't realize what it is. They [scientists] certainly know that they do anyway, you know, and we've got to believe them. "

Comments: Undoubtedly, the interviewees evaluated the constructiveness or destructiveness of archaeological/anthropological investigations very critically. 41 % of the Aborigines interviewed stated that those sciences could be both, destructive and constructive as well, while 27 % saw only the destructive side, one person (No.76) thought archaeology/anthropology to be solely constructive, while 32 % were unable to answer that question.

Although informant No.6 pointed out his inexperience with archaeological/anthropological research, be declared the main function of social sciences in preserving a state in cultural development, which has already changed. Anthropologists, he accused, help to maintain an Aboriginal cultural identity, which does not necessarily have to reflect the real world. Also interviewee No.20 drew a dark perspective upon the scientific investigation of Aboriginal culture. Too many unskillful people would write books

confirming their preconceived notion about how Aboriginal culture should be. They would obstinately disregard any "misleading" information.

Since interviewee No.16 has become disappointed with the habit of researchers in only recognizing their input on books written about Aborigines and not the Aborigines that have provided this information, she finds satisfaction only in reading books written by Aboriginal people. Following along the same lines, informant No.43 thinks that scientists would continue to conduct research in the conventional way and expect the people to believe them anyway. Only if the research confirmed his ideal of Aboriginality would informant No.111 consider it constructive, showing any other evidence, would be destructive.

Science, according to interviewee No.62, can only be destructive if the source of information is illegitimate. If this source is legitimate and properly stated, only the interpretation of it would show a few mistakes. Referring to Ms. Buchanans and the authors stay in their community, Informant No.13 criticized those scientists, who write books without proper fieldwork. She thinks that most authors enjoy creating a negative image of Aboriginal people, though they should know better.

Question No. 7 How do you think archaeologists and anthropologists could support the Aboriginal people ?

No.12 " First of all instead of sending a city slicker there is to send the bush people, regardless black or white, to talk to the people they meet there because they have a better contact with the bush than the city people. I'm pretty sure that we are able to achieve more than probably students and professors and other people from the universities or institutions or whatever. "

No.65 " I don't know, I can't answer that question. "

No.115 " Look at us people, look at me, look at my father you can write about it. Yeah, we need future work, we need people to take up for us, write our history, straighten things out. "

No.4 " For example, come to court, I think, yeah. "

No.53 " Well, that's a difficult question. The only way I can see where they would, would be the skill of people being able to carbon date paintings and the skill of people being able to interpret what these paintings were at that time, but they must first find a date, find the year to find the period of time in which these paintings were done. So that can get the dream side of the situation right. It is very difficult to move among Aboriginal people and get the correct story of a painting in a dream situation. Because in there might be something, who the person or Aboriginal elder or so might be telling someone, but the story is in the painting and might be leaving things out because it is not allowed to talk about them and there are a lot of secrets in these paintings they don't want people to talk about. It's a lot like bush tucker. If you ask Aboriginal people to show you bush tucker, they show you bush tucker and then you got another Aboriginal person to show you bush tucker and he is going past a three course meal more than the other person was willing to show you. And it is like that with all information coming from Aboriginal people. Some people like to talk about some parts of the painting, a painting which represents four skins of people so you only know a quarter of the painting afterwards... Scientifically, there is proof of people that go to communities and have an own interpretation of what they are going to explore. Scientists should listen to all the people and don't interpret too quickly. "

No.26 " It's up to every individual himself to support himself. "

No.97 " I think that it could show Australia and the Aboriginal's existence that the world knows and that they do have some right in what is going on. I think a lot of people in Australia in actual fact are not Aboriginal, they are white people, the settlers, the Chinese and so on, they find more consideration. "

No.36 " Getting fair knowledge of what happened, listening to the old people, you know. I mean say 20 years time it will be really beneficial to know to my son and for my grandchildren because there won't be any old people to pass that on to the anthropologists and the same thing will be written over and over again because it is more or less becoming a multi-cultural nation were the Aboriginal people are just degrading with European people and Vietnamese people and all sorts of people. So it will be beneficial to know at least for my grandchildren. "

No.70 " I know what this question is leading to in a political sense. It can be supportive if dealing with the colonial bureaucracy even today, especially in land claim processes and these sort of things. I mean the question of who we are and what we are gonna be is taken into the hands of present time authorities or political structures. You wouldn't assume that anthropologists and archaeologists have any central law to obey, you know, they sure had to do it in the past, we hope they won't in the future, since their view of Aboriginal culture becomes the world's view. I think they support us best, if listening to our ideas first and considering our knowledge. "

Comments: The main aim of this question was to attempt to find possible ways and research goals, which could support the Aboriginal people and keep anthropologists and archaeologists in business, so to speak. The answers to the previous question of the questionnaire did not lead to the assumption of a positive cooperation between scientists and Aborigines. Nevertheless, 92 % of the interviewees stated that they could enjoy the beneficial qualities of modern science in today's Australian society, if some basic rules were obeyed. Most frequently the scientists were advised to listen more careful to the people and not to interpret too quickly (No.70, 53, 36).

Informant No.12 regarded those urban scientists having little or no experience in the bush, as unsuitable for any kind of fieldwork with Aboriginal people living in a traditional way. "Bush people" conducting interviews within Aboriginal tribes would achieve more in terms of a truthful research outcome. Since the Australian society is ruled by people other than Aborigines, anthropologists and archaeologists have been asked to support the Aborigines in court (No.4) and create a positive public view, as Aboriginal people are still unable to defend themselves (No.115), though they should (No.26). Research projects should incorporate Aboriginal ideas and knowledge, although it might be divergent to prevailing opinions. Informant No.97 commented on the discrepancy of books showing the Aborigines' existence in Australia to other more recent settlers. The world should know about the circumstances Aborigines live with right now. Through the upcoming multi-cultural Australian society, where Aborigines have interbred with all other ethnic groups, interviewee No.36 fears a lost of knowledge, which can only be compensated for through careful and sincere research, in order to preserve this knowledge for future generations. An absolute dating method for paintings as well as the ability to interpret those paintings would truly uncover Aboriginal prehistory, though informant No.53 doubted that anyone would ever be able to do so.

Question No. 8 Original Question

No.70 " Well, I am aware of a number of theories having been around here in Australia. Lately there was one on TV talking about the apes and the relation to modern man, how they popped up all over the place and so on. You know there is one thing consistent about anthropologists there is only one thing I observed, which is consistent about anthropologists is that the one who is writing a new book is kind of embarrassed about what his colleagues of the last 50 years were saying [laughter] 50 years ago, so maybe you could put this to an anthropologist in 50 years time. The whole business about science of course is not about proof it is about disproof and the whole foundation of it is in saying out theories, but then actually do not buy them. So progress is mild, so the actually progressed thing you are doing is to disprove something, theories that once were accepted..., but that is European culture believe me or not. There are no anthropological theories that do not change, that just keeps going on and on, that's the nature of things. So if you ask me if I agree or disagree with theories you brought forward, I might reply, is it significant to know, if it changes anyway ? Or aren't our believes as significant than your theories, I sure don't need your theories. "

No.42 " Well, I firmly believe upon, that Aboriginal people were the first people that lived on earth, so I can only say: "Ask me in another 20 years and tell me one new story". "

No.26 " Yeah, I heard Aboriginals come from Asia somewhere, they come over in boats, that's all... [Supporting question] Well, Aboriginals they got some sort of religions than New Guinea. I met that New Guinea bloke and he had the same sort of things that we do. "

No.73 " Well, I believe that we were, em, my ancestors were the first Aboriginal people to be in Australia and I don't think we have no connection to people overseas like, hmm, places like Indonesia or Malaysia. I don't no relations there, I am a true, true Australian Aborigine. Because if we did have any, maybe some blood from overseas, Malaysia or anything like that, we should have any of these people here today in Australia. And for sure our coloring is so black we are so dark and the people from overseas are lighter and we've got no connection with that, no. That's what I think. "

No.118 " It is very logical, it is about as logical as the theory of the first seeding of the earth by a passing planet, ah, and starting a whole chain reaction. It is quite feasible, I have seen Aboriginal people, who look quite Asian and I have seen many, who aren't even similar to Asian people and I have seen the more robust type of Aboriginal people and I have seen the slimmer type and I have seen the intermingling of these two. I am not an expert of any field of archaeology, but as I mentioned earlier I saw a spearhead in New Guinea, of the people that look quite Asian and it was similar in shape and weight than the ones we used. So this is quite interesting, but this to me did not represent and archaeological find of any importance, it just confirmed my knowledge of what you can see already. I see no reason why these people did not come from that land. I went to a cave in Tasmania and found three teeth of a Tasmanian sabretooth tiger and those fellows must have come to such a cave and used them. I just can't say what is right, but my feeling is that it is the most logical theory. But those people wouldn't come in here because they are not a seafaring person, the only people who do any kind of boating in Aboriginal communities are Aboriginals at the west coast of West Australia and they make bark canoes and things like that, but they are not really seafaring. [Talk about the need to cross at least 80 sea miles with the boat, if coming from South East Asia] Well, maybe they came from New Guinea. In my knowledge there is no record of any dreaming talking about any seafaring boats. The only dreaming I heard about was in West Australia, but it was more recent. Also in rock and bark painting or carving you find no hint of a craft in any sense. My personal feeling is that there was no crossing of any water barrier. "

No.52 " I don't know, a lot of Aboriginal people are real Asian featured, some of it is correct and some is wrong as I feel, and I feel that as an Aboriginal bloke, so when you say full blood it matters if a white man has a baby with a real dark Aboriginal woman or a woman of my color has a baby with a white man, in many cases the baby is darker than the mother. It is true. And a friend of mine he is almost white and she is lighter than me and their boy is almost black. And another woman she is married to a Scandinavian bloke, they got three children, two are pretty fair, blond hair, blue eyes, but the one in the middle is darker than her. Yeah, I don't believe that, there are still throw backs. The other thing you said about Tasmania, their features are different. To me, I don't think they were 'cause I've met, maybe their skin is lighter, but their features are still there because I've met some Aboriginal Tasmanians. To me they look like white people except their features that are Aboriginal features, very Aboriginal. "

Comments: This question evoked the strongest responses of the interviewees because almost the majority found fault with several parts of the theories, many also commented on

previous results. The following examples contain a general overview of the more common answered. People, who believed that the Aborigines were the first people on earth made up a total of 58 %, similar to informant No.42. An important issue was the possible crossing of at least 80 sea miles. This, however, was not believed by most of the Aborigines who were interviewed (No.118), because there is no mention of it in any of the dreamtime stories and paintings.

The most creditable place of origin theory (if an immigration to Australia took place) would have been over New Guinea (No.26). The facial features of Aboriginal people were often compared to that of others in order to prove or disprove the respective theories (No.52, 118, 73). While some Aborigines saw similarities between Asian people and themselves (No.52, 118), others denied the existence of any similarities what so ever (No.33). The throw back theory was an issue of controversy. Some people encountered within their own circle of acquaintances, cases of throw back (No.52), others confirmed the prevailing theories. From an archaeological and anthropological perspective the ideas of informant No.70 are quite destructive. Because the main function of science is in trying to disprove rather then prove theories, there is little time for advances in scientific research. Knowing that, many theories will soon be replaced with newer ones, and none seems to be worth knowing. With this knowledge he refuses to accept modern theories and sticks with his own believes.

Question No. 9 Original question

No.73 " No, not without an Aboriginal deciding, to back up their theory or whatever they try to put across. "

No.16 " I can't answer that. I am not experienced enough to do that. I just know in certain years, and I don't know whether it was that the status of Aborigines was different constructed, there was a lot of hate against anthropologists, but now some people say they appreciate it. Let me put it this way, the only place were traditional ownership is a factor in land rights is in the Northern Territory, is that correct or not ? "

No.109 " During land rights cases ? Well, if anthropologists can tell the light people and show the light people how long the Aboriginal people have been there, then they should be considered as expert witnesses, again for the jury, for the people, who gonna make the decision, but I don't think they are more expert than the people, who come from the land. They are not more expert on Aboriginal themes than Aboriginal people. But, if the Aboriginal people in that court that need more conviction that the people came of the land and it takes an anthropologist to say, well these are the people that have legal rights of that land and what they say is right then, yes, they should be taken. No one is more expert than the people themselves, but if someone is helping the Aboriginal people this is not wrong. Probably the anthropologists, due to their western education can state things more properly in court terms, but this does not imply that they know more than Aboriginal people. "

No.22 " Oh yes, there should be because there were a lot of

white men that took the land and only over them you could get it back. And the Aboriginals have to recall certain places in the dreamtime, with some it is easier they have still the same name and there are records about. There is a lot of Australian country that belongs to Aboriginal people even though white man are living there, but some land never was of interest for the white man. This land we got back first. Unfortunately, for the white man you can find treasures there now like opals, diamonds, and gold. "

No.53 " No. [can you explain] Sure, because an anthropologist has been taught by an anthropologist. It is one of those things if you go back in time the memory gets diffuse as you progress further down the line teaching in anthropology, so the facts become clearer and clearer and there is more evidence like carbon dating, more evidence of things being found and so the evidence continues to grow, but if you go back the other way you almost come to a situation were you can't interpret things. So if you get a professor in those times you are going in a B line saying that this is what happened and passing it to the students, who might become professors as well taking up that line. And that's the way how you become an anthropologist and that to me smacks every discussion. I am very skeptical about people spending all their life going to school and their life going to University and afterwards teaching about life they have no idea about. I find that very hard to understand. I think life is in your eyes and life is in your hand, you can't get life behind the walls of any institution. No, I'm sorry, I find their attitudes most peculiar... [Talks about an anthropologist he met in Darwin. She admitted to have done no fieldwork, but was working as an anthropologist for almost 10 years now. A few weeks after the conversation she had to go to Brisbane in order to testify on Aboriginal land claims] Nevertheless, the Aboriginal people need anthropologists according to anthropologists, but not according to the Aboriginal people. That is the trouble with these people, they are very quiet and they don't like to make anybody unhappy, so rather than make them unhappy they tell them a lie and say:"Yes you'll helped us." But if you get the Aboriginal people away from the anthropologists they say:"Who are those people, why don't they go back to their own country ?" "

No.1 " Yes."

No.28 " Well, if they know something they should be in court 'cause that's were everything comes out about land rights, you know. So if someone has a land claim for one area they have gone through all this family tree, you know, to make sure that he comes from that area. [Supporting question] Yeah, they need someone to fight for them, you know, Aboriginal people. [Would you prefer an Aboriginal person or doesn't it matter] It doesn't matter as long as they are helpful. "

No.12 " No, not really, not really because most of these city slickers anyway don't know the Australian country, especially the Aboriginal people of course in the traditional way. They don't know the people, they don't know their needs. They really don't know the needs of the people, and the land, I suppose. "

No.105 " Well, I think because of their title people think that they know everything, but they don't, only the people themselves, they have to go to the ordinary people, the people, who live out in the bush. And sometimes it is really hard to, just to know because so many people are coming in and out and they take longer to come across than a town person, I suppose an urban person. And a lot of patience is needed, sit down there with them. (Some people do) rush them and rush them, you know, they'll come across eventually, but, you know, you just don't rush them. Lots of these people are white people like you [pointing to the author] not necessarily Australian people anyway, so they don't understand what is happening out in the land. I mean a lot of Australian people live out here all their life and still don't understand. And there is a lot of things they will never know because it is not taught, you know, if you are not initiated or something like that, you just don't know and that is how it stays. Some people go out there and just observe and get their conclusion out of air, most of them are just too pushy. They (Aborigines) just tell them what they want although most of the time they don't know what they are talkin' about and they just agree. Most of the time they (anthropologists) tell the people what they should want. Sometimes if there is another land rights issue, they come with a big truck and load the elders onto it. And they don't know what is going on. And they (anthropologists) tell them: "Oh, you are riding on the truck and then we are going to town and march for the land." And that is all they will ever know. There are a lot of things they don't know, but should know and no one tells them anyway. "

Comments: This question can be seen as complementary to the previous ones: No.6 and No.7. If question No.8 caused, quantitatively, the strongest response, question No.9 provoked the most vehement response. Only some informants showed insecurity in answering this question (No.16), but were well aware of the disparate opinions of Aborigines concerning scientists, ranging from appreciation for their work to hate. 45 % of the interviewees saw no need for scientists in land rights cases, for various reasons (See below), while another 45 % appreciated their involvement, as long as they helped the Aboriginal people (No.28). 10 % were either insecure or did not answer at all.

Again, several informants stated that no scientist will ever know more than the Aboriginal people, but because of their eloquence in court (No.109) and because of the structure of the legal/court system (No.22), they are needed. Since anthropologists, in particular, decide upon the validity of Aboriginal land claims, interviewee No.73 demanded an Aboriginal person to decide whether the anthropologist's statements were right or wrong. The jury in land right cases still seems to consist only of white people (No.109, 22), so that white people are needed to defend the Aborigines considering their higher status in society.

Some interviewees referred to the injustice in court, since some land can be claimed back easily, especially in desert or rural areas, while densely settled land will never be returned, even though the land claim might be valid (No.22, 91 next question). The University system which provides an education for future anthropologists was criticized by informant No.53. Time-honored theories would be passed from one scientific generation to the next. Life experience could not be taught behind the walls of institutions, but would have to be lived. Like several previous informants (see previous questions) he sees a basic difference in what Aboriginal people say about anthropologists and what they think. Basically, Aborigines would still hate anthropologists.

Often the author had the feeling that scientists, especially anthropologists are only needed if supporting the Aborigines in order to cope with modern Australian society (28) and all the rules, which were forcefully placed upon them. A possible way out of this dilemma seems to be the careful investigation of Aboriginal needs done by experienced fieldworkers (No.12) and the handling of Aboriginal people as being of equal status at least by those scientists (No.105). If scientists and Aboriginal people start working together, and this is a demand by both parties, then misunderstandings (No.105) and an unequal beneficial character of investigations of Aboriginal culture could be a relic of the past.

Question No. 10 Original Question

No.119 " Oh, the jail is full of them, are they recognized or what. Not until long, maybe 10 years, 4 years, not long ago, Aboriginal legal rights act was formed throughout Australia, until then, we had very little support in court. When they came to court defending themselves it was only them and no one else. You know we Aboriginals had a different law, we were not allowed to go into hotels, or liquor stores, and when we were found in town after dark, we could go to jail for 3 to 6 months. About 25 years ago I got what they used to call a citizenship role, just a little booklet, not a passport, you only can get it through law court and that made an Aboriginal person a citizen of Australia, but you needed it. I remember when I was a kid how they treated us. [Question about Aboriginal law versus westernized law] Some of our old laws are quite terrifying, if I got a court, I'd rather be judged by a white man's court. I know I get of quite fairly and not with a spear stickin' through one of my thighs. Some of the Aboriginal people might go to jail for a few years, but if they did something wrong traditional in their tribe it is hell to pay. I prefer the white man's law it is not as hard as the Aboriginal law. "

No.77 " Well there is two laws for us Aboriginals. Like if you do something wrong, if you murder someone, right, you go to jail, do so many years in jail, you come out, they are still punish you. [Which law do you prefer] Only Aboriginal law for Aboriginals, not by white's 'cause I have seen it myself, they go to jail, they come out, they got killed, so they get two punishments. "

No.33 " The Aboriginal people are sufficiently represented by Australian law in some areas, but in other areas they are hardly represented in whatsoever. Giving some examples, they are very, very strongly represented in land rights and unemployment benefits and all those sort of things, but inside that wheel of movement you will find someone in there, who is ripping them off, not necessarily a white person, but at least someone is ripping someone off. ... The first question I ask someone, who represents Aboriginal people is, what does this someone get for doing so ? I am really suspicious and I analyze this suspicion and I mostly find that someone is getting a great deal out of it. So the motivation of these people doing it is not as strong as I feel the motivation should be if handling these issues. It's only a question of money because my motivation comes out inside of me, not of my wallet. "

No.55 " Yes, I think so, yeah, I think they get a, if you get a pretty good lawyer you'll get a fair go, yeah. "

No.91 " In one way you get recognized by Australian law, but in other ways you don't, it is difficult, you know. I think if you want to claim land in New South Wales, you can in certain parts, but not in densely settled areas or those of industrial use. I think the Aboriginals should claim back as much as they can now because in a few years it's gonna be taken. Because those other people come and buy the country, but a lot of the land is ours, they can't buy because we don't sell our land. The country is owned by a lot of people, the Australian locals, the Japanese, French, British, and so on, but the Aboriginals up to now got the worst parts of the land. I see it a little like in America, where they put their houses everywhere and drove the locals in reserves. "

No.10 " Well, in the constitution, the whole business of people of an inferior race is quite consistent in the Australian constitution. They use phrases like the Aboriginal disadvantageous, bullshit like this. In 1967 or so, when they defined the Aboriginals as a race they should have rather chosen the term countryman and then consider the different tribes. Australia has a unique status, but we still rely on the old British imperial law system "

No.117 " No, we are not. Just look at the death rate in custody, look how they treat Aboriginal prisoners. How could they define a law, when they did not even recognize that this was our land, they took away, they should obey our laws or at least consider us, our feelings, believes and laws in the overall Australian one. They don't even take notice of our laws, that were long and strong, but justice. We are nothing but shit for them. "

No.21 " Yeah, I would say yes, even the Aboriginals own right of punishment has been recognized, they have been told that they can't practice pay-back law anymore, this is being considered now as murder. So if they practice that, they go to jail. "

Comments: Although this question does not seem to fit in with the theme of this thesis, most of the answers given refer to important issues of Aboriginal status (No.119, 117) and their attitude towards modern Australian society (No.33, 10), which archaeology/anthropology is a product of. Referring to governmental administration and state-owned institutions in which teachers work together with scientists, informant No.33 declared that those representatives of Aboriginal people would be guided by profit rather than by idealism. 25 % of the informants answered yes, referring mostly to their treatment in court (No.21), while 37.5 % replied no since both institutions of punishment, the white man's court and the Aboriginal one would still be valid (No.77). Another 37.5 % thought the recognition to be sufficient in some areas, while others were poorly represented. One informant also saw a weakness in the reliance on the "Old British Imperial Law System" that is not applicable to the country of Australia (No.10).

8. STONE TOOL EXPERIMENTS

8.1 Physical properties of stone material

When dealing with stone tools of any kind, the researcher should conduct a careful analysis of the mineralogical components of the tool in order to state the usefulness of the material to be worked further as a stone tool. The pedrographic analysis may also help, if previously unknown, to assign the material to known quarries in nearby regions. A third, commonly underestimated factor is the development of patina on the tool's surface causing full or partial destruction of use-wear. Some mineralogical components might enhance the development of patina and others might impede it. These factors should be considered before making blanket statements about the presence or absence of use-wear.

The two different materials (quartzitic sandstones), estimated as sandstone and basalt, encountered in the present analysis were thin-sectioned for further mineralogical investigations. Prof. Dr. Vinx of the Mineralogical Department, University of Hamburg, as well as Geology students at the University of Darwin were kind enough to conduct microscopic examinations of the stone material for each case. Both analysis shall not be withheld from the reader. Prof. Dr. Vinx, who investigated the samples concluded the following:

Sandstone Australia
Well-sorted and mature.
Grain size 50 microns - 5 mm.
Detritic components: quartz (>99 %), zircon, tourmaline, all grains are well-rounded
Cement: chalcedony/microcrystalline quartz. Locally open voids.
Comment: The detritic components are within the range of normal sandstones, this applies to the minerals, their grain size and shape.
Far from normal is the cement of chalcedony/microcrystalline quartz which can best be explained by some sort of hydrothermal action, not by normal diagenetic processes. (Photo 1)
The Geology students in Darwin were less determined in their analysis of the tool samples: a) Relatively coarse-grained (84 grains/mm) pyroclastic basalt with minor lenses of tuffaceous sandstone.
b) Sandstone as analyzed by Prof. Dr. Vinx
Both materials can be found in several quarries in nearby locations in the area where they were collected. The sandstone seems to be far more useful for the purpose of stone tool manufacturing than the relatively brittle basalt.

8.2 Multi-purpose stone knife manufacturing

Since the following experiments were rather self determined much less performed by the author, neither was the chipping floor previously prepared, nor could a selection of usable anvils, hammerstones and working material be influenced. The chipping took place either at old traditional tool manufacturing sites or directly at the quarry where the working

material was obtained from. In order to reach these places, quite often next to old, already deserted settlements, hours of bushwalking or, when lucky, rough four-wheel drives had to be endured. As an additional precaution next to the authors promise not to publicly state the location of these sites, maps, aerial photographs and compasses were not allowed to be taken on the trip. Follow-up examinations were almost made impossible through these precautionary steps.

Only once was the author able to reach a site on his own, which involved a four-day search through semi-arid regions. Fortunately, this site was used over an extended period of time so that limited excavations added a time component (at least 400 years) to the hitherto modern tool manufacturing process. At other sites presumably "older" tools were often just dug up (with a stick) from sediments that might have been disturbed or undisturbed and where post depositional alterations could not be excluded.

Seldom, could the author find the time to collect all the data he would have wished to obtain, (48) since his "tour guides" soon lost interest, preferring rather to go kangaroo or guana hunting and subsequently asking the author to speed up his investigations. Figuring that the tool production sequences and techniques showed little distinctions between the different groups, disparate data were collected in detail during every manufacturing experiment. One single reduction sequence consisting of one or two reduction phases was identified as the main, if not, the only known method.

A) Primary reduction

a) Pre-manufacturing

As earlier stated, these stone tool experiments were comprised of several different stone tool manufacturing campaigns, carried out in various locations (Photo 2) and by stone tool workers with disparate technological sophistication and skill. The time and energy expended to make these stone tools have varied considerably too. If particular weight and dimension measurements are mentioned in the following then they represent mean values established through comparative analysis of the data collected in the experiments. Precondition for every successful knapping is the careful selection of the raw material being used to strike from flakes. Mostly the Australian knapper, the author encountered only one exception, has the infallible ability to select those lithic materials that fracture easily (See also Flaking attributes of... Sec.8.1). Seldom was an initial reduction conducted to test the quality of the stone intended for use (Photo 3). High quality, conchoidally fracturing materials, generally selected by Aboriginal stone workers,

---

(48) Extension of chipping floor, sizes and weight of hammerstones, block and anvil measurements, photographic documentation, percentage calculations, etc.

(Photo 1: Thin sectioning of Sandstone)

(Photo 2: Typical knapping location)

(Photo 3: Testing the raw material)

(Photo 4: Raw material block)

included quartzite, basalt, jasper, silcrete, chert, chalcedony though seldom silicified wood. In addition to the flaking quality of the raw material other selection criteria were taken into consideration. These were the weight and dimension of the stone material, its relative thickness and the existence of a natural platform on the future proximal end of a block. The general rule for the weight and dimension of the stone material is that the stone weight should not exceed the physical lifting abilities of the stone tool worker and the size should not be too unwieldy or too small to work with. The thicker the stone, the harder the intender has to hit the stone in order to strike a flake. The most desirable form would be thin, but longish. The platform as a future location to apply force to is desirable, saving the energy to establish one by a percussion technique. Even though rounded and subrounded raw material shapes were considered, angular or sub-angular shapes were preferred (Photo 4). Securely also the hammerstones were selected, amazingly displaying a bigger hardness after Mohs', therefore the hammerstones seldom cracked or broke during the manufacturing process.

Since previous knapping locations were chosen, an anvil had already been provided (Photo 5). The two main characteristics of such an anvil were a flat, even platform on one side and a steep, pointed "nose" on the other side. At least one platform edge had to display a 90 degree to 120 degree angle in order to accurately support those parts of the block that were intended to flake. The "nose" is thought to split boulders in half to make them more handy for the subsequent preparation. Usable blocks weighing between 750 - 4000 gr, depended also on the material used and varied between 40 x 35 x 20 cm to 18 x 16 x 14 cm in dimensions. The sizes of the hammerstones employed range from 20 x 10 x 7 to 9 x 7 x 6 cm and weigh between 1494.7 gr and 365.5 gr.

Previous heat treatment, as indicated by some researchers (Flenniken/White 1985:133) could not be observed, but was mentioned by some Aborigines as a possible preparatory step.

b) Manufacturing

The main intention of the primary reduction is the production of macro-flakes and cores, either to be used as tools, or to be refined in the secondary reduction. If only a rounded or subrounded block was available, the first move would be the preparation of a flaked or faceted platform by a percussion technique. The author himself observed only two kinds of possible percussion techniques employed by the Aboriginal stone tool workers. Flenniken and White (1985:133-34) mentioned four possible techniques from which only one can be positively confirmed at this point. A single facet platform preparation was performed by simply throwing "the potential core onto a stationary rock in the ground, then selecting suitable fragments as cores." (Source, see above) Bipolar on-anvil, block on-block, or free-hand percussion techniques using a hammerstone to prepare the working platform were never observed even though they seem like useable, alternative techniques. Another, more controllable technique than the "throwing" approach represents a technique where the pointed "nose" of the anvil is used as a

reverse striker. The splitting block is held with either both hands or only one hand and beaten on the anvil nose, a force due to which the block cracks leaving a single facet platform (Photo No. 6). The skilled Aboriginal stone tool worker knows of the consequences of a varying impact angle. If the anvil platform(nose)-to-block working-face angle is 90 degrees then a potential working platform of the core providing an angle of 90 degrees or less to the working face can be expected. Although Flenniken and White (1985:133) note that the shape of the block dictates the primary reduction stage, the main intention of the knapper is rather, the production of macro-flakes for immediate use or those core shapes where blades can be struck from, than the production of a core displaying a platform. These macro-flakes were either produced through an on-anvil bipolar flaking or free-hand percussion technique, in both cases using a hammerstone or the variation of impact angles when using the nose of the anvil. The relative thickness of the block and its bulky shape were responsible for the rough shape of the makro-flakes. Those flakes were often wider than longer, therefore especially suitable for scraping, but seldom usable for even simple cutting purposes. Amazingly, the "anvil nose" technique (49), if skillfully applied delivered, admittably rough, blades with fairly sharp cutting edges. These stone tools, called stone knives by the Aborigines, often represented the end product and no further reduction was undertaken (Photo 7). The frequent finding of cores, only reduced towards this stage, support the statement. If finer blades were the aim to produce, a secondary reduction had to be conducted. Often it is arbitrary to separate the reduction stages as platform preparation. Flake or blade removal occurred alternately throughout the entire reduction sequence due to raw material shape.

c) Post Manufacturing

As earlier mentioned, a careful selection and preparation of the chipping floor was not possible due to the fact that the actual place of manufacturing was not previously known when the experiments started. It would have been a meticulous job to clean a chipping floor, probably used for some hundred years, from any previously chipped flake in order to establish a flake scatter pattern or to provide any weight loss considerations. A photographic documentation of the chipping floor before and after the experiments as well as the careful observation of the main directions, the flakes fell to, enable the author to state the differences in flake scatter patterns occurring through disparate working techniques (Fig. 12 -14). In order to provide the dimensions of the flake scatter pattern, single flakes were measured in distance to the anvil. In the event that the primary and secondary reduction stage would be clearly separable, the experiment was stopped after the primary reduction. The Aboriginal stone tool workers as well as bystanders were asked to select those macro-flakes they would consider suitable for those purposes previously defined by them (See section 8.5).

----

(49) Own nomenclature

(Photo 5: Typical anvil)

(Photo 6: Anvil nose technique)

(Photo 7: Typical stone knife)

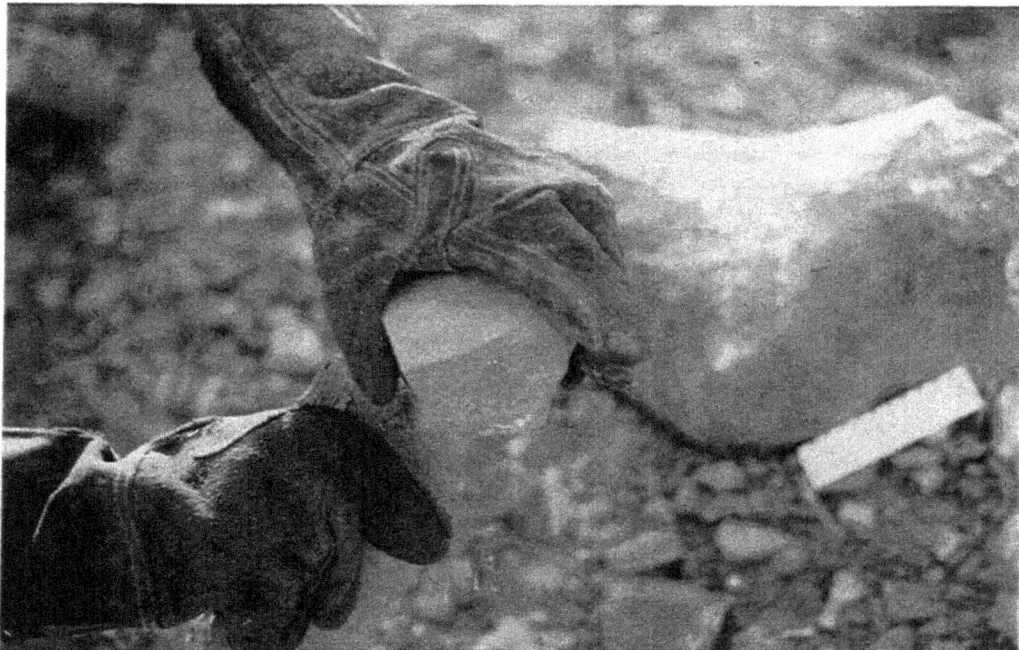

(Photo 8: Free-hand percussion)

These macro-flakes were photographed, singly bagged, and handled with extreme care. Those macro-flakes that could either be used as they were or refined in a secondary reduction were photographed and measured before they were further reduced. When possible the handling was also demonstrated and photographed (50). Only those where the bare skin does not show (wearing a long glove) might be publicly shown.

In some experiments a superficial cleaning of the chipping floor was possible mostly accompanied by surly remarks of the Aborigines who wanted to carry on. If this cleaning uncovered older, earlier produced flakes, which seemed to be usable, those were also selected and singly bagged. In order to avoid confusion the newly produced flakes were named FN (Flakes new) and the older ones FO (Flakes old). The experiments were numbered so that an old flake obtained from experiment No.B would be FOB1. The 1 indicated if this flake was the first, second, etc. found.

B. Secondary Reduction

a) Pre-manufacturing

The primary reduction delivered two types of possible cores usable for further processing. At first, the actual nodule being previously reduced and those macro-flakes whose shape made them especially usable for refined blade production. If the primary reduction did not lead to the production of a core with straight ridges and a rounded working face the core would not be usable for the successful production of blades. Since the newly struck flake (blade) will splinter along the straight ridges of the core (later margins of the blade) and a less rounded working face would establish flakes that are wider than longer, cores not displaying the above mentioned features can be seen as discarded. Surprisingly, stone tool workers, who have not manufactured blades for almost 30 years still know about this important fact and securely selected those cores or macro-flakes showing these features. Worn out intenders were replaced with those that were pointed in order to hit the proximal end of the core more accurately.

b) Manufacturing

Three different techniques were observed to produce the multi-purpose tool "stone knife" within the secondary reduction stage. The on-anvil flaking method was the direct continuation of the technique used in the primary reduction stage. The dexterous variation of the impact angle as well as the deliberate selection of the impact point steered over the anvil nose made it possible to strike high quality blades.

----

(50) Some of the photos can not be released since they have been even strictly forbidden by the respective Aboriginal groups.

The unsuccessful attempt of the author to produce similar blades using the same technique made it obvious that practice and skill is needed to obtain similar results. The author found this technique to be one of the most simple looking but hardest to perform. The second technique observed was the free-hand percussion technique. The intentionally reduced core was held with one hand and struck with the intender held in the other one (Photo No.8). The disadvantage to the previously mentioned technique is that the intender has to hit very hard in order to strike a flake. This lowered the accuracy so that often the core broke in an unintended way. The on-anvil method uses the natural weight of the core to reinforce the applied power of the blow. The advantage of the free-hand percussion technique is the permanent visibility of the working platform and working face in order to decide the location of the subsequently applied forces. It has to be noted here that the free-hand percussion technique seems to be one of the more seldom used stone working techniques also because of the enhanced danger of injuries as some Aborigines have stated. The most commonly applied technique is represented in the on anvil bipolar technique. The core was held at an angle of 35 degrees to 50 degrees towards the platform working edge of the anvil so that one side of the core was fully supported by the anvil edge. The angle of blows (blow angle) employed to the proximal end of the core varied from 50 degrees to 70 degrees. The on-anvil bipolar technique is also and maybe especially be employable when a core becomes exhausted or in other words too small to be worked with any of the other techniques mentioned (Photo 9). The chipping off of two flakes, a primary flake with negative as well as a positive percussion bulb and a secondary flake with only a positive percussion bulb was recognizable when the striker did not exactly hit the marginal region of the core platform and the blow angle was 90 degrees. (Secondary-multiple-flakes) In general the chipped off blades displayed straight, feather terminated margins, crushed distal ends and normally shaped proximal ends. If using this technique, blades could be produced without a huge production of waste material as well as, in a little time, consuming manner.

c) Post manufacturing

The post manufacturing phase was characterized through overhasty data recording and little time consuming activities, since most of the Aboriginal knappers and bystanders reacted with little appreciation (sympathy) towards these procedures. Still, the Aborigines were asked to select those flakes and blades they found most suitable for the purposes stated in section 8.5. Again, the chipping floor was photographed and the author attempted to establish a flake scatter pattern. The selected flakes were singly bagged and inscribed in the usual way. The letter b was added to all flake number, in order to show that it was manufactured in the secondary reduction phase. When possible also the hammerstones and the anvil were photographed to show their wear. It has to be noted that some of the stone knives, even those that turned out extremely well were taken home by the Aboriginal children or the stone tool workers.

Fig.14 On-anvil technique

Key

Location of knapper facing north

- Location of knapper facing north
- 50% og flakes
- 25% of flakes
- 15% of flakes
- 5 – 10% of flakes

N

Fig.13 Anvil-nose technique

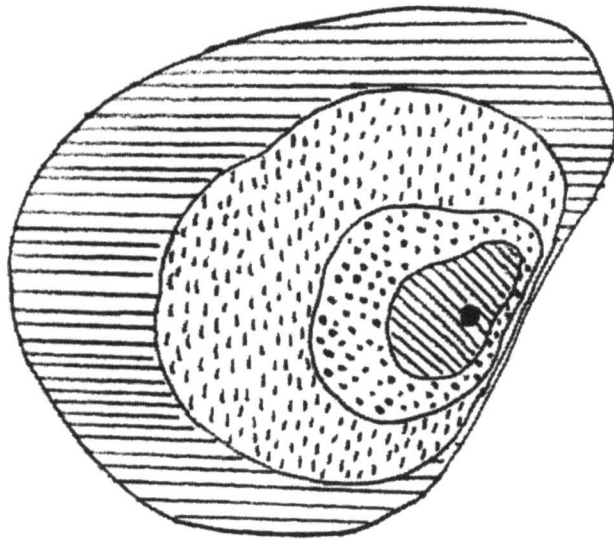

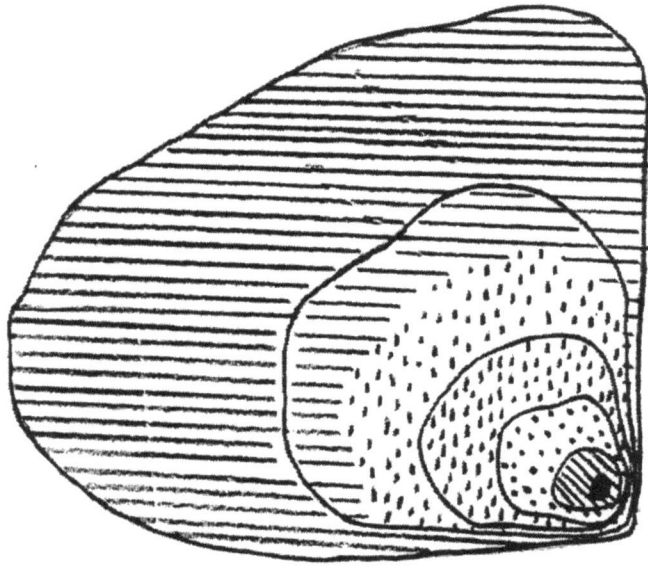

Fig.12 Free-hand percussion

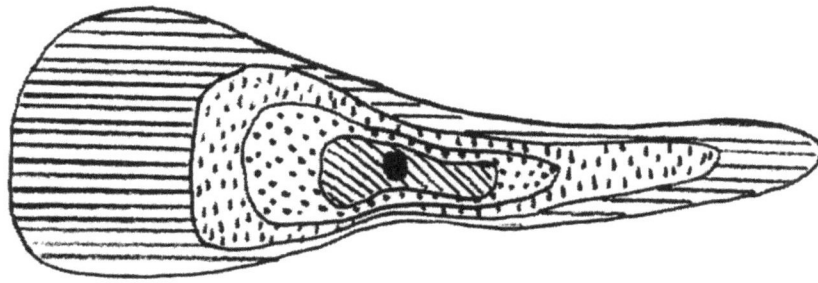

1 m

Fig. 12 – 14 Flake scatter patterns occurring through disparate working techniques

(Photo 9: Refinement)

(Photo 10: Rough tools/Preforms)

(Photo 11: Stone knifes and scrapers produced)

(Photo 12: Adze preform, Hammerstone)

C) Local differences in the manufacturing process

Although some local differences were observed, the main differences in stone tool manufacturing obviously were related to the personal skill and craftsmanship of the single knapper. The local factors were solely related to the raw material at hand. If only basaltic rock material was available the stone tool worker had to choose such a technique that would give him/her the ability to use his/her individual physical strength most efficiently. In order to reach the critical point beyond the elasticity of the basaltic material, which means to break it, the stone tool worker had to hit harder and with higher velocity. The only technique that promises somewhat satisfying possibilities to manage both the material being struck harder and controlled to avoid unintended breakage is the on-anvil bipolar technique. Even though this technique has its weaknesses (Deunert 1990:49-60), the free-hand percussion and on-anvil technique would deliver worse results. In case quartzitic raw materials could be obtained, the on-anvil technique was the most preferred, albeit free-hand percussion as well as on-anvil bipolar techniques were applied. One Western Australian knapper, working with quartzitic material in the Alice Springs region did solely work with the free-hand percussion technique after he had established a core in the desired dimensions and with a platform through a block-on block technique.

When working with the on-anvil technique some knappers preferred to use both hands to hold the block with, while most stone tool workers chose the one handed blow. The selection of a suitable anvil also varied considerably. Knappers who intended to exclusively work the core through the on-anvil technique chose those anvils showing a "nose" not considering an eventual platform. The main feature of anvils used for the on-anvil bipolar technique was the platform without such a "nose".

When employing the free-hand percussion technique to the stone material, short blows struck with high velocity, were preferred, while long blows were seldom applied. One knapper even moved both hands towards each other, attempting to smash both stone parts, core and striker, against each other. When using the on- anvil bipolar technique some stone tool workers preferred heavy pointed hammerstones, while others chose those of rounded and medium size.

8.3 Flaking attributes of different raw material

Two different raw materials were used for the experiments carried out in the Northern Territory of Australia. Naturally, the quartzitic material displayed different flaking attributes than the basaltic material. Since the author has already given the flaking attributes of basalt (Deunert 1990:65) only the main characteristics will be summarized here. Although the Australian basalt (5,5 on the Moh's scale) was not quite as hard as the Hawaiian Mauna Kea basalt (7 on the Moh's scale) it displayed similar flaking attributes. In order to reach the critical point beyond the elasticity of the brittle material the stone worker has to hit the material harder, faster or with a heavier striker, compared to the flint for example. In order to work the Mauna Kea basalt either the blow velocity or the force had to be increased, while the Australian basalt tended to break easier.

Experienced knappers know that the obtained accuracy in stone tool working is directly proportional to the applied efforts to reach the breakage point of the material being worked. The elastic property of the material used is of decisive importance since the dynamic load induced by the striker might be absorbed or only partially absorbed. If it is fully absorbed, the knapper has to hit harder or with higher velocity. In case it is only partially absorbed unintended breakage occurs. Both basaltic as well as quartzitic material demand an accurate blow on the marginal region of the working platform if reduced with the on-anvil bipolar technique. Since the production of longish and slightly rounded flakes was especially the main intention of the stone tool workers, the core had to be split longitudinally unless a thick block was previously selected. The longitudinal split as well as the controlled splitting of a thick block is a difficult and often frustrating enterprise. This was particularly true when basaltic raw material was chosen. Quartzitic material tended to chip naturally so that little to medium force was necessary to launch the intended breakage. As stated earlier (Section 8,2) the establishment and maintenance of straight ridges in addition to a concave shape on the working face of the core was a necessity for producing successful blades. Quartzitic material was easily shaped this way, so that sharp and longish blades could be manufactured.

Basalt, on the other hand, tended to break without leaving the desired ridges on the working face of the core. Albeit some high quality basalt flakes were produced so the amount of debitage accumulated, was twice as high as when quartzitic material was used.

8.4 Tool Measurements

Since the replica tools were not employed for any of the possible materials which could have been worked with, only a few measurements were needed to clarify stone technological aspects. Most importantly a distinction had to be made between those tools being reproduced and the ones being excavated or otherwise collected in order to state possible technological changes. The basic flake extension measurements were needed in order to relate them to special manufacturing techniques (Such as: wide flake interprets: no ridges were previously produced on core). The length of the stone knives was measured from the proximal end to the distal one. The width was measured from the most distant points of the lateral margins. The thickness was gauged at the thickest part of the cross-section. The measurements of the platform thickness were important since they showed the carefulness of the production and the skill of the stone tool worker.

If a thin platform was present, the striker hit the exact marginal region of the working platform of the core the flake was struck from. Edge angle measurements were undertaken to clarify technological perspectives rather than to indicate possible tool functions. The edge curvature and the edge morphology using a hand lens with 10x magnification was also noted. The edge curvature indicated the efficient or non-efficient establishment of ridges on the working face of the core the flakes were obtained from. If the edge is straight a successful establishment of those ridges can be implied. Finally, any visible peculiarities were mentioned.

It has to be noted that only complete flakes were taken into consideration. A complete flake is defined as having a single interior surface and an intact striking platform intersected by the bulb of percussion. Intact margins displaying a hinge or feather termination as well as no lateral breaks inferring with accurate width measurements were required.

c) Comparison of results

It was generally noticed that the quartzitic stone tools developed patina even after a short time, which might also have covered parts of the cutting edge. It will be interesting to see if the patina destroys the use-wear when chemically building up on the tool surface. In section 8.6 an attempt will be made to exfoliate this patina, especially from those areas of the stone tool cutting edge were use-wear is discernible and supposedly extends under the patina layer. When comparing previous investigations of stone tools of different material using a 10x magnifying hand lens, the author has to note the absence of clearly recognizable use-wear either observed with the naked eye or the hand lens. Edge smoothing or rounding was the only observable characteristic which eventually pointed to tool strain while being used. The basaltic material used, at least in the stone tool experiments, brittled easily.

Even if the author had the intention to develop use-wear, little of it would be observable afterwards under the microscope. The basalt of some of the tools either collected or given by the Aborigines was harder and more complex, with these tools the most promising previous use-wear was observed. The quartzitic material was as easy to flake as it was hard to scratch. The edge surely was rounded but did not show obvious polish or striation as is sometimes observed on other materials that have been, for example, worked with extremely hard materials. These early observations predicted a negative outcome of the subsequent low and high power use-wear examination.

After having compared the single dimension measurements of the tools, there seemed to be no preferred length, width or thickness of the stone knives. The length ranged from 8 - 16 cm, while 10 - 12 cm was the average. The width did not exceed 5 cm and was not smaller than 1.9 cm. Tools thicker than 2 cm were rare, while 1,4 to 1,6 cm were relatively common. The edge angle measurements uncovered edge angles ranging from 30 - 40 degrees as the most common type while smaller and especially larger angles were rare. When comparing the measurements of the experimentally produced flakes to the given or earlier manufactured ones, one becomes aware of the conformity of the data. It seems that the immediately visible edge damage of the experimentally produced stone tools is heavier than to the comparable

older tools. This might indicate the little practice of the stone tool workers when asked to manufacture the 41 tools considered in this thesis.

8.5 Blade usage stated by the Aborigines

The stone knife appears to have been used for various purposes. Most commonly stated was the use of the stone knife to cut a kangaroo in the traditional way. This process involved the cutting through of sinews along the jumping joint in order to twist the ankle bone in the anatomically opposite direction. The kangaroo blood, which is drunk to enhance sexual potency, was drained through a cut of the main blood veins. Both techniques involve the cutting through skin, fresh flesh and eventually sinews. Often too, the tail was cut off before cooking the kangaroo in an earth oven, exposing the tool to friction against cartilage and bone. The actual cutting up of the kangaroo into handy parts was done in a cooked state. The skilled Aboriginal hunter cut the kangaroo in a traditionally defined way avoiding cutting through bones or other hardly manageable parts.

It was said that the stone knives were so durable that a whole kangaroo could be cut up without the tool becoming dulled. Another function of the stone knives was its use as a carving tool for deliberate wood working. This process involved the whittling, scraping, planing, and drilling of those woods that were endemic to this specific region. At first, the wood had to be obtained, since already seasoned wood is a lot harder to work with. If a small tree was needed, a stone hatchet was used to cut it, but if only smaller branches were needed, the stone knife served as a little saw. Branches were especially cut for the thatching of a shelter to protect against the sun and eventually the rain. The wood and branches obtained were formed into the desired shape and state through whittling and sometimes the wood was split by using the stone knife as a cleaver or chisel. The bark was either whittled or scraped, while a plain and smooth surface was obtained through planing. The finished tool was decorated with carvings of dreamtime events or tribal signs.

Stone knives were also used for the care of the body. This involved hair cutting, eventually shaving, but also used as a tool for surgery, wherewith clots of blood, abscesses, etc. were operated on. Seldom, if at all, was the stone knife used as a weapon. It was only used for defense, when no other weapon was at hand. The knife was also needed to collect and cut herbs and fruits, as well as, to dig up roots. Often it was used as a knife for eating or for the preparation of food.

8.6 High an low power examination of the stone material

a) Introductory remarks

Every usable edge of the flakes either found or given by the Aborigines was examined under 20x, 60x, 90x, and 120x magnification. A binocular C.H.Schröder 6078 microscope was used for the examination. Since the only light source of

Flake	Weight in gr	Length in cm	Width in cm	Thickness in cm	Relative Angle in degrees	Absolute Angle in degrees	Edge Curvature	Retouch / Comments
FNA 1	73.25	13.5	4.0	1.7/PL 1.1	30 - 35	35	Irregular; Rough	2 natural retouches
FNA 2	60.56	11.0	4.7	1.3/PL 0.7	35 - 40	30 - 35	Slightly convex; Rough	Thick layer of crust adherent
FNA 3	21.95	10.1	3.3	0.9/PL 0.9	25	25	Strongly concave: Rough	Patinated; damaged cutting edge
FNA 4	88.74	16.3	1.9	1.8/PL 1.3	40	30 - 35	Straight; Even	Rounded; smooth cutting edge
FNA 5	28.08	8.0	3.9	0.9/PL 0.4	15 - 20	20	Irregular; Even	1 groove; rounded
FNA 6	59.39	9.2	4.2	1.1/PL 0.6	35	30 - 35	Strongly convex; Even	1 notch; natural retouches
FNA 7	75.09	12.9	3.1	0.5/PL 0.3	10 - 15	10	Straight; Rough	
FNA 8	36.76	8.9	4.3	1.4/PL 1.1	40 - 45	40	Slightly concave; Rough	Heavy edge damage; Crushing Notches
FNA 9	56.98	9.8	3.1	2.0/PL 1.2	20 - 25	25 - 30	Slightly convex; Rough	
FNA10	84.32	13.1	2.6	1.2/PL 0.6	35 - 40	30	Irregular; Rough	2 natural retouches
FNB20	29.01	8.4	2.4	1.5/PL 0.8	30	30 - 35	Slightly convex; Even	
FNB21	64.38	11.1	3.3	1.2/PL 0.5	15 - 20	20	Irregular; Rough	
FNB22	87.64	13.4	3.9	1.7/PL 0.6	30 - 35	30 - 35	Concave; Rough	Crushing of the forward edge
FNB23	61.26	12.3	4.0	2.2/PL 1.0	35 - 40	35	Slightly concave; Rough	1 deep groove
FNB24	47.84	9.2	3.5	1.4/PL 0.9	20	20	Convex; Rough	1 notch; natural retouches
FNC25	64.83	11.5	3.4	1.5/PL 1.2	30 - 35	35 - 40	Straight; Rough	Rounded; smooth cutting edge
FNC26	45.97	8.5	2.7	1.2/PL 0.8	25 - 30	30	Slightly concave; Even	
FNC27	39.65	12.0	2.4	1.2/PL 0.5	35	30 - 35	Slightly concave; Rough	
FNC28	53.61	12.6	3.1	1.4/PL 1.0	45	40	Slightly convex; Rough	1 natural retouch
FNC29	71.96	11.1	2.0	0.9/PL 0.6	35 - 40	35	Convex; Rough	
FNC30	65.70	10.6	4.7	0.8/PL 0.9	20 - 25	20 - 25	Straight; Even	Crushing; damaged cutting edge parts
FND36	56.96	10.2	4.1	1.9/PL 1.0	40	40 - 45	Irregular; Rough	2 notches;crushed edge
FND37	42.03	9.7	4.3	1.3/PL 0.7	35 - 40	30 - 35	Slightly convex; Rough	Heavy edge damage; several retouches
FND38	75.06	13.8	3.2	2.1/PL 1.2	35 - 40	35 - 40	Slightly concave; Rough	1 groove
FND39	80.10	15.9	3.7	1.4/PL 1.2	25	25	Irregular; Even	1 natural retouch
FND40	43.58	12.9	3.5	1.9/PL 0.4	15 - 20	20	Irregular; Rough	
FNE45	51.92	11.2	2.3	1.3/PL 0.3	25 - 30	30 - 35	Straight; Rough	
FNE46	39.61	12.7	1.9	1.1/PL 0.8	30 - 35	30 - 35	Slightly concave; Rough	Crushing of the forward edge
FNE47	46.06	11.5	4.1	0.8/PL 0.6	35	25 - 30	Slightly concave; Rough	2 natural retouches
FNE48	68.03	8.4	3.5	2.2/PL 1.3	25 - 30	30 - 35	Slightly convex; Rough	1 deep groove; notches
FNF52	36.35	11.3	2.3	1.4/PL 1.0	30	25 - 30	Irregular; Rough	
FNF53	74.83	14.6	2.7	1.0/PL 0.5	35	30	Convex; Rough	
FNF54	71.94	13.7	4.8	1.2/PL 1.1	35 - 40	40 - 45	Straight; Even	Several notches
FNF55	47.90	9.8	3.4	2.3/PL 0.7	40 - 45	35 - 40	Straight; Rough	Crust reaching parts of the forward edge
FNF56	57.32	12.6	2.1	1.5/PL 0.4	50	45	Irregular; Rough	
FNF57	79.64	15.6	3.7	0.9/PL 0.7	15 - 20	15 - 20	Slightly convex; Rough	1 natural retouch

Table 1: Measurements of tools manufactured

Flake	Weight in gr	Length in cm	Width in cm	Thickness in cm	Relative Angle in degrees	Absolute Angle in degrees	Edge Curvature	Retouch / Comments
FNF58	60.25	9.4	2.5	1.2/PL 0.9	30 - 35	35	Strongly concave; Rough	1 natural retouch
FNG68	35.66	8.4	3.4	1.1/PL 1.0	40 - 45	35 - 40	Convex; Rough	
FNG69	72.89	12.1	4.8	2.0/PL 1.3	15 - 20	20 - 25	Irregular; Rough	Crushing; notches
FNG70	55.92	10.2	4.2	1.8/PL 1.2	35	35	Slightly concave; Rough	Heavy edge damage; crushing
FNG71	48.62	8.9	3.2	1.2/PL 0.8	25 - 30	25 - 30	Irregular; Rough	1 notch
Given Flakes								
FO74	64.78	11.4	2.8	1.2/PL 0.5	35	30 - 35	Slightly concave; Even	Edge smoothing; rounding
FO75	43.61	9.3	3.5	1.4/PL 0.8	35 - 40	25 - 30	Irregular; Even	
FO76	77.43	12.3	4.6	1.1/PL 0.6	25	25 - 30	Convex; Rough	Slight edge rounding
FO77	82.67	14.6	4.3	1.4/PL 1.2	25 - 30	30	Concave; Even	New breakage; retouches
FO78	53.82	10.0	3.9	1.9/PL 1.0	35 - 40	30 - 35	Slightly convex; Even	Strongly patinated cutting edge

Table 2: Measurements of tools either manufactured or obtained from Aborigines

Flake	Weight in gr	Length in cm	Width in cm	Thickness in cm	Relative Angle in degrees	Absolute Angle in degrees	Edge Curvature	Retouch / Comments
FOA11	64.45	11.1	3.0	1.4/PL 0.8	30	30	Irregular; Rough	Definite edge rounding;1 natural retouch
FOA12	37.92	8.5	1.9	0.8/PL 0.7	15 - 20	15 - 20	Slightly concave; Even	
FOA13	47.12	10.9	3.6	1.5/PL 0.5	35 - 40	35	Convex; Rough	
FOA14	57.10	11.3	3.4	1.7/PL 1.2	30 - 35	25 - 30	Slightly convex; Rough	New breakage;Notch
FOA15	51.00	11.0	3.3	1.8/PL 0.8	25 - 30	30	Slightly concave; Even	Edge smoothing;Rounding
FOA16	27.37	7.5	2.2	1.2/PL 0.7	35	30 - 35	Concave; Even	
FOA17	72.14	15.3	4.7	1.7/PL 1.0	40 - 45	35 - 40	Straight; Rough	Sharp undisturbed edge
FOB18	80.04	13.4	4.1	1.6/PL 0.6	25	25 - 30	Irregular; Rough	Crust adherent to the cutting edge
FOB19	32.65	10.2	3.3	1.2/PL 1.1	25 - 30	30	Strongly convex; Rough	1 deep groove
FOC31	41.88	10.9	3.1	0.9/PL 0.8	30 - 35	30 - 35	Slightly convex; Even	
FOC32	59.23	11.4	3.5	1.4/PL 0.9	30 - 35	25 - 30	Strongly convex; Rough	
FOC33	75.91	13.7	4.0	2.1/PL 1.4	40	35 - 40	Straight; Even	st.patinated;ifedge discernable/smooth
FOC34	29.99	10.0	2.6	1.2/PL 0.9	30 - 35	35	Irregular; Rough	Crushing;Notches
FOC35	44.21	11.3	3.4	1.6/PL 0.7	25 - 30	25 - 30	Slightly concave; Rough	
FOD41	46.75	10.7	2.9	1.4/PL 0.8	15 - 20	20 - 25	Slightly concave; Rough	
FOD42	61.63	12.2	3.3	1.6/PL 0.6	30 - 35	25 - 30	Slightly convex; Rough	2 natural retouches;Notch
FOD43	58.82	11.9	3.6	1.6/PL 0.7	10 - 15	20 - 25	Irregular; Rough	Damaged and patinated cutting edge
FOD44	37.56	10.4	3.4	1.4/PL 0.5	35 - 40	35 - 40	Straight; Rough	Heavy edge damage;Groove;Notches
FOE49	29.89	9.8	2.3	1.3/PL 0.6	35	35	Strongly convex; Even	
FOE50	49.11	10.1	3.2	1.7/PL 0.8	25	20 - 25	Irregular; Even	Rounded;Smooth cutting edge
FOE51	41.74	9.9	2.8	0.9/PL 0.9	40 - 45	35 - 40	Straight; Rough	
FOF59	83.01	14.7	4.5	2.0/PL 1.2	35 - 40	35 - 40	Slightly convex; Rough	
FOF60	55.26	12.2	3.4	1.9/PL 0.5	30 - 35	25 - 30	Strongly concave; Rough	Crushing of the forward edge
FOF61	57.02	11.9	3.1	1.7/PL 0.4	25 - 30	30 - 35	Irregular; Rough	
FOF62	63.47	13.6	3.3	1.4/PL 0.6	35	30 - 35	Straight; Even	
FOF63	51.73	10.9	3.0	1.4/PL 0.7	25 - 30	30	Slightly concave; Even	Definite edge rounding;Smoothing
FOF64	49.88	9.7	2.8	0.8/PL 0.4	30 - 35	35	Slightly convex; Rough	1 retouch supposedly natural
FOF65	53.97	11.4	3.2	1.7/PL 0.8	35 - 40	30 - 35	Irregular; Rough	
FOF66	72.67	13.7	3.6	1.6/PL 0.5	15 - 20	20 - 25	Slightly convex; Rough	Patinated areas;Covering cutting edge
FOF67	70.20	14.1	4.2	1.4/PL 0.7	40 - 45	35 - 40	Strongly concave; Rough	Crushing; Damaged cutting edge parts
FOG72	59.87	12.4	3.0	1.4/PL 0.5	35 - 40	35 - 40	Straight; Rough	Retouches/Natural
FOG73	62.55	12.0	3.3	1.5/PL 1.1	25 - 30	30	Slightly concave; Even	

Table 3: Measurements of tools either excavated or collected

(Page 82)

this microscope was transmitted light a different source had to be used. A Hertel & Reuss MKL 200 glasfiber lamp with adjustable light intensity and three different tentacles to be turned towards the investigating object was employed. The foot of the microscope was taken off and the optical part was mounted on a stable stand in order to enable the investigator to observe the top of the edge, since there was not sufficient space for the tool in the original arrangement.

Unfortunately, the microscope was not equipped with any filters used to screen the brightness of the light reflected from the highly reflective quartzitic stone tools. Such tools could only be examined when lowering the light intensity of the glasfiber lamp or turning its tentacles to the margin regions of the tool. Additional difficulties occurred when attempting to photograph through the microscope. At first the exposure time could not be automatically steered over a exposuremeter so that standard adjustments had to be developed depending on the grade of reflectivity of the respective tool. Generally the shutter time varied from ¼ sec to 1 second when the use of the non-sensitive 100 Asa film was taken into account.

Since there was no fitting adapter to mount the camera on the tube of the microscope it had to be fitted to one of the eyepieces. Wishing to employ a higher or lower magnification, the camera had to be removed and another ocular had to be chosen, which extended the examination time for every tool immensely. The photos were shot with the aid of the selftimer, in order to avoid any blurring. A Minolta SRT101 camera was employed for the photographic documentation. Some photographic examples can be seen in the appendix A.

The outcome of the high and low power use-wear analysis is listed in a tabular form and can be seen in table 3. Unfortunately, only a few of the tools displayed use-wear, even those, that were definitely used over a longer period of time (Tool FO75). Already before his close investigation of the quartzitic material Prof.Dr.Vinx remarked that little use-wear might be found due to the hardness and complex morphological structure of the material. Since only 9 out of the 37 investigated tools displayed some kind of use-wear a descriptive explanation of these tools seems to be appropriate in order to acquaint the reader with the meager findings which were grounds for subsequent conclusions.

b) Tool interpretation

FOA12: Three microflake scars were observed on the basaltic tool. Two of them were found on the ventral and one on the dorsal side of the stone knife. This involved mainly feather (66,7 %), but also step (33,3 %) terminated scars. Due to their small number the microflake scars were scattered along the tool edge. Other than one scar, which was quite large, the microflake scars were small in size. The dorsal edge aspect was slight, while the ventral one was partially unmodified to slightly rounded. The polish observed on both edge aspects was dull to bright, grainy, and not very smooth. Striation as well as denticulation was absent. The arrangement

of the microflake scars pointed to bi-directional motion whereas the equal strain of both edge aspects rather implied a cutting/slicing motion than whittling or scraping/planing. Medium to soft material was thought to have been used.
Evaluation: Insecure (vague) interpretation

FOA16: This basaltic tool displayed feather (40 %) and step (40 %) terminated scars to equal numbers. Additionally one dorsal snap terminated (20 %) scar was present. Slightly more dorsal than ventral scars were found. Due to the smallness of the scars their configuration was scattered along the tool's edge. Even though the dorsal as well as ventral edge aspect was only slightly rounded, polish was observable on both sides. The polish was dull, grainy and mostly pitted. Unfortunately, no striation or denticulation was detectable. Also here, the arrangement of the microflake scars pointed to a motion where the tool was used sideways so that whittling of medium-hard material was concluded.
Evaluation: Secure interpretation

FOC33: This quartzitic tool showed only one dorsal, hinge terminated (100 %) microflake scar. Neither edge rounding/smoothing nor denticulation or striation was observed. This stone knife was either not used at all or only over a short period of time on soft material, while the direction of use or the action performed is impossible to state.
Valuation: Insecure (vague) interpretation

FOE50: The highest amount of microflake scars was found on this quartzitic tool, displaying slightly more dorsal scars than ventral ones. This stone knife represented at the same time the only securely interpretable quartzitic tool since it showed strong edge rounding, as well as, polished areas, at least on the dorsal side. Feather (44,4 %) and step (44,4 %) terminated microflake scars were documented,while snap (11, 2 %) terminated ones were meagerly represented. None of the scars overlapped leaving the scar configuration scattered on the dorsal and ventral edge side. The edge rounding could be considered strong, since it is already discernible with a 10x magnifying hand lens. Amazingly, only the dorsal side seemed to have areas that could be defined as polished. The polish was bright, extremely smooth and non-pitted. Striation and denticulation was absent. The one sided polish would rather point to a scraping and planing motion than to the interpreted whittling one, but the arrangement of the microflake scars was decisive for the statement of the action. Medium- hard contact material may have caused the traces observable on the stone tool.
Evaluation: Secure interpretation

FOF62: This little stressed basaltic stone knife displayed dorsal and ventral microflake scars. The scars were exclusively feather (100 %) terminated ones, which obviously were scattered along both edge

sides. Slight edge rounding was observed on the dorsal edge side, while unmodified to slight rounding was characteristic for the ventral side. Polish and striation were absolutely absent. The microflake scars as well as the intermittent and shallow denticulation pointed to a bi-directional cutting or slicing motion with ripping along the tool edge. The use of soft contact material seemed to be fitting in view of the number and appearance of the microflake scars.
Evaluation: Secure interpretation

FOG73: The five observed microflake scars were mainly found on the dorsal side of the basaltic tool edge, almost firmly indicating a scraping or planing motion. The scars were mainly composed of step (60 %) terminated scars, but also lesser amounts of snap (20 %) and feather (20 %) terminated microflake scars. Due to their number and size the scars were scattered along the tool's edges. Strong edge rounding, as well as, dull, grainy and pitted polish was observed on the dorsal side of the tool, while only slight rounding and no polish occurred on the ventral side. No striation and denticulation were found. Knowing that scraping as well as planing motions develop similar use- wear traces, a distinction between these actions would only be made possible through extension measurements of the polish or striation. This would imply that charts with these measurements considering the different materials of the tool and the contacted items would have to be established and still only an vague interpretation would be possible. Scraping/planing can be firmly stated though the contact material was assumed to be medium-soft because of the few traces that were observable.
Evaluation: Secure interpretation

FO 74: This quartzitic tool displayed, similar to the previously mentioned one, a relatively high amount of scars on one side of the tool. Three dorsal feather (75 %) and step (15 %) terminated scars were opposed one ventral, feather terminated scar. The scars were scattered along both edges which were also slightly rounded. Polish, striation and denticulation were absent. A scraping, maybe planing motion was simply concluded because of the unequal dorsal/ventral distribution of the microflake scars. The contact material may have been medium-soft.
Evaluation: Insecure (vague) interpretation

FO 77: The basaltic tool FO 77 displayed dorsal and ventral scars in equal numbers. Snap (50 %), feather (25 %), and hinge (25 %) terminated scars were present. The scars were small in size and scattered along the tool edge. The dorsal and ventral edge rounding seemed to be slight, while polish, stria-

tion, or denticulation were absolutely absent. Even though the supposedly well executed action did not leave many traces, a whittling motion was interpreted because of the arrangement of the microflake scars. Medium contact material could have caused the present use-wear.
Evaluation: Insecure (vague) interpretation

FO 78: This quatzitic tool was rather more interesting because of its crust than because of its use-wear. A few (two) observable microflake scars were found on the dorsal side of the tool consisting of feather (50 %) as well as step (50 %) terminated scars. The scar configuration was scattered and only slight edge rounding was observed. Polish and denticulation were absent. Interesting was the possible striation observed on the tool partially covered by a thick crust. Mineralogical examinations verified the crust/patina as having been developed through chemical processes within the stone as well as chemical or bacteriological processes from the surrounding environment. In order to test the hypothesis that this crust might destroy the use-wear, while accumulating on the tool's surface, this layer had to be exfoliated. Other tools that did not show any kind of use-wear were chosen to derive and execute possible exfoliation techniques. The following techniques were tested:
a) An electrolytic bath did not remove any crust particles, even when the tool was kept in it for several hours. b) Soaking it in water over several days lead to similar non-sufficient results. c) Doing the same in a saline solution did partially remove some of the crust. d) Brushing or scraping off of the crust was possible but considered to be too aggressive for the tool's surface. e) The same was true for acids when laid on, in a non-dissolved state. f) Most efficient was the boiling of the tool in water enriched with a few drops of household cleaner with organic acids to dissolve lime. Technique f) was applied to tool FO 78 in order to exfoliate the crust at least on the area were use-wear was assumed. After microscopically investigating the tool, it could be stated that the striation either never continued under the crust or was destroyed by it. The crust exfoliation technique could not have destroyed the use-wear since the previously observed striation was still present. Other researchers may be advised to conduct a careful use-wear analysis of the investigating tool before the boiling procedure, since the tool might receive additional use-wear through the movement in the water (hitting the pot) Tool FO 78 was thought to have been used in a scraping motion on soft contact material.
Evaluation: Insecure (vague) interpretation

Table 4: Results of the microscopic investigation of the collected stone knifes

Tool	Total Micro-flake Scars D	V	Snap D	V	Feather D	V	Step D	V	Hinge D	V	Configuration D	V	Edge Rounding D	V	Polish/Smoothing D	V	Striation D	V	Denticulation	Action	Contact Material
FOA11	-	-	-	-	-	-	-	-	-	-	-	-	-	-	-	-	-	-	None	Not used	Not used
FOA12	1	2	-	-	1	1	-	1	-	-	SC	SC	SL	SL;UN	Yes	Yes	-	-	None	Cut /Sli	Soft-Medium
FOA13	-	-	-	-	-	-	-	-	-	-	-	-	-	-	-	-	-	-	None	Not used	Not used
FOA14	-	-	-	-	-	-	-	-	-	-	-	-	-	-	-	-	-	-	None	Not used	Not used
FOA15	-	-	-	-	-	-	-	-	-	-	-	-	-	-	-	-	-	-	None	Not used	Not used
FOA16	3	2	1	-	1	1	1	1	-	-	SC	SC	SL	SL	Yes	Yes	-	-	None	Whittling	Medium-Soft
FOA17	-	-	-	-	-	-	-	-	-	-	-	-	-	-	-	-	-	-	None	Not used	Not used
FOB18	-	-	-	-	-	-	-	-	-	-	-	-	-	-	-	-	-	-	None	Not used	Not used
FOB19	-	-	-	-	-	-	-	-	-	-	-	-	-	-	-	-	-	-	None	Not used	Not used
FOC31	-	-	-	-	-	-	-	-	-	-	-	-	-	-	-	-	-	-	None	Not used	Not used
FOC32	1	-	-	-	-	-	-	-	1	-	-	SC	-	-	-	-	-	-	None	Not used	Not used
FOC33	-	-	-	-	-	-	-	-	-	-	-	-	-	-	-	-	-	-	None	Not used	Not used
FOC34	-	-	-	-	-	-	-	-	-	-	-	-	-	-	-	-	-	-	None	Not used	Not used
FOC35	-	-	-	-	-	-	-	-	-	-	-	-	-	-	-	-	-	-	None	Not used	Not used
FOD41	-	-	-	-	-	-	-	-	-	-	-	-	-	-	-	-	-	-	None	Not used	Not used
FOD42	-	-	-	-	-	-	-	-	-	-	-	-	-	-	-	-	-	-	None	Not used	Not used
FOD43	-	-	-	-	-	-	-	-	-	-	-	-	-	-	-	-	-	-	None	Not used	Not used
FOD44	-	-	-	-	-	-	-	-	-	-	-	-	-	-	-	-	-	-	None	Not used	Not used
FOE49	-	-	-	-	-	-	-	-	-	-	-	-	-	-	-	-	-	-	None	Not used	Not used
FOE50	5	4	1	-	2	2	2	2	-	-	SC	SC	ST	ST	Yes	-	-	-	One Notch	Whittling	Medium-Hard
FOE51	-	-	-	-	-	-	-	-	-	-	-	-	-	-	-	-	-	-	None	Not used	Not used
FOF59	-	-	-	-	-	-	-	-	-	-	-	-	-	-	-	-	-	-	None	Not used	Not used
FOF60	-	-	-	-	-	-	-	-	-	-	-	-	-	-	-	-	-	-	None	Not used	Not used
FOF61	-	-	-	-	-	-	-	-	-	-	-	-	-	-	-	-	-	-	None	Not used	Not used
FOF62	1	1	-	-	1	1	-	-	-	-	SC	SC	SL	SL;UN	-	-	-	-	Interm/Shallow	Cut / Sli	Soft (Flesh?)
FOF63	-	-	-	-	-	-	-	-	-	-	-	-	-	-	-	-	-	-	None	Not used	Not used
FOF64	-	-	-	-	-	-	-	-	-	-	-	-	-	-	-	-	-	-	None	Not used	Not used
FOF65	-	-	-	-	-	-	-	-	-	-	-	-	-	-	-	-	-	-	None	Not used	Not used
FOF66	-	-	-	-	-	-	-	-	-	-	-	-	-	-	-	-	-	-	None	Not used	Not used
FOF67	-	-	-	-	-	-	-	-	-	-	-	-	-	-	-	-	-	-	None	Not used	Not used
FOG72	-	-	-	-	-	-	-	-	-	-	-	-	-	-	-	-	-	-	None	Not used	Not used
FOG73	4	1	1	-	1	-	2	1	-	-	SC	SC	ST	SL	Yes	-	-	-	None	Scra / Pla	Medium-Soft
FO74	1	3	-	-	1	2	-	1	-	-	SC	SC	SL	SL	-	-	-	-	One Notch	Scraping	Medium-Soft
FO75	-	-	-	-	-	-	-	-	-	-	-	-	-	-	-	-	-	-	None	Not used	Not used
FO76	-	-	-	-	-	-	-	-	-	-	-	-	-	-	-	-	-	-	None	Not used	Not used
FO77	2	2	1	1	-	1	-	-	-	1	SC	SC	SL	SL	-	-	-	-	None	Whittling	Medium
FO78	2	-	-	-	1	-	1	-	-	-	SC	-	SL	-	-	-	-	-	None	Scraping	Soft

(Page 85)

c) Summary

The high and low power examination established that 9 out of 37 tools were used. Only four times was a secure interpretation of the executed action and the contact material was possible. A vague interpretation was possible only five times. Only firm basaltic tools could be interpreted, while only one quartzitic tool displayed sufficient use-wear allowing a secure statement about its use. The possible uses of stone knives previously stated by the Aborigines could be confirmed as whittling, cutting/slicing, planing, and scraping was recognized through the traces these actions left on the tool surface. A definite recognition of the contact material was not possible. Crust, built up on quartzitic tools was found to destroy use-wear, which might have been present in the form of polish or striation even though the author has to admit that he could only test this theory on one tool. The author would have also liked to examine the tools with a magnification up to 350x, since previous studies (Deunert 1990:203-205) showed that polish and especially striation was often only visible between 200x and 350x magnification. A limiting factor for the investigated stone knives was the lack of comparable data from either previous studies or replicative experiments.

8.7 Evaluation of the experiments considering the cooperation and interest of the Aborigines

When Howard Creamer, working with the National Parks and Wildlife Service in New South Wales, published his paper (1980:10-17) about the possible cooperation of archaeologists and Aborigines he probably had the vision of a publicly interesting archaeological enterprise. Even though he published a photo (Fig 3:14) where Aborigines seemed to gather around out of interest for the explanations of an archaeologist dealing with stone tools, there was no way that these people could be kept in the hot sun for longer than 10 - 15 minutes without loosing the interest. This does not imply that Aborigines may have a short attention span, on the contrary, they measure their possible benefits arising from their involvement in public and academic archaeology. The only benefit seems to be the explanation of a history/prehistory they already know, mostly in a different way, from their dreamtime stories. Archaeology does not give them considerable support in court with regards to their land claims. Archaeologists continue to excavate even in sacred places. Further more, most Aboriginal people do not even know or want to know what archaeology is. These and similar reactions and comments the author experienced when he tried to relate to pure archaeological problems, especially in his stone tool technological part. Although some interesting results were obtained in the above analysis, a close cooperation with the Aborigines would made things more efficient. It would have been desirable to collect more data, i.e. through partial excavation of the chipping floor or a lengthier tool manufacturing experiment. The author would have also liked to have been allowed to investigate some of the stone knives that are occasionally in use even today. The author personally had the feeling that the Aborigines showed interest in the general idea of this thesis, to be a de facto decision maker of what should be investigated in Australian prehistory, but considered the exemplary chosen stone tool analysis unimportant and of little benefit.

9. SUMMARY AND CONCLUSION

Initially it was stated that the Aborigines, mainly those who live on their traditional land, seem not to be interested in their cultural heritage as possibly uncovered through scientific research. Even obviously biased results are not contradicted in writing. Australia, as a whole, and Aboriginal history and prehistory in detail, evolved into a worldwide field of interest in search of a commonly applicable theory of settlement, subsistence, migration, and development in early times of humankind. Similar to other countries, in Australia the indigenous inhabitants have received more rights, especially concerning their once traditionally owned land. This, admittedly honorable and justifiable development did not cause positive intercultural relations in the respective areas. Trespassing warnings and a ban on all scientists in some areas, was the consequence, perhaps this was a reaction to colonial scientific investigations. Since anthropology, more than archaeology, needs steady communication with groups to be investigated, their main investigational tools, observation, interviewing, and recording became useless. But also, archaeologists had to face consequences which mainly occurred during long and often unsatisfactory negotiations of possible excavations in prehistorically interesting areas. Not only did the scientists and Aborigines living on their traditional land became opposing parties, but also those Aborigines, who had moved further in the assimilation process towards the western culture, opposed to those Aborigines, whose traditional knowledge and conservational mechanisms were still intact. Urban Aborigines especially, lost contact to their traditional life and its values and became more and more interested in their cultural heritage. The outlined, already massive, but steadily reinforcing discrepancies represent a major factor that had to be overcome in the following years. In order to investigate the problems occurring and eventually finding a satisfying solution, one had to become aware of their full extend as well as the numerous factors involved.

The beginning of the present thesis deals with methodological considerations. It was decided to use a continuously developing and even altering question catalogue since the full extend of a problem can never be grasped unless actively involved in its solution, in this case, the active interplay of the interviewer and the respective interviewee. The following application of this question catalogue has proved the truthfulness of this assumption. Another, even more important pre-investigational decision was the use of a middleperson, who would develop more easily a closer relation to Aboriginal people through her ethnic background and in some cases, gender differences. The consequently excellent cooperation with most Aborigines made the author believe that the right person was chosen. Experience showed the research manipulating influence of any kind of dependency of the researcher towards the interviewee and vice versa. The author tried to avoid any dependencies, and when existent, the interview results were either biased or not considered at all.

The outline of the archaeological/anthropological interpretation of prehistoric Australia - pre 1770, revealed the importance of such an enterprise and showed the necessity of future research projects. The short history of Australian archaeological investigations shows the time related developmental stages and the modern conflict between scientists exploring Australia's prehistory. Phrased differently, this outline was also needed for the interviews conducted in order to examine possible differences in historical and prehistorical perspectives. Personally, the author regards Australian archaeology as excellent, however, it is meagerly supported by government or university administrations. Also within the Australian population archaeology seems to have no lobby in general, not to mention, within Aboriginal groups, who often mistake archaeology for anthropology.

Although generations of scientists have tried to develop and prove theories of possible places of origin of the Aboriginal culture, none of them have been convincing up to now. Also migrational patterns within Australia are ambiguous though unitarily stating an immigration from regions in the north. This statement, by the way, does also comply with several dreamtime stories. Since biological, cultural, and linguistical research has failed to provide data useable for derivational interpretations archaeology should and could provide comparable data. With the knowledge that the human occupation of continental Australia is at least 40.000 years old, a date has been obtained to connect early Australian cultures to the already known and dated ones in South East Asia. Unfortunately, little research has been done so far in comparing i.e. the inventories of sites in South East Asia and Australia. More excavations have to follow in both regions in order to prove early hypotheses.

Another problem is the obvious lack of boats, today and in the archaeological record, as well as of Aborigines, who could skillfully operate them in aquatic environments. These boats would have been needed to cross the sea-barrier between South East Asia and continental Australia.

Far more secure than the vague investigations of the Aborigine's origin are the archaeological statements about Australian settlement and early subsistence strategies established through even early inland sites. It becomes obvious that the earliest human occupants of Australia must have successfully endured the moist coastal and arid desert environments equally as successful, albeit eventually two different groups, the gracil and the robust type, settled Australia simultaneously. Scientists tend to believe that the earliest settling society was highly adaptive and sophisticated, though it left its impact on the Australian continent through hunting, especially with fire. In the future more sites have to be uncovered and excavated to allow the researchers more reliable statements about the time, distribution, and variety of settlements.

By interpreting Aboriginal prehistory archaeology also has its limits, especially when being approached ethnoarchaeologically, experiencing little or no support through Aboriginal groups. In an attempt to actively involve Aboriginal people in a scientific project replicative stone tool experiments have been conducted using the locally available raw materials of each area being investigated. Commonly applied standard procedures were employed for the gathering and recording of data needed for subsequent interpretations.

Major problems already occurred when trying to approach an Aboriginal community. Permission is always needed to even trespass on Aboriginal, land not to mention, living within an Aboriginal community. The normal procedure would be to submit of an application to the land council. This detailed application should contain personal data, educational background, any research proposals, and any affiliations with institutions, and should indicate the possible beneficial features for the group to be investigated. The researcher might have to wait about 4 weeks to 3 months for approvals or mostly rejections. If approved it does not imply that the chosen community knows about his/her research or even expects his/her appearance since it is not announced by the council. The researcher is better off establishing personal contacts to Aboriginal people in and around the cities and receiving invitations to their communities. This way the researcher has at least one contact person on the day of arrival and the "oral press" would work for him/her. Still, the researcher would have to propose his/her project to the respective community council, but now, at least, the researcher has the opportunity to actively take part in the decision making process through clear arguments. Once the community council approves, the rest of the community will know about the researcher and his/her project within a few days. Although an approval was obtained, in this case, the researcher should not imply that there is a common interest in his/her studies. Most Aborigines are only interested in partial aspects, in the present case, the solution of some subproblems, of the respective research project.

Based on personal experience, the author feels that the Aborigines are more interested in special questions relating more to the question catalogue, since they referred to actual problems that Aborigines face today, than the stone tool experiments. Nevertheless, some interesting results have been obtained. Special consideration found the multipurpose stone knife, whose manufacturing sequences could clearly be stated. Along with the already known knapping techniques like free-hand percussion and on-anvil bipolar flaking, a third one was observed. The author called it the anvil-nose technique, since a little ledge of the anvil was used as a reverse striker. The splitting block is held with either both hands or only one and beaten on the anvil nose, a force due to which the block cracks leaving a single facet platform. Often the rough outcome of stone knives with fairly sharp edges was the end product. Only when more deliberate tools were needed, was a secondary reduction conducted.

The tool measurements and outer appearance considerations established a continuity of homogeneous stone knives throughout the last few hundred years; also local variations were few. It became obvious that the quartzitic material was easy to flake but extremely hard to even scratch. Patina, previous edge damage and eventually visible use-wear was also noted since the following use-wear analysis should confirm or deny the actual stone knife usages stated by Aboriginal people. 9 out of 37 tools, either obtained, collected, or excavated were established as being used and has

confirmed the previously stated employment. Crust, built up on quartzitic tools was found to destroy previously present use-wear, though this theory could only be tested on one tool.

Again the author has to place emphasize on the little interest shown of Aboriginal people in the stone tool manufacturing part though the author tried everything to state the importance of such an enterprise. As earlier mentioned, most Aborigines were gladly willing to have their say in several questions asked, since they liked the general idea of being a de facto decision maker of what should be investigated on, in Australian prehistory. The elaborate and eloquent answers obtained by some questions showed the direct involvement in the problems mentioned. The opinions expressed were often extremely diverse and can not be summarized here, but could guide future researchers to a better understanding of today's Aboriginal people and enhance the ability to develop future research projects.

With respect to this, it should be mentioned that the present research has a somewhat exceptional characteristic through the use of an obviously fitting middleperson. Most interviewees did not like their name being publicly stated and would never give an honest interview to a person who did not belong to a minority or oppressed group, that has endured a similar fate as they have. This conflict is explainable through Aboriginal history of the last few hundred years. Traditionally, the Aborigines determined their own fate and development, however, with the arrival of the Europeans, it became more foreign determined. First treated like animals, then tried to be "domesticated" and "brain washed" on missions and reserves and finally given some rights adherent to diverse conditions, the Aborigines still living on their traditional land developed a mistrust of almost all new projects.

Australians today turn a blind eye to the conditions the Aborigines live in, even blame them for the financially depressed state of Australia. Since the Aborigines can not return to their traditional life style, but will not be accepted as full members of the new Australian society, displacement and uprooting have caused major problems. The psychological effect is dejection and depression, using alcohol to drown themselves in, hoping to, in the short term, give themselves a spiritual push. We have to face the fact that the treatment of the Aborigines is equally bad, if not even worse than, in some points (health care) the treatment exercised in the old Apartheid regime in South Africa. The health status, infant mortality, and juvenile hearing or vision loss, is comparable to third, forth, and even fifth world countries.

In recent years Aboriginal groups have tried to reestablish Aboriginal confidence and power, pointing out traditional values. Factually, most Aborigines lost their traditional cultural identity, since a process of successful knowledge conservation, the oral tradition, is not being practiced anymore. As regards this, it is extremely ambiguous to think that the newly propagated Aboriginal awareness can purely rely on their own knowledge of pre-/history and leave out any scientific research. It becomes apparent that the stated pre-/history might be a newly created one. The outline of the archaeological/ anthropological interpretation of prehistoric Australia shows that archaeology especially, is needed in this process of identification, though archaeology is still in its beginning stages. Archaeologists and especially anthropologists have to be conscious of their delicate situation and immense responsibility when dealing with cultures other than their own. It is adequate to explore a culture, grown up in, since being well aware of its respective value system and thinking. Every other prehistoric or contemporary culture can only be explored fragmentary and the results will always be ambiguous if an "interpretive tool" is used. Such an interpretive tool can be, the cultural background, method, and theory, but also the experience.

The literary outcome especially of anthropological research might enhance the reading skills and expressiveness of the students working in this field. It might even involve them in the process of broader thinking and encourage them to be culturally aware of their own and other societies, but it can not reflect the original ideas, thoughts and modes of behavior even less so when being expressed in a language of a person with a different cultural background.

It has become obvious now that there is a mutual dependency between scientists exploring Australian prehistory and Aborigines. Measures have to be found to involve both sides, who will benefit equally from the investigations. The Aborigines need scientists who will show proof of the vague prehistory that they are aiming to identify with and scientists need Aborigines to fully understand and interpret prehistoric findings. If this thesis has given a stimulus of working together and reduced conflicts, then it has not failed in its purpose.

Summary in German

DEUTSCHE ZUSAMMENFASSUNG

Zu Anfang dieser Arbeit wurde festgestellt, daß die Aborigines, hauptsächlich diejenigen, die noch auf ihrem angestammten Land leben, offenbar kein Interesse an ihrer kulturellen Herkunft haben, als diese möglicherweise durch wissenschaftliche Forschung herausgefunden werden könnte. Auch offensichtlich fragwürdige Resultate werden nicht schriftlich widerlegt. Australien, als ganzes, und die Geschichte und Urgeschichte der Aborigines im speziellen, entwickelte sich zu einem weltweiten Interessensfeld, um anwendbare Besiedlungs-, Daseins-, Migrations- und Entwicklungstheorien in frühester Menschheitsgeschichte zu suchen. Ähnlich wie in anderen Ländern haben auch in Australien die indigenen Bewohner mehr Rechte erhalten, im besonderen Maße ihr traditionell besessenes Land betreffend. Diese, zugegebenermaßen ehrbare und gerechtfertigte Entwicklung hat dennoch keine positiven, interkulturellen Beziehungen hervorgerufen. Im Gegenteil, wurden einige Gebiete nun für Wissenschaftler unzugänglich erklärt, vielleicht nur erklärbar durch schlechte Erfahrungen mit kolonialwissenschaftlichen Forschungen. Da Ethnologie, mehr als Archäologie, die ständige Kommunikation mit denjenigen Gruppen braucht, welche Untersuchungsgegenstand sind, schien der Ethnologie wichtigste Forschungs-

technik, die Beobachtung, das Interview und die Aufzeichnung hinfällig geworden zu sein. Doch auch Archäologen spürten negative Auswirkungen, was sich hauptsächlich in langen, wenig zufriedenstellenden Verhandlungen über mögliche Ausgrabungen in prähistorisch interessanten Gegenden äußerte. Am Kulminationspunkt dieser Entwicklung war es nicht nur so, daß die Wissenschaftler und Aborigines gegnerische Parteien wurden, sondern auch diejenigen Aborigines, welche stärker in die westliche Kultur integriert waren, sich gegen solche Aborigines, deren traditionelles Wissen und dessen Konservierung intakt war, wendeten. Besonders städtische Aborigines haben den Kontakt zu ihrem traditionellen Lebensstil und dessen Werten verloren und interessierten sich daher mehr und mehr für ihre kulturelle Herkunft. Die eben beschriebenen, massiven, jedoch sich noch verstärkenden Diskrepanzen stellen einen wichtigen Faktor dar, welcher in den nächsten Jahren überwunden werden muß. Um die auftauchenden Probleme zu untersuchen und diese eventuell zu einer zufriedenstellenden Lösung zu führen, mußte man sich ein möglichst genaues Bild des Ausmaßes und der zahlreichen, abhängigen Faktoren machen.

Der Anfang der vorliegenden Arbeit beschäftigt sich mit methodologischen Problemen. Es wurde beschlossen einen sich ständig entwickelnden und sogar verändernden Fragenkatalog zu benutzen, da die ganze Bandbreite einer speziellen Problematik niemals ganz erfaßt werden kann, wenn man sich nicht aktiv mit deren Lösung beschäftigt, in diesem Fall die aktive Zusammenarbeit zwischen dem Interviewer und dem entsprechenden Interviewpartner. Die nachfolgende Anwendung dieses Fragenkataloges hat die Richtigkeit dieser Annahme bestätigt. Eine andere, noch wichtigere Entscheidung vor der eigentlichen Untersuchung war die Verwendung einer Mittlerperson, die, bedingt durch ihre kulturelle Herkunft und manchmal durch den Geschlechtsunterschied, schneller und leichter eine enge Beziehung zu den Aborigines entwickeln würde. Die sich daher ergebende hervorragende Zusammenarbeit mit den meisten Aborigines, scheint der Entscheidung rechtzugeben. Erfahrung zeigt auch, daß jede Art der Abhängigkeit vom Wissenschaftler zum Interviewer und umgekehrt, sich manipulierend auf die Forschung auswirken kann. Es wurde daher versucht, jede Abhängigkeit zu vermeiden, und sollte sie dennoch vorhanden gewesen sein, so wurden die Ergebnisse des Interviews entweder angezweifelt oder überhaupt nicht herangezogen.

Der Abriß der archäologischen/ethnographischen Interpretation von Australiens Prähistorie - vor 1770, zeigte die Wichtigkeit einer solchen Unternehmung und zukünftiger Forschungsprojekte. Die kurze Einführung in die Geschichte der australischen Archäologie zeigt die historisch bedingten Entwicklungsstadien und den zeitgenössischen Konflikt zwischen Forschern der australischen Prähistorie. Anders ausgedrückt, wurde dieser Überblick für die Interviews benötigt, um mögliche Unterschiede in historischen, prähistorischen Perspektiven aufzuzeigen. Persönlich ist der Autor der Meinung, daß die australische Archäologie als ausgezeichnet anzusehen ist, lediglich zu wenig von Regierung und Universitätsverwaltung unterstützt. Ebenso scheint Archäologie unter der australischen Bevölkerung keine Lobby zu haben, besonders bei aboriginal Gruppen, die Archäologie häufig mit Ethnologie verwechseln.

Auch wenn Generationen von Wissenschaftlern versucht haben, Theorien über die Herkunft der Aborigines zu erstellen und zu beweisen, so war bisher keine absolut überzeugend. Auch Migrationsmuster in Australien sind zweifelhaft auch wenn einheitlich eine Einwanderung aus dem Norden angeführt wird. Diese Aussage, übrigens, stimmt mit mehreren Traumgeschichten der Aborigines überein. Da biologische, kulturelle und linguistische Forschungen versagt haben, brauchbare Daten für Herkunftsinterpretationen zu liefern, sollte und könnte die Archäologie solche Daten bereitstellen. Durch das Wissen, daß die menschliche Besiedlung von kontinental Australien mindestens 40.000 Jahre zurückliegt, wurde ein Datum gewonnen, um frühe australische Kulturen mit jenen schon datierten in Süd-Ost Asien zu verknüpfen. Leider wurde bisher wenig über den Vergleich von Inventarien süd-ost asiatischer und australischer Ausgrabungen gearbeitet. Mehr Ausgrabungen in beiden Regionen müssen die Folge sein, um frühe Hypothesen zu überprüfen.

Wesentlich konkreter als die unsicheren Interpretationen über die Herkunft der Australier sind die archäologischen Aussagen über die frühen australischen Besiedlungs- und Unterhaltsstrategien, untermauert sogar durch frühe Inlandplätze. Es scheint nun offensichtlich, daß die frühesten, menschlichen Bewohner von Australien sowohl die feuchten Küsten- als auch die trockenen Wüstenregionen gleichermaßen erfolgreich besiedelten, obwohl wahrscheinlich zwei verschiedene Gruppen, die "Grazilen" und die "Robusten", Australien gleichzeitig besiedelten. Wissenschaftler glauben heute, daß die frühest besiedelnde Gruppe sehr adaptiv und fortschrittlich gewesen sein muß, die jedoch einen nachhaltigen Eindruck auf den australischen Kontinent hinterlassen hat, besonders durch das Jagen mit Feuer. In der Zukunft müssen mehr Siedlungsplätze entdeckt und ausgegraben werden, um den Forschern sicherere Aussagen über die Zeittiefe, Verteilung und Vielfalt der Besiedlung zu ermöglichen.

Bei der Interpretation der Vorgeschichte der Aborigines ist jedoch auch die Archäologie beschränkt, besonders wenn ethnoarchäologisch gearbeitet wird und wenig Unterstützung von aboriginal Gruppen erfahren wird. In einem Versuch, die Aborigines aktiv in einem wissenschaftlichen Projekt mitwirken zu lassen, wurden Experimente zur Herstellung von Steingeräten, unter Verwendung der jeweils vorhandenen Steinmaterialien, durchgeführt. Generell angewendete Standardprozeduren wurden für das Sammeln und Aufnehmen von Daten verwendet, um diese für spätere Interpretationen verwenden zu können.

Grundlegende Probleme tauchten schon bei dem Versuch auf, eine aboriginal Gemeinde zu besuchen. Eine formelle Erlaubnis, um Aboriginal Land zu überqueren, geschweige denn in einer Aboriginal Gemeinde zu leben, ist von Nöten. Der normale Vorgang zur Erlangung einer solchen Erlaubnis wäre die zeitige Einreichung einer Bewerbung an das "Land Council". Diese detaillierte Bewerbung sollte alle persönlichen Daten, den Bildungsweg, jegliche Forschungsvorhaben

und jegliche Verbindung zu Institutionen, wie auch den möglichen benefiziellen Charakter für die zu untersuchende Gruppe aufzeigen. Der Forscher muß dann ungefähr 6 Wochen bis 3 Monate auf die Zusage, jedoch meist Ablehnung, warten. Wenn angenommen, besagt dieses noch lange nicht, daß die ausgewählte Gemeinde über das Forschungsvorhaben Bescheid weiß, noch daß sie den Forscher in irgendeiner Form erwartet, da dieses vom "Land Council" nicht weitergeleitet wurde. Der Forscher wird besser daran tun, persönliche Kontakte zu Aborigines in und um die Städte zu knüpfen und persönliche Einladungen zu erhalten. Auf diese Art hat der Forscher wenigstens eine Kontaktperson am Tage der Ankunft und die "mündliche Presse" hat schon für ihn gearbeitet. Dennoch müßte und sollte der Forscher sein Forschungsvorhaben dem jeweiligen "Community Council" näher erklären, doch wenigstens jetzt hat der Forscher die Möglichkeit, durch klare Argumente aktiv in dem Entscheidungsprozeß mitzuwirken. Wenn einmal das "Community Council" das Projekt genehmigt hat, weiß spätestens 1 oder 2 Tage später die ganze Gemeinschaft darüber Bescheid. Auch wenn eine Genehmigung erteilt wurde, sollte der Forscher nicht davon ausgehen, daß die gesamte Gemeinschaft uneingeschränktes Interesse in das Forschungsvorhaben zeigt. Die meisten Aborigines werden nur in Teilaspekten, im vorliegenden Fall der Lösung einiger Unterprobleme, des jeweiligen Forschungsvorhabens interessiert sein.

Basierend auf persönlicher Erfahrung, ist der Autor der Meinung, daß die Aborigines wesentlich mehr an den speziellen Fragen im Fragenkatalog interessiert waren, da sie sich auf die tatsächlichen Probleme der Aborigines heute beziehen, als an den Steingeräteexperimenten. Es wurden jedoch einige sehr interessante Ergebnisse erzielt. Besondere Erwähnung fand das Mehrzweck Steinmessser, dessen Herstellungsstadien klar erkannt werden konnten. Neben den bereits bekannten Schlagtechniken, wie der Freihandschlag und die bipolar Amboßtechnik, wurde auch eine dritte beobachtet. Der Autor hat diese Technik die Amboß-Nasen-Technik genannt, da ein kleiner Vorsprung am Amboß als ein umgekehrter Schlagstein genutzt wurde. Der zu bearbeitende Block wurde entweder mit beiden Händen oder nur mit einer Hand gehalten und auf die Amboßnase geschlagen, eine Kraft, durch welche der Block zersprang, eine unifaciale Plattform hinterlassend. Meist wurden so grobe Steinmesser mit beachtlich scharfen Ecken produziert. Lediglich wenn feinere Werkzeuge benötigt wurden, wurde eine weitere Bearbeitung durchgeführt.

Die Gerätemessungen und äußere Formbetrachtungen weisen auf eine Homogenität und Kontinuität von Steinmessern über die letzten Jahrhunderte hin; auch lokale Varianten waren beschränkt. Früh wurde erkannt, daß das quarzitische Material zwar leicht zu schlagen war, jedoch zu hart, um es auch nur einzuritzen. Patina, vorherige Beschädigungen der Schneidekante und eventuell sichtbare Gebrauchsspuren wurden ebenso notiert, da die folgende Gebrauchsspurenanalyse die eigentliche Steinmesserverwendung, hervorgehoben von den Aborigines, bestätigen oder widerlegen sollte. 9 der 37 entweder erhaltenen, aufgesammelten oder ausgegrabenen Steingeräte wurden als im Sinne der vorher angenommenen Verwendung benutzt. Kruste, welche sich auf quarzitischen

Steingeräten abgelagert hatte, wurde als Gebrauchsspuren zerstörend herausgefunden, auch wenn dieses nur an einem Gerät nachgewiesen werden konnte.

Nochmals muß der Autor das geringe Interesse der Aborigines an der Herstellung von Steingeräten hervorheben, auch wenn die Wichtigkeit solcher Untersuchungen ständig betont wurde. Wie schon früher erwähnt, waren die meisten Aborigines gerne bereit auf viele Fragen zu antworten, da sie die Idee mochten, die eigentlichen Entscheidungsmacher über das zu sein, was in Australiens Prähistorie erforscht werden sollte. Die ausführlichen und durchdachten Antworten erhalten bei einigen Fragen, zeigten die direkte Beteiligung an den angesprochenen Problemen. Die ausgedrückten Meinungen waren oft extrem divers und können hier nicht zusammengefaßt werden, doch könnten sie zukünftige Forscher zu einem besseren Verständnis mit Aborigines führen und die Möglichkeit steigern, neue Forschungsprojekte zu erschließen.

In diesem Zusammenhang soll erwähnt werden, daß die vorliegende Forschung einen Ausnahmecharakter hatte, da eine offenbar günstige Mittlerperson herangezogen wurde. Die meisten Interviewpartner wollten ihren Namen nicht öffentlich preisgeben und würden ein ehrliches Interview keiner anderen Person geben, als derjenigen, die auch zu einer Minderheiten- oder Unterdrückten-Gruppe gehört und als solches ein ähnliches Schicksal wie sie erfahren hatte. Dieser Konflikt scheint durch die aboriginal Geschichte der letzten Jahrhunderte erklärbar. Hatten die Aborigines traditionellerweise ihr Schicksal selbst bestimmt, so wurde es nun mehr und mehr von anderen beeinflußt. Behandelt zuerst wie die Tiere, dann zu "domestizieren" versucht und einer Gehirnwäsche auf Missionen und Reservaten unterzogen, gab man den Aborigines einige Rechte, jedoch mit diversen Konditionen verbunden, Daher entwickelten die Aborigines, welche noch auf ihrem angestammten Land leben, Mißtrauen gegenüber fast allen neuen Projekten.

Das heutige Australien scheint blind der Bedingungen in denen die Aborigines heute leben, scheint sie sogar für die finanzielle Depression in Australien verantwortlich zu machen. Da die Aborigines nicht zu ihrem traditionellen Lebensstil zurückkehren können, auf der anderen Seite jedoch nicht als vollwertige Mitglieder der australischen Gesellschaft akzeptiert werden, stellen Entwurzelung und Unzugehörigkeitsgefühl ein großes Problem dar. Der psychologische Effekt ist Niedergeschlagenheit und Depressionen oft einhergehend mit Alkoholmißbrauch, in der Hoffnung wenigstens für kurze Zeit einen spirituellen Schub zu erleben. Wir müssen uns heute klarmachen, daß die Behandlung der Aborigines mindestens ebenso schlecht, wenn nicht schlechter in einigen Punkten (medizinische Versorgung) ist, als jene Behandlung der Schwarzen im alten Apartheid System in Süd Afrika. Der Gesundheitszustand, die Kindersterblichkeit, kindlicher Gehör- und Sehverlust sind vergleichbar mit dritt, viert und sogar fünft Welt Ländern.

In den letzten Jahren haben aboriginal Gruppen versucht ihr Vertrauen und ihre Stärke wiederzugewinnen durch die Rückbesinnung auf traditionelle Werte. Tatsächlich jedoch, haben die meisten Aborigines ihre traditionell, kulturelle Identität verloren, da der bisher erfolgreiche, wissenskonservierende Prozeß, die orale Tradition, nicht mehr praktiziert wurde. In diesem Zusammenhang ist es sehr zweifelhaft zu glauben, daß die neu propagierte aboriginal Bewußtheit sich nur auf eigenes Wissen der Vor- und Frühgeschichte stützen kann und wissenschaftliche Forschung vernachlässigt. Es wird offensichtlich, daß diese propagierte Vor- Frühgeschichte eine neu kreierte sein mag. Die Beschreibung der archäologischen und ethnologischen Interpretation von Australien zeigt, daß besonders die Archäologie in diesem Identifikationsprozeß gebraucht wird, obwohl jene Forschung noch an Anfang steht. Archäologen, und besonders Ethnologen müssen sich ihrer delikaten Situation und immensen Verantwortung bewußt sein, wenn sie mit anderen Kulturen als der eigenen umgehen. Es ist angemessen eine Kultur zu erforschen, in der man aufwuchs, da man sich des jeweiligen Wertesystems und des Denkens bewußt ist. Jede andere prähistorische und zeitgenössische Kultur kann nur fragmentarisch ergründet werden und die Resultate werden immer fragwürdig sein, sofern ein "interpretatives Werkzeug" benutzt wurde. So ein interpretatives Werkzeug kann die kulturelle Herkunft, die Methode, Theorie, doch auch die eigene Erfahrung sein.

Besonders in ethnographischer Forschung kann das literarische Endprodukt die Lesekenntnisse und Ausdruckskraft der Studenten, welche in diesem Feld arbeiten, steigern. Es kann den Studenten sogar neue Horizonte öffnen und ihn/sie anreizen kulturell aufgeschlossen gegenüber anderen Kulturen zu sein, doch es kann niemals die ursprünglichen Ideen, Gedanken und Verhaltensweisen ausdrücken, zumal auch noch niedergeschrieben in einer Sprache einer Person mit unterschiedlicher, kultureller Herkunft.

Es scheint nun offensichtlich, daß es eine gegenseitige Abhängigkeit zwischen Wissenschaftlern, welche die australische Prähistorie erforschen und den Aborigines gibt. Wege müssen gefunden werden, beide Seiten gleichermaßen heranzuziehen, um von den Forschungen gleichermaßen zu profitieren. Die Aborigines brauchen Wissenschaftler, welche die vage Vorgeschichte untermauern, mit welcher sich die Aborigines identifizieren und die Wissenschaftler brauchen die Aborigines, um prähistorische Befunde vollständig zu interpretieren. Wenn diese Dissertation eine Stimulans zur Zusammenarbeit gegeben und Konflikte reduziert hat, dann hat sie nicht ihren Zweck verfehlt.

10. BIBLIOGRAPHY

Abbie,A.A. The original Australians. Sydney,A.H. & A.W.Reed, 196

Aboriginal Land Rights (Northern Territory) Act 1976, Section 23e, 51 and 54Allbrook,D.B. The human biology of the western Pacific basin: asurvey of the physical anthropology and relationshipsof peoples within Australia, Melanesia, Micronesia, Philippines and Polynesia. In:Yearbook of Physical Anthropology 18, 1974:202-45

Allen,F.J. The first decade in New Guinea archaeology. In: Antiquity 46, 1972:180-90

(the same) When did humans first colonize Australia ? In: Search 20(5), 1989:149-154

Allen,F.J., Golson.J., Jones,R. (eds) Sunda and Sahul, Prehistoric studies in South East Asia, Melanesia and Australia. London, Academic Press, 1977

Allen,J. Excavations at Bone Cave, South Central Tasmania, January -February 1989 In: Australian Archaeology 28, 1989:105-6

(the same), Gosden,C., Jones,R., White,J.P. Pleistocene dates for human occupation of New Ireland, northern Melanesia In: Nature 331, 1988:707-709

Altman,J.C. Hunter-Gatherers today: An Aboriginal economy in North Australia. Australian Institute of Aboriginal Studies,Canberra 1987

(the same) Economic status In: Jupp, J. (ed.) The Australian people North Ryde 1988:201-7

(the same) Hunter-gatherer subsistence production in Arnhem Land:The original affluence hypothesis re-examined.In: Mankind 14(3), 1984:179-90

(the same), Taylor,L. Marketing Aboriginal art in the 1990s. Canberra, Aboriginal Studies Press, 1990

Anthropological Forum Symposium on the uses and misuses of anthropology. In: Anthropological Forum 1(2) 1964,5(2) 1983-4, University of Western Australia

Appell,G. Ethical dilemmas in anthropological inquiry: a case bookWaltham, Massachusetts, Crossroad Press, 1978

Ascher,R. Analogy in archaeological interpretation In: Southwestern Journal of Anthropology 17, 1961:317-25

Atlas, Australians: a historical atlas Broadway, Fairfax, Syme&Weldon Associates, 1987

Australian Academy of Science. Committee on climatic change Report 21, 1976

Australian South Sea Islanders: A report of the current status of South Sea Islanders in Australia prepared by: The Evatt Foundation 750a George St. Sydney 2000, Feb. 1991

Bachman,J.G.; O'Malley, P.M. Yea-saying, nay-saying, and going to extremes: black-white differences in response styles.In: Public Opinion Quaterly 48, 1984:491-501

Bailey,G.N. The role of shell middens in prehistoric economies Cambridge University Press, Cambridge 1975

Bailey,K.D. Methods of social research The Free Press, New York 1987

Baldock,C.V.; Lally,J. Sociology in Australia and New Zealand: theory and method, Greenwood Press, Westport 1974

Balme,J., Merrilees,D., Porter,J.K. Late Quaternary mammal remains, spanning about 30.000 years, from excavations in Devil's Lair, Western AustraliaIn: Journal of the Royal Society of Western Australia 61, 1978:33-65

Barbetti,M.F. Archaeomagnetic and radiocarbon studies of Aboriginal fire-places. Australian National University, Canberra, 1974

Barbetti,M.F., Allen,H. Prehistoric man at Lake Mungo, Australia, by 32.000 years B.P. In: Nature 240, 1972:46-8

Barham,A.J., Harris,D.R. Prehistory and paleoecology of Torres Strait.In: Masters,P.M., Flemming,N.C. (eds) Quaternary coastlines and marine archaeology: towards the prehistory of land bridges and continental shelves. London, Academic Press 1983:530-57

Barley,N. The innocent anthropologist. Notes from the mud hutMiddlesex, Penguin Books 1986

Barwick,D., Urry,J., Bennett,D. Aselected bibliography of Aboriginal history and social change:thesis and publishes research to 1976. In Aboriginal history 1, 1977:111-69

Basedow,H. The Australian Aboriginal Adelaide, F.W.Preece, 1925

Bayne,P. Legal status In: Crowley,F.K. (ed.) A new history ofAustralia, Melbourne 1974:212-16

Becker,H. Die Ureinwohner Australiens Dresden, 1872

Bell,C.; Collins,H.; Jupp,J.: Rubinstein,W.D. Ethnic minoritiesand Australian foreign policy. Canberra, Australian National University, 1983

Bell,D.R. Daughter of the dreaming, Melbourne, McPhee Gribble/Allen and Unwin 1983, based on Ph.D Thesis, Australian National University, Canberra, 1980

(the same) Going it alone: practizing applied anthropology, In: Anthropological Forum 5, 1983-84:176-81

(the same) Have anthropologists had their day in court ? Typescript, Canberra 1985 and Australian Anthropological Society Newsletter 28, 1985:18-27

(the same) In the case of the lawyers and anthropologists, In: Journal of intercultural studies 7(1), 1986a:20-9

(the same) The Warumungu claim: a view from the research ranks, In: Australian Institute of Aboriginal Studies Library, 1986b:PMS 5047

Bell,J.H. The culture of the Aborigines.
In: Mc Leod,A.L. (ed.) The pattern of Australian culture. Melbourne, Oxford University Press, 1963:441-77

Bell,W.T. Studies in thermoluminescence dating in Australia. PhD Thesis, Australian National University 1978

Bengtsson,H. Australiens svarta ste stenaldersfolk. Stockholm, Natur och Kultur 156, 1947

Bennett,D. World catalogue of theses and dissertations about theAustralian Aborigines and Torres Strait Islanders:second update. In: Australian Aboriginal studies 1, 1985:46-61

Berndt,C.M. Uses and misuses in anthropology, In: Anthropological Forum 1(2), 1964:168-87

Berndt,R.M. The Cove Dispute: the question of the Australian Aboriginal land and the preservation of sacred sites, In: Anthropological Forum 1(2) 1964:258-95

(the same) Australian Aboriginal religions, Leiden 1974

(the same) The world of the first Australians London: Angus & Robertson 1965

Berndt,R.M., Berndt,C.M. The world of the first Australians, Sydney, Ure Smith, 1964

Birdsell,J.B. Some environmental and cultural factors influencing thestructuring of Australian Aboriginal populations. In: The American Naturalist 87, 1953:171-207

(the same) Some problems involving Pleistocene man. Cold Spring Harbour Symposium on Quantitative Biology 22, 1957:47-69

(the same) Preliminary data on the trihybrid origin of the Australian Aborigines. In: Archaeology and Physical Anthropology in Oceania 2, 1967:100-55

(the same) The problem of evolution of human races: classification or clines In: Social Biology 19, 1972:136-62

(the same) The recalibration of a paradigm for the first peopling in Greater Australia. In: Allen,J. (ed.) Sunda and Sahul, London 1977:113-67

(the same) Physical anthropology in Australia today.
In: Annual Review of Anthropology 8, 1979:417-30

Black,E.C. The canoes and canoe trees of Australia.
In: Mankind 3, 1947:351-61

Borofsky,R. Making history, Cambridge University Press, Cambridge 1987

Bourke,C.J. and Coutts,P.J.F. Were Australias Aborigines the first Asian migrants ? In: Asian 1(2), 1977:12-13

Bowdler,S. Bass Point: The excavation of a south-east Australian shell midden showing cultural and economic change. B.A. (Hons.) University of Sydney, 1970:141 leaves

(the same) The coastal colonisation of Australia In: Allen,J. (ed.) Sunda and Sahul, London 1977:205-46

(the same) (ed.) Coastal archaeology in eastern Australia Australian National University, Canberra, 1982

Bowler,J.M. The Keilor Terraces: an assessment of geological problems In: The Artefact 14, 1969:1-16

(the same) Alluvial terraces in the Maribyrnong Valley near Keilor, Victoria. In: Memoirs of the Natural Museum of Victoria 30, 1970:15-58

(the same) Recent developments in reconstructing late Quaternary environments in Australia. In Kirk,R.L., Thorne,A.G. (eds) The origin of the Australians, Canberra, Australian Institute of Aboriginal Studies, 1976:55-77

Bowler,J.M., Jones,R., Allen,H., Thorne,A.G. Pleistocene human remains from Australia: a living site and human cremation from Lake Mungo, western New South Wales. In: World Archaeology 2, 1970:39-60

Bowler,J.M., Thorne,A.G. Human remains from Lake
Mungo. Discovery and excavation of Lake Mungo
III. In: Kirch,R.L., Thorne,A.G. (eds) The origin of
the Australians, Canberra, Australian Institute of
Aboriginal Studies, 1976:127-38

Bowler,J.M., Hope,G.S., Jennings,J.N., Singh,G., Walker,D.
Late Quaternary climates of Australia and New
Guinea. In: Quaternary Research 6, 1976:359-94

Boyce,M.W. The Australian Aboriginal child: bibliography
and abstracts, part 1; physical and intellectual
development. Malvern, Victoria 1975

Brace,C.L. Australian tooth-size clines and the death of a
stereotype In: Current anthropology 21(2),
1980:141-64

Bradburn,N.M.; Sudman,S. Improving interview method and
questionnaire design, San Francisco 1979

Braunstein,S. Land rights legislation: a selected bibliography
Darwin, Community College 1981

Broom,L.; Jones,F.L.; McDonnell,P.; Williams,T. The
inheritance of inequality. London: 1980

Broom,R. Aboriginal Australians. Black response to wite
dominance1788 - 1980, Sydney, Allen & Unwin,
1982

Browne,K. An introduction to sociology.
Polity Press, Cambridge 1992

Bulmer,M. (ed.) Social research ethics
New York, Holmes and Meier Publishers,
Incorporated, 1982

Bulmer,S. Radiocarbon dates from New Guinea
In: Journal of the Polynesian Society 73, 1964:327-
28

Burnum Burnum Burnum Burnum's Aboriginal Australia a
travellers guide North Ryde, Angus and Robertson
Publishers, 1988

Calaby,J.H. Some biogeographical factors relevant to the
Pleistocene movement of man in Australia. In:
Kirch,R.L., Thorne,A.G. (eds) The origin of the
Australians, Canberra, Australian Institute of
Aboriginal Studies, 1976:23-27

Camm,J.C. Australian census maps 1901
Kensington, McQuilton & Yorke, 1983

Campbell,J.B. Settlement patterns of offshore islands in
northeasternQueensland.In: Australian Archaeology
9, 1979:18-32

Campbell,T.D., Grag,J.H., Hackett,C.J. Physical
anthropology of the Aborigines of central Australia.
In: Oceania 7(1), 1936:106-261

Cann,R. Mitochondrial DNA variation and the spread of
modern population. In: Kirk,R.L., Szathmary,E.
(eds) Out of Asia: peopling the Americas and the
Pacific. Canberra, Journal of Pacific History,
1985:113-22

Chappell,J. Aspects of late Quaternary paleogeography of
the Australian-East Indonesian region. In:
Kirk,R.L., Thorne,A.G. (eds) The origin of the
Australians, Canberra, Australian Institute of
Aboriginal Studies, 1976:11-22

Charleux,M. 40.000 ans déjà.
In: Australie noire, Paris, Autrement Revue,
1989:70-73

Clark, C. Australian hopes and fears
London, Hollis & Carter, 1958

Clark,G. World prehistory.
Cambridge University Press, 1962

Collingridge,G. The discovery of Australia. A critical
documentaryand historic investigation. Sydney,
Hayes, 1895

Colliver,F.S. The rain forest Aborigines and their artifacts.
Brisbane, Typescript, 1976

Connah,G. Australian field archaeology: a guide to
techniques 1982

(the same) Of the hut I builded. The archaeology of
Australias' history. Cambridge University Press,
1988

Cooper,C. Aboriginal and Torres Strait Islanders collection
Canberra, Aboriginal Studies Press, 1989

Cooper,H.M. Large stone implements from South Australia.
In: Records of the South Australian Museum 7,
1943:343-69

Coppell,W.G. Audio-visual resource materials relating to the
Aboriginal Australians. Canberra, Curriculum Dev.
Ctr. 1978

Cornelius,J. Le peuplement de l'Australie. In: Bulletin Museé
Anthropologie prehistoire Monaco 22, 1978:119-25

Cotterell,B., Kamminga,J. Mechanics of pre-industrial
echnology: an introduction to the mechanics of
ancient and traditional material culture. Cambridge
University Press, 1989-1990

Craig,B.F. Arnhem land peninsular region (including Bathurst and Mellville islands) Canberra, Australian Institute of 1966

(the same) Cape York, Canberra, Australian Institute of Aboriginal Studies, 1967

(the same) Kimberley region: an annotated bibliography, Canberra, Australian Institute of Aboriginal Studies, 1968

(the same) Central Australian and Western desert regions: an annotated bibliography, Canberra, Australian Institute of Aboriginal Studies, 1969

(the same) North-West-Central Queensland; an annotated bibliography, Canberra, Australian Institute of Aboriginal Studies, 1970

Crocker,R.L. Post-Miocene climatic and geologic history and its significance in relation to the genesis of the major soil types of South Australia. In: Commonwealth Scientific and Industrial Research Organization Bulletin 193, 1946:7-56

Cromwell,L. Consulting and no client constituency, In: Anthropological Forum 5, 1983-84:240-53

Crowley,F. (ed.) A new history of Australia. Richmond, William Heinemann Australia, 1988 (1974)

Cuddy,D.L. Contemporary Australian-American relations Saragota, 1981

Curr,E.M. The Australian race (3 vols.) Melbourne, John Ferres, 1886

Curry,F. Breach of confidence, Oxford, Clarendon Press, 1984

Curtain,C.C., vanLoghem,E., Schanfield,M.S. Immunoglobulin markers as indicators of population affinities in Australasia and the Western Pacific. In: Kirk,R.L., Thorne,A.G. (eds) The origin of the Australians, Canberra, Australian Institute of Aboriginal Studies, 1976:347-55

Davidson,J.P.S. The chronology of Australian watercraft. In: Journal of the Polynesian Society 44, 1935:1-16

Davidson,D.S., McCarthy,F.D. The distribution of some important types of stone implements in Western Australia. In: Anthropos 52, 1957:390-458

Davidson,G.R., Kearney,G.E., Delacey,D.R. The psychology of Aboriginal Australians. Sydney, Wiley, 1973

Davies,A.F., Encel,S. (eds.) Australian Society London, Pall Mall Press, 1965

Deacon,H. How did past climates affect prehistoric people in Australia and South Africa ? In: Digging Stick 2(2), 1985:5-6

Deunert,B. A fundamental basalt flake analysis based on experimentally produced and used flakes as well as the prehistoric Waikalua material. Masters Thesis, Hamburg 1993

Dorn,R.I., Nobbs,M.F., Cahill,T.A. Cation-ratio dating of rock engravings from Olary province of arid South Australia. In Antiquity 62(237), 1988:681-9

Dorst,J. Kookaburas, wombats et cie. In: Australie noire, Paris, Autrement Revue, 1989:62-69

Dortch,C.E. Early and late stone industrial phases in Western Australia. In: Wright, R.V.S. (ed) Stone tools as cultural markers: change, evolution and complexity, Canberra, Australian Institute of Aboriginal Studies, 1977:104-32

Dortch,C.E., Bordes,F. Blade and Levallois technology in Western Australian prehistory. In: Quartär 27(8), 1977:1-19

Dortch,C.E., Muir,B.G. Long range sightings of bush fires as possible incentive for Pleistocene voyagers to Greater Australia. In: W.A. Naturalist 14(7), 1980:194-8

Douglas,L., Roberts.A., Thompson,R. Oral history: a handbook Sydney, Allen and Unwin, 1988

Doutch,H.F. The palaeogeography of northern Australia and New Guinea and its relevance to the Torres Strait area. In: Walker,D. (ed) Bridge and barrier: the natural and cultural history of Torres Strait, Canberra, Australian National University, 1972:1-10

Dragovich,D. Minimum age of some desert varnish near Broken Hill, New South Wales In: Search 17, 1986:149-51

Dubois,M.J. Le peuplement du Pacifique. In: La Recherche 8(74), 1977:47-50

Du Cros,H. Skeletons in the closet: A history of the prehistoric archaeology of N.S.W. (c:1890 - 1940) B.A.(Hons.), University of Sydney, 1983

Dunlop,I. Ethnographic film-making in Australia: the first seventy years. In: Aboriginal history 3(2), 1979:111-17

Dunlop,M., Kirkpatrick,B. A listing of Aboriginal periodicals. In: Aboriginal History 3(2), 1979:120-27

Dunn,F., Dunn,D.F. Maritime adaptions and exploitation of marine resources in Sundaic southeast Asian prehistory. In: Bartstra,G.J. et al (eds) Modern Quaternary research in southeast Asia, Rotterdam, Balkema,A.A., 1977:1-28

Dyen,J. Language distribution and migration theory. In: Language 32, 1956:611-26

Earl,G.S.W. On the characteristics of the Papuan, Australian and Malayu-Polynesian nations. In: Journ. Ind. Archipel. east Asia.Nov.1849, 3(II):682-9, Jan.1850, 4:1-10, Feb.1850, 4:66-74, Apr.1850, 4:172-81

Eddy,J. Britain and the Australian colonies 1818 - 1831. The technique of government. Oxford, Clarendon Press, 1969

Elkin,A.P. The Australian Aborigines: How to understand them. Sydney, Angus and Robertson, 1938 (First publ.)

(the same) The threefold use of anthropology, In: Anthropological Forum 1(2), 1964:152-67

(the same) Equality and authority. A study of class, status and power in Australia. London, Tavistock, 1970

Ellis,R.W. The Aboriginal inhabitants and their environment. In: Twindale,C.R., Tyler,M.J., Webb,B.P. (eds) Natural history of the Adelaide region. Adelaide, Royal Society of South Australia, 1976:113-20

Favenc,E. The history of Australian exploration from 1788 to 1888 Amsterdam, Meridian Pub.Co., 1888

Fenner,F.J. The Australian Aboriginal skull: its non-metrical morphological characters. In: Transactions of the Royal Society of South Australia 63(2), 1939:248-306

Finn,P.P. Confidentiality and the "public interest" In: ALI 497:1984

Flenniken,J., White,J.P. Australian flaked stone tools: a technological perspective. In: Records of the Australian Museum 36(3), 1985:131-51

Flood,J.M. Archaeology of the dreamtime Sydney, William Collins, 1983 (reprint 1989)

(the same) Sites and bytes Canberra, Australian Government Publishing Service, 1989

(the same) The riches of ancient australia St. Lucia, University of Queensland Press, 1990

Florek,S. Fire in a quarry. In: Australian Archaeology 29, 1989:22-27

Flowers,R. Who are Aboriginal community adult educators ? What they do and what skill do they need ? Department of Community and Aboriginal Education. Faculty of Education. University of Technology, Sydney 1990

Foley,G.; Flowers,R. Strategies for self-determination. Aboriginal adult education training and community development in N.S.W. A national research fellowship scheme research project. Final report. Faculty of Education. Universty of Technology, Sydney 1990

Foley,W.A. Papuan languages and New Guinea prehistory. In: Foley,W.A. The Papuan languages of New Guinea. Cambridge, Melbourne, C.U.P., 1986:269-83

Frankel,D. et al.Aboriginal landscapes. In Camm,J.C.R., Mc Quilton,J.Australians: a historical atlas. Broadway, Syme and Weldon Associates, 1987:27-44

Freckleton,J. The role of anthropologists as expert witnesses, Paper prepared for the Australian Law Reform Commission, 1984

Friedman,L.M. Expert testimony, its abuses and reformation, In: Yale Law Journal 19, 1910:247-57

Fritzpatrick,B. The Australian people 1788 - 1945 Mellbourne, University Press, 1947

Gale,F. Urban Aborigines. ANU Press, Canberra, 1972

Gallus, A. Vorläufiger Bericht über paläolithische Funde in gesicherter Fundlage aus Australien. In: Mitteilungen der anthropologischen Gesellschaft in Wien 83, 1954:131-134

(the same) Excavations at Keilor. In:The Artefact 7, 1967:1-2, 24, 1971:1-12, 27, 1972:9-15, 8(1-2), 1983:11-41

(the same) A summary of the results of excavations by the Archaeological Society of Victoria at Keilor (near Melbourne) as per april 1974. In:The Artefact 33, 1974-1-9

(the same) The Middle and Early Upper Pleistocene stone industries at Dry Creek archaeological sites near Keilor, Australia. In: The Artefact 1(2), 1976:75-108

Galloway,R.W. Late Quaternary climates in Australia. In: Journal of Geology 73, 1965:603-18

Garanger,J. Les premiers Australiens. In: L'Histoire 1, 1978:46-53

Geddes,W.R. Anthropology and native policy, In: Anthroplogical Forum 1(2), 1964:188-94

Gill,A.M., Groves,R.H., Noble,I.R. (eds) Fire and the Australian Biota. Australian Academy of Science, Canberra 1981:23-54

Goede,A. Electron spinresonance - A relative dating technique for Quaternary sediments near Warranambool, Victoria. In: Australian Geographical Studies 27, 1989:14-30

Goldie,T. Fear and temptation: The image of the indigene in Canadian, Australian and New Zealand literatures Kingston, Mc Gill - Queens Uni.Press, 1989

Goldkins,V. Anthropologists, informants and the achievement of power in Chan Kom, In: Sociologus 20(1), 1970:30-42

Gojak,D. Culture and tradition in Australian prehistory: the core tool and scraper tradition. University of Sydney, B.A. (Hons.) 1982

Golson,J.Both sides of the Wallace Line: Australia, New Guinea and Asian prehistory. In: Archaeology and Physical Anthropology in Oceania 6 (2), 1971:124-44

(the same) Land connections, sea barriers and the relationship of Australian and New Guinea prehistory. In: Walker,D. (ed) Bridge and barrier: the natural and cultural history of Torres Strait. Canberra, Australian National University, 1972:375-95

Gorden,R. Interviewing: Strategy, techniques, and tactics. Homewood III. Dorsey 1969

Gould,R.A. The archaeologist as ethnographer: a case from the Western Desert of Australia, American Museum Novitates, N.2403, 1971

(the same) Use-wear on Western Desert Aboriginal stone tools: a reply to Messrs. In: Hayden,B., Kamminga,J. Newsletter of Lithic Technology 2(1-2), 1973:9-13

(the same) Australian archaeology in ecological and ethnographical perspective. Warner Modular Publications, Module 7, 1973

Graeme,H. Australia's changing population: Trends and implications Melbourne, Oxford Uni.Press, 1986

Graetz,B., McAllister,I. Dimensions of Australian society Melbourne, Macmillan 1988

Gray,A. Demographic and social history. In: Jupp,J. (ed.) The Australian people, North Ryde 1988:135-40

Greenberg,J. Social scientists take the stand. In: Michigan Law Review 54, 1956:953-70

Greenway,J. Bibliography of the Australian Aborigines and the native people of Torres Strait to 1959. Sydney, Halstead Press 1963

Griffiths,T. Contemporary Australia New York, 1979

Groube,L., Chappel,J., Murke,J., Prince,D. A 40.000 year old occupation site at Huon Peninsula, Papua New Guinea. In: Nature 324, 1986:453-55

Crowley,F.K. (ed.) A new history of Australia, Melbourne 1974

Gruhn,R. On Brace's Australian tooth-size thesis: a closer look at the linguistic evidence. In: Current Anthropology 21(6), 1980:804-6

Gumbert,M. Paradigm lost: an analysis of anthropological models and their effects on Aboriginal land rights, In: Oceania 52(2), 1981:103-23

(the same) Neither justice nor reason: a legal and anthropological analysis of Aboriginal land rights. University of Queensland Press, St. Lucia, 1984

Habgood,P.J. The origin of the Australians: a multivariate approach. In: Archaeologica Oceania 21(2), 1986:130-7

Hale,H.M., Tindale,N.B. Notes on some human remains in the lower Murray Valley, South Australia. In: Records of the South Australian Museum 4, 1930:145-218

Hallam,S. Fire and hearth. Australian Institute of Aboriginal Studies, Canberra, 1975

Hammond,G.N. The Indian connection: A study of anthropological opinion and evidence suggesting that the origin of the Australian Aborigines is to be found on the Indian sub-continent. Sydney, B.A.(Hons.), Typescript 1979

Harding,J.; Spence,B. An annotated bibliography of Aboriginal-controlled justice programs in Canada. School of Human Justice. Univerity of Regina, Saskatchewan 1991

Hawke,E.N. Archaeological resource management: a legal perspective.Australian National University 1975

Hayden,B. Palaeolithic reflections: lithic technology and ethnographical excavation among Australian Aborigines Canberra, Aboriginal Studies Press, 1979, amended reprint 1981

(the same) Australian Western Desert technology: an ethno-archaeological study of variability in material culture. Doctoral dissertation, University of Toronto 1976

Hiat,L.R. Local organization among the Australian
    Aborigines,
    In: Oceania 32 (4), 1962:267-86

Horton,D.R. Water and woodland: the peopling in Australia.
    In: Australian Institute of Aboriginal Studies
    Newsletter 16, 1981:21-27

Howells,W.W.; Warner,W.L. Anthropometry of the natives
    of Arnhem Land and the Australian race problem.
    In: Papers of the Peabody Museum 16, 1937:1-97

Howitt,A.W. The native tribes of South-East Australia
    London, Macmillan, 1904

Hrdlicka,A. the peopling of the earth. In: Proceedings of the
    American Philosophical Society 65, 1926:150-56

Irving,T.H. 1850-70 In: Crowley,F.K. (ed.) A new history of
    Australia, Melbourne 1974:124-164

Isaacs,J. Australian dreaming: 40.000 years of Aboriginal
    history. Lansdowne Press, Sydney 1980

Janson,S., Macintyre,S. (eds.) Through white eyes
    Australian Historical Studies, Sydney, Allen &
    Unwin, 1990

Jaspan,M.A. Anthropology and commitment to political
    causes,
    In: Anthropological Forum, 1(2), 1964:212-19

Jennings,J.N. Sea level changes and land links. In:
    Mulvaney, D.J.; Golson,J. (eds.) Aboriginal man
    and environment in Australia, Canberra, 1971:1-13

Jennett,C. Modern politics/The mass media In: Jupp, J. (ed.)
    The Australian people, North Ryde 1988:228-
    33/252-55

Jones,R. Fire-stick farming.
    In: Australian National History 16, 1969:224-8

(the same) Rocky Cape and the problem of the Tasmanians.
    Ph.D Thesis, University of Sydney, 1971

(the same) Emerging picture of Pleistocene Australians.
    In: Nature 246, 1973:275-81

(the same) The fifth continent: problems concerning the
    human colonization of Australia. In: Annual
    Reviews of Anthropology 8, 1979:445-66

(the same) ed. Archaeological research in Kakadu National
    Park. Australian National Parks and Wildlife
    Service, Canberra, 1985

(the same) The alligator rivers: a mirror to a continental
    prehistory. In: Wade-Marshall,D., Loveday,P. (ed)
    Floodplains research, Northern Australia: Progress
    and prospects 2. Darwin, Australian National
    University, North Australian Research Unit,
    Appendix 1, 1988:1-26

Jones,R., Meehan,B. Floating bark and hollow trunks.
    In: Hemisphere 21(4), 1977:16-21

Jones,R., White,N. Point Blank: stone tool manufacture at
    the Ngilipilji Quarry, Arnhem Land, 1981 In:
    Meehan,B. Jones,R. (eds) Archaeology with
    Ethnography, Canberra, Australian National
    University, 1988:51-93

Jones,P.G. A bibliography of Aboriginal archaeology in
    South Australia. In: Records of the South Australian
    Museum 19(1), 1985:1-14

Joyce,E.B., Anderson,J.R. Late Quaternary geology and
    environment at the Dry Creek archaeological sites
    near Keilor in Victoria, Australia. In: Artefact 1,
    1976:47-74

Jupp,J. (ed.) The Australian people: An encyclopedia of the
    nation, its people and their origions
    North Ryde, Angus & Robertson, 1988

Kamminga,J. Microscopic and experimental studies of
    Australian Aboriginal stone tools.
    B.A.(Hons.), University of Sydney, 1971

(the same) A functional study of an Australian tool type: the
    elouera In: Wright,R.V.S. (ed) Stone tools as
    cultural markers: change, evolution and complexity,
    Australian Institute of Aboriginal Studies, Canberra,
    1978:205-12

(the same) Mechanics of pre-industrial technology.
    Cambridge University Press, 1990

Kabo,V.R. Tasmaniitsy i Tasmaniiskaya problema.
    Izdatel'stvo Nauka, Glavnaya Redaktsiya
    Vostochnoy Literatury, Moskva, 1975

Keast,A., Crocker,R.L., Christian,C.S. (eds) Biogeography
    and ecology in Australia. The Hague, 1959

Keen,I. (ed.) Being black: Aboriginal cultures in settled
    Australia Canberra, Aboriginal Studies Press, 1988

(the same) Kinship In: Berndt,R.M.; Tonkinson,R. (eds.)
    Social anthropology and Australian Aboriginal
    studies: acontemporary overview.
    Canberra,1988:77-124

Kennedy,M. Born a half-caste
Canberra, Australian institute of Aboriginal Studies,
1985

Kenyon,A.S., Stirling,D.C. Australian Aboriginal stone
implements. A suggested classification. In:
Proceedings of the Royal Society of Victoria 13,
1901:191-200

Kershaw,A.P. Quarternary vegetation and environments. In:
Keast,A. (ed.) Ecological bibliography of Australia.
The Hague 1981:81-101

Kenyon,A.S., Mahoney,D.J. Stone implements of the
Australian Aborigines. A guide.
Melbourne, Arnell & Jackson, 1914

Kerr,C.R., Carroll,J.D. Social scientists and the courts: the
development of testimonial privilege
In: Social Science Journal 15(1), 1978:103-13

Kirk,R.L. Serum protein and enzyme markers as indicators
of population affinities in Australia and the Western
Pacific. In: Kirk,R.L., Thorne,A.G. (eds) The origin
of the Australians, Australian Institute of Aboriginal
Studies, Canberra, 1976:329-46

(the same) Physiological, demographic and genetic
adaptation of Australian Aboriginals. In; Keast,A.
(ed) Ecological Bibliography of Australia, The
Hague 1981:1801-15

Kirk,R.L., Thorne,A.G. (eds.) The origin of the Australians
Australian Institute of Aboriginal Studies, 1976

Klaatsch,H. Der Werdegang der Menschheit und die
Entstehung der Kultur. Bong, Berlin 1922

(the same) Die Steinartefakte der Australiaer und Tasmanier
verglichen mit denen der Urzeit Europas. In:
Zeitschrift für Ethnologie 40, 1908:407-28

Knott,J. Settlement 1851-1880 In: Jupp,J. (ed.) The
Australian people. North Ryde 1988:48-54

Köpping,K.P. Ethnographic collections and the new identity
of native populations. In: Occasional Papers in
Anthropology 2, 1973:9-23

(the same) Ist die Ethnologie auf dem Wege zur Mündigkeit.
In: Paideum 26, 1980:21-40

Labaw,P.J. Advanced questionnaire design.
Abt Books, Cambridge 1980

Laidlaw,R. Aboriginal society before European settlement.
In: The European Occupation, Heinemann
Educational, Richmond, 1981:1-43

Lancaster,L. Recruitment and retention of special education
teachers on Native American reservation schools.
Ann Arbor, Michigan 1992

Lampert,R. The great Kartan mystery. In: Terra Australis 5,
The Australian National University Press, Canberra,
1981, 210p

(the same) Trends in Australian prehistoric research.
In: Antiquity 49, 1975:197-206

Lawrence,R. Aboriginal habitat and economy. In: Occasional
Papers 6, Department of Geography, Australian
National University Press, Canberra, 1968, 290p

Lesson,A. Les Polynesians Vol.1, Librairie de la Société
Asiatique de Paris, Paris, 1880

Lie-Injo,J.E. Genetic relationship of several Aboriginal
groups in South East Asia. In: Kirk,R.L.,
Thorne,A.G. (eds) The origin of the Australians,
Australian Institute of Aboriginal Studies, Canberra,
1976:277-306

Lightfoot, R. Archaeology of the house and household: a
case study of assemblage formation and household
organization in the American southwest. Ann Arbor,
Michigan, 1992

Lohrey,A. Australian studies overseas: a guide.
Australian Government Publishing Service,
Canberra, 1988

Love,W. Was the dreamtime ever a realtime? In:
Anthropological Society of Queensland Newsletter
196, 1989:1-14

Macintosh,N.W.G. Anthropological study; part 1. Human
grouping and the background of prehistoric man.
Part 2. Critical studies of the antiquity of man in
Australia. In addition some facts relating to the
possible origin, migration and affinities of the
Australians and Tasmanians. University of Sydney,
1950

(the same) The Australian Aboriginal: the world's first
mariner? In: University of Sydney Gazzett 3,
1975:15-16

Macintosh,N.W.G.; Larnach,S.L. Aboriginal affinities
looked at in world context. In: Kirk,R.L.;
Thorne,A.G. (eds.) The origin of the Australians,
Canberra, 1976:113-26

Maddock,K. The Australian Aborigines: A portrait of their
society
Ringwood, Penguin Books Australia Ltd., 1974

Maiden,J.H. The useful native plants of Australia (including
Tasmania) Sydney, Turner and Henderson, 1889

Marchant,L.R. A list of french naval records and illustrations
relating to Australain and Tasmanian Aborigines,
1771 - 1828 Canberra, Australian Institute
of Aboriginal Studies, 1969

Massola,A. Australian fish hooks and their distribution. In: Memoirs of the National Museum of Victoria 22, 1956:1-17

(the same) Bibliography of the Victorian Aborigines. From the earliest manuscripts to 31. Dec. 1970. Melbourne, The Hawthorn Press, 1971

Mathews,R.H. Ethnological notes on the Aboriginal tribes of the Northern Territory. In: Queensland Geographical Journal (N.S.) 26, 1901:69-90

Mayne, T. Aborigines and the issues information and resources catalogue. Australian Council of Churches, Sydney, 1986

McArthur,M. Food consuption and dietary levels of groups of Aborigines living on naturally occuring foods. In: Mountford,C.P. (ed) Records of the American - Australian scientific expedition to Arnhem Land (vol.2), Melbourne University Press, Melbourne, 1960:90-135

Mc Bryde,I. Records of times past. Ethnohistorical essays on the culture and ecology of New England tribes Canberra, Australian Institute of Aboriginal Studies, 1978

McCarthy,F.D. Comparison of the prehistory of Australia with that of Indo-China, the Malay Peninsula and Netherlands East Indies. In: Proceedings of the Third Congress of Prehistorians of the Far East, 1940:30-50

(the same) Some unusual stone artefacts from Australia and New Guinea. In: Records of the Australian Museum 21(5), 1944a:264-6

(the same) Some unusual, cylindro-conical, stones from New South Wales and Java. In: Records of the Australian Museum 21(5), 1944b:257-60

(the same) Nomenclature of Australian stone implements: the 1964 classification, Australian institute of Aboriginal Studies, conference on nomenclature of implements and culture, Sydney April 25th to 28th, Typescript, 1963

(the same) Australian Aboriginal stone implements. Australian Museum, Sydney, 1967 and 1976

McCarthy,F.D., Bramell,E., Noone,H.V.V. The stone implements of the Australian museum, No.19, Sydney 1946

McCovell,P. The linguistic prehistory of Australia: opportunities for dialogue with archaeology. Paper presented May 1990

Meehan,B.F. The form, distribution and antiquity of Australian Aboriginal mortuary practice, being a study of their material culture and the manner in which they untilized their physical environment. University of Sydney 1971

Meehan,B.F., Jones,R. (eds.) Archaeology with ethnography: an Australian perspective Canberra, Department of Prehistory, 1988

Megaw,J.V.S. Archaeology, art and Aborigines; a survey of historical sources and later Australian prehistory. In: Royal Australian Historical Society Journal 53(4), 1967:277-94

(the same) Art styles and analysis. In: Mankind 6(9), 1967:393-402

Memmott,P. Bibliography on Aboriginal settlement and housing. University of Queensland, Department of Architecture, Aboriginal Data Archive 1977

Merlan,P. Gender. In: Berndt,R.M.; Tonkinson,R. (eds.) Social anthropology and Australian Aboriginal studies: a contemporary overview. Canberra, 1988:15-74

Merriless,D. Man the destroyer: later Quaternary changes in the Australian marsupial fauna. In: Journal of the Royal Society of Western Australia 51, 1968:1-24

Middleton,H. Aborigines. In: Encel,S., Berry,M. (eds.) Selected readings in Australian society Melbourne, Longman Cheshire, 1987

Moodie,P.M., Pedersen,E.B. The health of Australian Aborigines: an annotated bibliography, AGPS, Canberra, 1971

Morrison,J. The biracial origin of the Australian Aborigines. In: Medical Journal of Australia 2, 1967:1054-6

Moyle,A.M. Source materials: Aboriginal music of Australia and New Guinea. In Ethnomusicology 15(1), 1971:81-93

Mulvaney,D.J. The stone age of Australia. In: Proceedings of the Prehistoric Society, (N.S.) 27, 1961:56-107

(the same) Classification and typology in Australia: the first 350 years. In: Wright,R.V.S. (ed), Stone tools as cultural markers, Australian Institute of Aboriginal Studies, Canberra, 1978:263-268

(the same) Blood from stones and bones. In: Search 10, 1979:214-18

(the same) Encounters in place: Outsider and Aboriginal Australians 1606 - 1985. St. Lucia, Uni. of Queensland Press 1989

Mulvaney,D.J., Golson,J. (eds) Aboriginal man and environment in Australia, Australian National University Press, Canberra, 1971

Mulvaney,D.J., Joyce,E.B. Archaeological and geomorphological investigations on Mt. Moffatt Station, Queensland, Australia. In: Proceedings of the Prehistoric Society 31, 1965:147-212

Murray,P.F. Australian megamammals: restorations of some late Pleistocene fossil marsupials and a monotreme.In: Artefact 3(2), 1978:77-99 (the same) Australian prehistoric animals, Methuen, 1985

Murray,T., White,J.P. Archaeology in Australia and New Guinea.
In: World Archaeology 13(2), 1981:255-63

Nadel,G. Australia's colonial culture. ideas, men and institutions in mid-nineteenth century eastern Australia Cambridge, Mass., Harvard Uni.Press., 1957

Nadel,S.F. Interview technique in social anthropology.
In: Bartlett,F. et al (eds.) The study of society, London, Routledge and Kegan Paul Ltd., 1939:317-27

Nanson,G.C., Young,R.W., Stockton,E.D. Chronology and palaeoenvironment of the Cranebrook Terrace (near Sydney) containing artefacts more than 40.000 years old.
In: Archaeologica Oceania 22, 1987:72-78

Neate,G.J. The Aboriginal land rights (Northern Territory) act 1976 and its effect on the usage on Aboriginal land, Typescript, Australian Institute of Aboriginal Studies, Canberra, 1977

(the same) Keeping secrets secret,
In: Aboriginal Law Bulletin 5, 1982:1ff

Nejelski,P., Peyser,H. A researchers' shield statute: guarding against the compulsory disclosure of research data.
In: National Research Council 1975:B1-B86

Nicholas,S.; Shergold,P.R. The convict period. In: Jupp,J. (ed.) The Australian people,North Ryde 1988:23-31

Nobbs,M.F., Dorn,R.I. Age determinations for rock varnish formations within petroglyphs: cation-ratio dating of 24 motifs from Olary region, South Australia.
In: Rock Art Research 5(2), 1988:108-124

O'Brian, M. The legend of the seven sisters
ISBN:0855752165, 1990

O'Connell,J.F. Aspects of variation in central Australian lithic assemblages. In: Wright,R.V.S. (ed.) Stone tools as cultural markers: change, evolution and complexity. Australian Institute of Aboriginal Studies, Canberra, 1977:269-82

O'Connor, R. A case of might-have-been: some reflections on the new "two kilometre law" in the Northern Territory,
In: Anthropological Forum 5(2), 1983-84:201-7

Orton,C. Mathematics in Archaeology, London, Collins, 1980

Oswald,W., Schoepfle,M. Systematic fieldwork Newsliary Park, Sage Publishing, 1087

Palmer,I. Buying back the land: Organizational struggle and Aboriginal land fund commision Canberra, Aboriginal Studies press, 1988

Palmer,K., Brady,M. Diet and lifestyle in the desert: A profile of an Aboriginal community at Maralinga Canberra, Aboriginal Studies Press, 1991

Parsons,P.A., White,N.G. Variability of anthropometric traits in Australian Aboriginals and adjacent populations: its bearing on biological origin of the Australians.
In: Kirch,R.L., Thorne,A.G. (eds.) The origin of the Australians, Australian Institute of Aboriginal Studies, Canberra, 1976:227-44

Pearce,R.H. Uniformity of the Australian backed blade tradition. In Mankind 9, 1973:89-95

Perkins,C. Political objectives. In Jupp,J. (ed.) The Australian people, North Ryde, 1988:233-39

Peterson,N. (ed.) Aboriginal land rights: A handbook Canberra, Australian Institute of Aboriginal Studies, 1981

(the same) Tribes and boundaries in Australia. In: Social Anthropology Series No.10, Canberra, Aboriginal Institute of Aboriginal Studies, 1976

Pevar, S.L. The rights of Indians and tribes: the basic ACLU guide to the Indian and tribal rights.
Southern Illionois University Press, Carbondale 1992

Pewewardy,G. Relationships among labor force status, wages, and participation in vocational education among young American Indians. Ann Arbor, Michigan, 1992

Pilling,A.R. Aborigine culture history: a survey of publications 1954-1957. Detroit, Wayne State University Press, 1962

PM, Peter Moosleitners interessantes Magazin, Gruner + Jahr AG + Co Druck- und Verlagshaus, Verlagsgruppe München, Dec. 1978 - today

Prado y Tovar, D.D. de New light on the discovery of Australia asrevealed by the Journal of Cpt. Prado y Tovar (transl. from spanish) London, Hakluy & Soc., 1930

Price, C.A. The ethnic character of the Australian population. In: Jupp,J. (ed.) The Australian people, North Ryde, 1988:119-28

Prince,J. The Aborigines: Where do they come from ? In: Australian Outdoors and Fishing, 1976:52-65

Prokopec,M., Sedivy,V. Australian Aboriginals and the outer world: dermatoglyphical evidence. In: Kirk,R.L., Thorne,A.G. (eds) The origin of the Australians, Australian institute of Aboriginal Studies, Canberra, 1976:215-26

Radcliffe-Brown,A. Three tribes of Western Australia. In: Journal of the Royal Anthropological Institute 42, 1913:146 ff

(the same) Former numbers and distribution of the Australian Aborigines. Official Yearbook of the Commonwealth of Australia, No. 23, Melbourne, 1930

(the same) The social organization of Australian tribes In: Oceania 1, 1930-31

Ranft-Panek,B. Anpassung und Konfrontation: Sozio-ökonomische Veränderungen und ihr Einfluß auf den Kulturwandel bei den Australischen Aborigines. Bonn, Holos, 1990

Reim,H. Die Ureinwohner Australiens. In. Habel,R. (ed) Völkerkunde für jedermann, Leipzig, VEB Haack,H. 1966:317-27

Reynolds,B. Material culture. In: Jupp,J. (ed.) The Australian people. North Ryde, 1988:196-201

Reynolds,H. The other side of the frontier. Aboriginal resistance to the European invasion of Australia. Penguin Books, Victoria, 1982

(the same) Dispossession. Black Australians and white invaders Sydney, Allen & Unwin Australia PtyLtd., 1989

(the same) With the white people. Penguin Books, Victoria, 1990

Rivet,P. Les Australiens et les Malayo-Polynésiens en Amérique. In: Anthropologie 35, Paris 1925

Robert,W.C.H. Explorations Dutch 1605 Amsterdam, Philo. Press, 1973

Robinson,P. The hatch and brood of time: A study of the the 1. generation of native-born white Australians 1788 - 1828 Melbourne, Oxford Uni. Press, 1982

Robson,M.K., Parsons,P.A. Fingerprint studies on four Central Australian Aboriginal tribes. In: Archaeology and Physical Anthropology in Oceania 2(1), 1967:69-78

Rose,A.M. The social scientist as an expert witness. In: Minnesota Law Review 40, 1956:205-218

Rose,D.B. Aboriginal Australia. In: Jupp,J. The Australian people: an encyclopedia of the nation, its people and their origins. North Ryde, Angus & Robertson, 1988:9-13

Ross,L. Mothers behind bars: a comparative study of the experiences of imprisoned American indian and white women. Ann Arbor, Michigan 1992

Rowley,C. Aboriginal policy and practice. Vol. 1 - 3 Canberra, Australian national University Press, 1970 - 71

Rozen,L. The anthropologist as expert witness, In: American anthropologist 79(3), 1977:555-78

Schilder,G. Australia unveiled: The share of the Dutch navigators in the discovery of Australia Amsterdam, 1976

Schmidt,W. Grundlinien einer Vergleichung der Religionen und Mythologien der Austronesischen Völker. In: Denkschrift der Kaiserlichen Akademie der Wissenschaften, Wien, 1910

Schnell,R.; Hill,P.B.; Esser,E. Methoden der empirischen Sozialforschung. Oldenburg, 1989

Schoetensack,O. Die Bedeutung Austaliens für die Heranbildung der Menschen aus einer niederen Form. In: Zeitschrift für Ethnologie 33, 1901:127- 54

Schott,L. Zur Bedeutung odontologischer Befunde bei australiden Bevölkerungsgruppen. In: Ethnographisch-archäologische Zeitschrift 24(4), 1983:675-80

Schrire,C. Ethno-archaeological models and subsistence behaviour in Arnhem Land. In: Clarke, D.L. (ed) Models in archaeology, London, Methuen, 1972:653-70

(the same) The Alligator rivers: prehistory and ecology in western Arnhem Land. Australian National University, Canberra, 1982

Schulze,L. The Aborigines of the upper and middle Finke River: their habits and customs, with introductory notes on the physical and natural history features of the country. In: Transactions of the Royal Society of South Australia 14, 1891:210-46

Shanghvi,L.D. Comparative genetic studies between some groups of Australian Aboriginals and certain tribal peoples of India. In: Kirch,R.L., Thorne,A.G. (eds) The origin of the Australians, Australian Institute of Aboriginal Studies, Canberra, 1876:401-14

Sharpe,C.E. Prehistoric art in Australia Melbourne College of Education, 1972

(the same) Prehistoric art in Australia: a teacher's guide Fine Arts Tesis, Typescript, Boston, 1976

Sharpe,M.C. Bundjalung settlement and migration. In: Aboriginal History 9(1), 1985:101-24

Shaw,A.G.L. The story of Australia London, Faber and Faber Limited, 1955

(the same) 1788 - 1810. In: Crowley,F.K. (ed.) A new history of Australia, Melbourne 1974:1-44

Silver Digest The Australian Aborigine: customs of yesterday and today. Avalon, Silver Digest Publishing, 1970

Simmons,R.T. The biological origin of Australian Aboriginals. In: Kirch,R.L., Thorne, A.G. (eds) The origin of the Australians, Australian Institute of Aboriginal Studies, Canberra, 1976:307-28

Singh,G., Kershaw,A.P., Clark,R. Quaternary vegetation and fire history in Australia. In: Gill,A.M.G., Groves,R.H., Noble,I.R. (eds) Fire and the Australian biota. Australian Academy of Science, Canberra, 1981:23-54

Smith,B. The spectre of Truganini. 1980 Boyers lectures Sydney, The Australian Broadcasting Commision, 1980

Smith,H.M.; Biddle,E.H. Look forward not back. Australian National University Press, Canberra, 1975

Smith, M. Late pleistocene zamia exploitation in outhern Western Australia. In: Archaeology in Oceania 17 1982:117-21

Smith,M.A. Central Australia: preliminary archaeological investigations. In: Australian Archaeology 16, 1983:27-38

(the same) Pleistocene occupation in arid Central Australia. In: Nature 328, 1987:710-11

(the same) Central Australian seed grinding implements and Pleistocene grindstones. In: Meehan,B., Jones,R. (eds) Archaeology with ethnography, Australian National University, Canberra, 1988:94-111

(the same) The pattern and timing of prehistoric settlement in Central Australia. Unpublished Ph.D. Thesis, University of New England, 1988

(the same) The case for resident human population in the Central Australian Ranges during full glacial aridity.
In: Archaeology in Oceania 24(3), 1989:93-105

Snyder-Joy,Z.K. American Indian education in the southwest: issues of self-determination and local control Ann Arbor, Michigan, 1992

Speiser,F. Melanesien und Indonesien.
In: Ethnologische Zeitschrift 70, 1938:463-81

Spencer,W.B. Native tribes of the Northern Territory of Australia, London, 1914, 516p.

Spradley,J.P. The ethnographic interview New York, Holt, Rinehart and Winston, 1979

Sollas,W.J. Ancient hunters and their modern representatives. London, Macmillan, 1911

Stanner,W.E.H. Durmugam, a nangiomeri In: Casagrande,J.B. (ed.) In the company of man, New York, Harper and Brothers, 1960:63-100

(the same) Aboriginal territorial organization: estate, range, domain and regime. In: Oceania 36 (1), 1965:1-26

Stephens,E. The Aborigines of Australia. In: Journal and Proceedings of the Royal Society of New South Wales 23, 1819:476-503

Stone,S.N. Aborigines in white Australia: A documentary history of the attitudes affecting official policy and the Austalian Aborigine 1697 - 1973, South Yarra, 1974

Struwe,R. Forschungsgeschichte und Forschungsstand der Archäologie zur ursprünglichen Besiedlung Australiens, Humbolt Universität, Berlin, 1968

(the same) Untersuchungen zum älteren Abschnitt der Urgeschichte Australiens aufgrund einer Analyse der Steinindustrien Australiens und dreier Fundkomplexe aus Neuguinea und Indonesien. Ph.D. Thesis, Humboldt Universität zu Berlin, 1974

(the same) Überblick zum gegenwärtigen Stand der archäologischen Forschungen in Australien. In: Ethnographisch,- archäologische Zeitschrift 19(4), 1978:699-705

(the same) Zur Besiedlungsgeschichte Australiens.
In: Altertum 27(4), 1981:217-23

Tattersall,J., Delson.E., Couvering,J.V. Encyclopedia of
human evolution and prehistory.
New York, London, Garland Publishing, 1988

Tatz,C. Race politics in Australia: Aborigenes politics and
the law Armidale, University of the New England
Publishing Unit 1979

(the same) Aborigines and uranium and other essays
Victoria, Heinemann Educational Australia, 1982
Taylor,P. (ed.) After 200 years. Photographic essays
of Aboriginal and Islander Australia today
Canberra, Aboriginal studies Press, Canberra, 1988

Terrill,R. The Australians
Simon and Schuster, New York 1987

Thawley,J., Gauci,S. Bibliographies on the Australian
Aborigine: an annotated listing. Second edition
La Trobe University, Borchardt Library, 1987

The Heritage of Australia/Enzyclopedia
The Maximilian Company of Australia PtyLtd,
1981

Thomas, N.W. Australian canoes and rafts.
In: Journal of the Anthropological Institute 35,
1905:56-79

Thomson, N. Health In: Jupp, J. (ed.) The Australian people.
North Ryde, 1988:248-52

Tindale,N.B. Relationship of the extinct Kangaroo Island
culture with cultures of Australia, Tasmania and
Malaya. In: Records of the South Australian
Museum 6, 1937:39-60

(the same) Palaeolithic Kodj Axe of the Aborigines and its
distribution in Australia. In: Records of the South
Australian Museum 9, 1950:257-74

(the same) Culture succession in eastern Australia from Late
Pleistocene to the present In: Records of the South
Australian Museum 13, 1957:1-49

(the same) Radiocarbon dates of interest to Australian
archaeologists.
In: Australian Journal of Science 27, 1964:24

(the same) Nomenclature of archaeological cultures and
associated implements in Australia. In: Records of
the South Australian Museum 15, 1968:615-640

(the same) Aboriginal tribes of Australia.
Berkeley, University of California Press, 1974

(the same) Aboriginal tribes of Australia; their terrain,
environment controls, distribution, limits and proper
names. Canberra, Australian National University
Press, 1974

(the same) Progress in Australian archaeology. Archaeology
and the living people in Australia.
3p. roneo. South Australian Museum, n.d.

(the same) Desert Aborigines and the southern coastal
people: some comparisons. In: Keast, A. (ed.)
Ecological biogeography of Australia, The Hague
1981:1853-84

Tonkinson,R. working for the judge: role and responsibility,
In: Anthropological Forum 5, 1983-84:182-88

Toohey,J. Anmatjirra and Alyawarra land claims to Utopia
pastoral lease, Canberra, AGPS, para.89, 1980 see
also pages 105-8

(the same) Daly River (Malak Malak) land claim,
Canberra AGPS, 1982,86-89

(the same) Seven years on,
Canberra AGPS, para.880, 1983

Topinard,P. Etude sur les Tasmanians. In: Memoirs of the
Society of Anthropology of Paris, Series 1, 3,
1872:307-29

Trembley,M.A. The key-informant technique: a non-
ethnographical application In: American
Anthropologist 59(4), 1957:682-94

Tugby,D.J. Toward a code of ethics for applied
anthropology,
In: Anthropological Forum 1(2), 1964: 220-231

Turner,W. Report on the human crania and other bones of
the skeletons collected during the voyage of
H.M.S.Challenger, in the year 1873-1876. Part 1 -
The crania. In: Report of the scientific results of the
exploring voyage of H.M.S. Challenger 1873-
1876, Zoology 10, 1884:1-30

Vachon,D.A. Essay of passion, Imagination and striving:
Aboriginal responses to the anthropological
enterprises, In: Anthropological Forum 5, 1983-
85:221-30

Vos,G., Kirk,H.R.L., Steinberg,A.G. The distribution of the
gamma globulin types Gm(a), Gm(b), Gm(x) and
Gm-like in South and Southeast Asia and Australia.
In: American Journal of Human Genetics 15(1),
1963:44-52

Wade-Marshall,D., Loveday,P. (eds.) Contemporary issues
in development. Northern Australia: Progress and
prospects Vol.1, Darwin, Australian national
University, North Australia Research Unit, 1988

Wallace,V.H. Women and children first. An outline of a population policy for Australia. Melbourne, Oxford Uni.Press, 1946

Wax,R. Doing fieldwork. Warnings and advice Chicago, Midway Reprints from 1971, 1985

Webb,C., Allen,J. A functional analysis of Pleistocene bone tools from two sites in southwestern Tasmania. In: Archaeology Oceania 25(2), 1990:75-79

Wells,E. Reward and punishment in Arnhem land 1962 - 1963. Canberra, Australian Institute of Aboriginal Studies, 1982

Wharton,W.J.L. (ed.) Captain Cook's journal during the first voyage round the world made in H.M. bark Endeavour 1768 - 1771. Australian Facsimile Edition, No.188, 1966

White,C. Early stone axes in Arnhem Land. In: Antiquity 41, 1967a:149:52

(the same) Plateau and Plain: Prehistoric investigations in Arnhem Land, Northern Territory, Unpublished Ph.D. Thesis, Australian National University, Canberra, 1967b

(the same) The prehistory of the Kakadu people. In: Mankind 6(9), 1967c:426-31

White,J.P. Typologies for some prehistoric flaked stone artefacts of the Australian New Guinea Highlands. In: Archaeology and   Physical Anthroplogy in Oceania 4, 1969:18-46

(the same) Early man in New Guinea. In: Elkin,A.P., Macintosh,N.W.G. (eds) Grafton Elliot Smith: the man and his work. Sydney University Press, Sydney, 1974:109-13

White,J.P., O'Connell,J.F. Australian prehistory: new aspects of antiquity. In: Science, 1979:21-28

(the same) A prehistory of Australia, New Guinea and Sahul. Academic Press Australia, 1982

White,M.E. Australias prehistoric plants and their environment. Methuen, 1984

Whitehead,T.L., Connaways,M.E. (eds.) Self, sex, gender in cross-cultural fieldwork. Chicago, University of Illinois Press, 1986

Wigge-Caase,M. Zur wirtschaftlichen Entwicklung der Aborigines im Nordterritorium. Universität Göttingen, Master Thesis, 1983

Williams,J.A. Interview-respondent interaction: A study of bias in the information interview. In: Sociometry 27, 1964:338-52

Williams,N.W. Two laws managing disputes in a contemporary Aboriginal community. Canberra, Australian institute of Aboriginal Studies, 1987

Willmot,E. Education In: Jupp, J. (ed.) The Australian people. North Ryde, 1988:244-47

Wilpert,C.B. Kosmogonische Mythen der australischen Eingeborenen. Das Konzept der Schöpfung und Anthropogenese. München, Ph.D. Thesis, 1970

Wolfgang,M.E. The social scientist in court, In: Journal of the Criminal Law and Criminology 65, 1974:239-47

Wood-Jones,F. Australia's vanishing race. Sydney, Angus and Robertson, 1934

Wright,R.V.S. (ed.) Stone tools as culture markers: change, evolution and complexity Australian Institute of Aboriginal Studies, Canberra, 1977

Wurm,S.A. Languages of Australia and Tasmania. The Hague, Mouton, 1972, 208p.

Wyndham,W.T. The Aborigines of Australia. In; Journal and Proceedings of the Royal Society of New South wales 23, 1889:36-42

Ziegert,H. Objektorientierte und problemorientierte Forschungsansätze in der Archäologie. In: Hephaistos 2, 1980:57-65

(the same) Wissenschaftliche Arbeitstechniken in den Kulturwissenschaften. In: Reihe Kulturwissen-schaften 12, München 1986

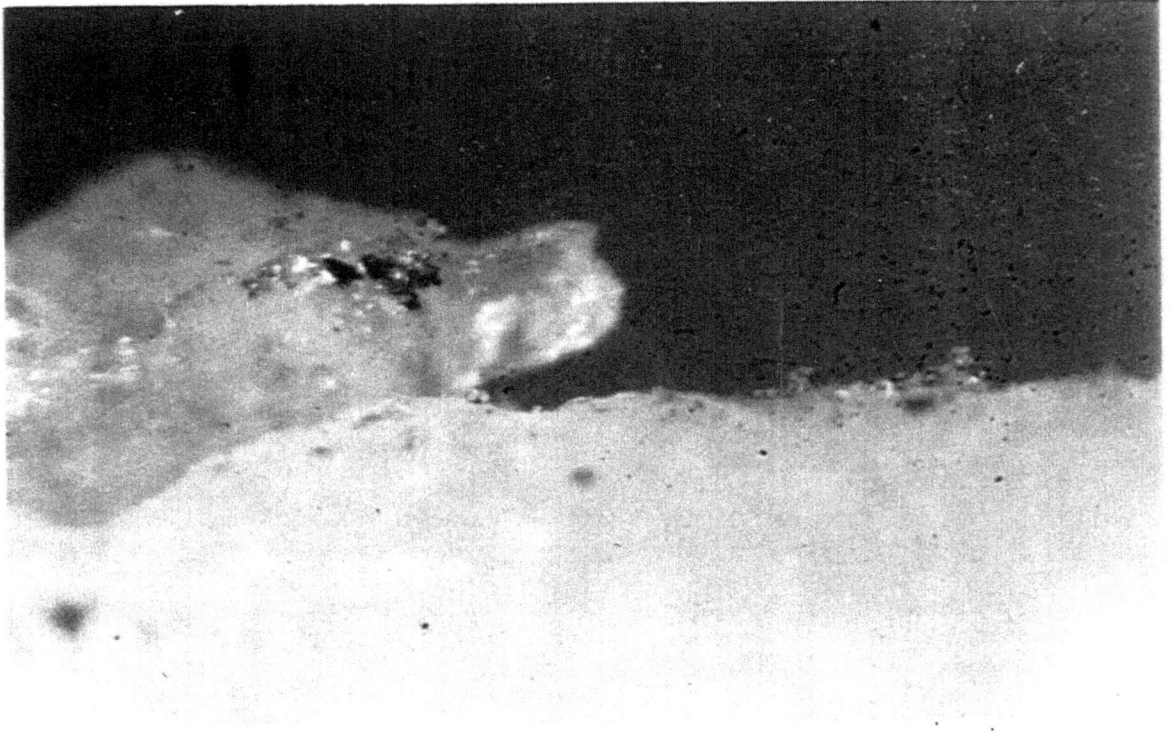

(Tool FOF62 displaying slight denticulation at 120x magnification)

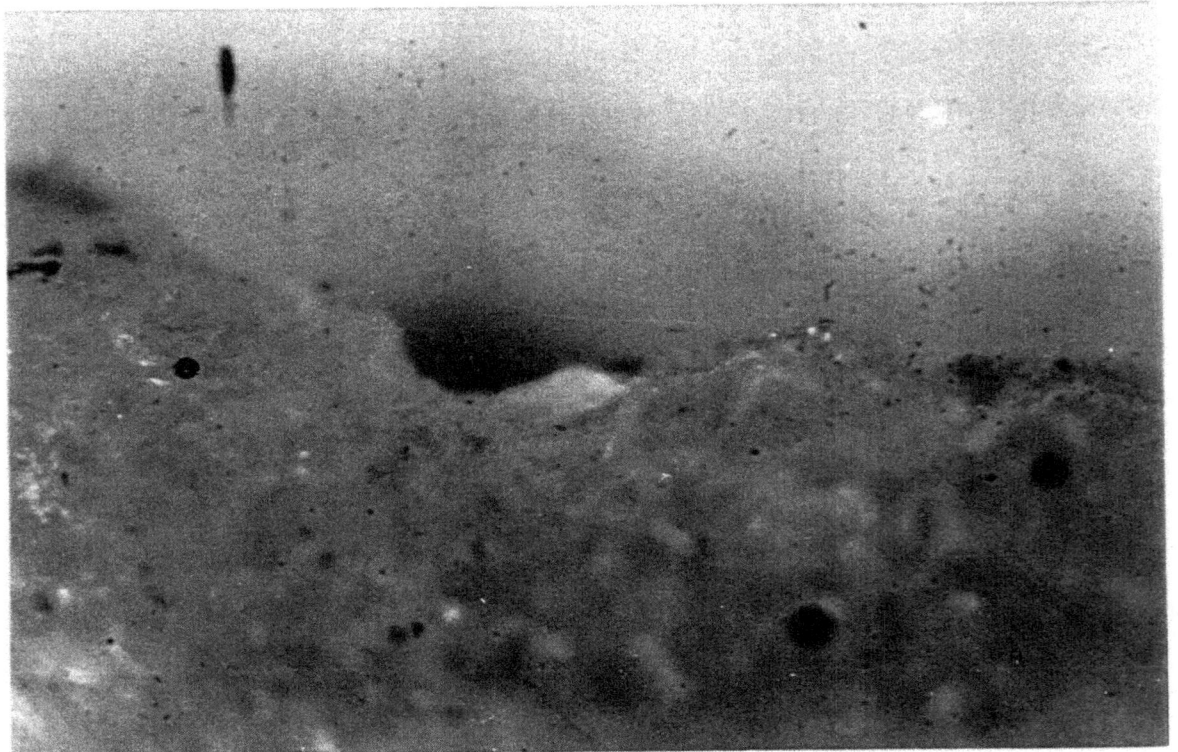

(Tool FOA16 displaying mikroflake scars at 90x magnification)

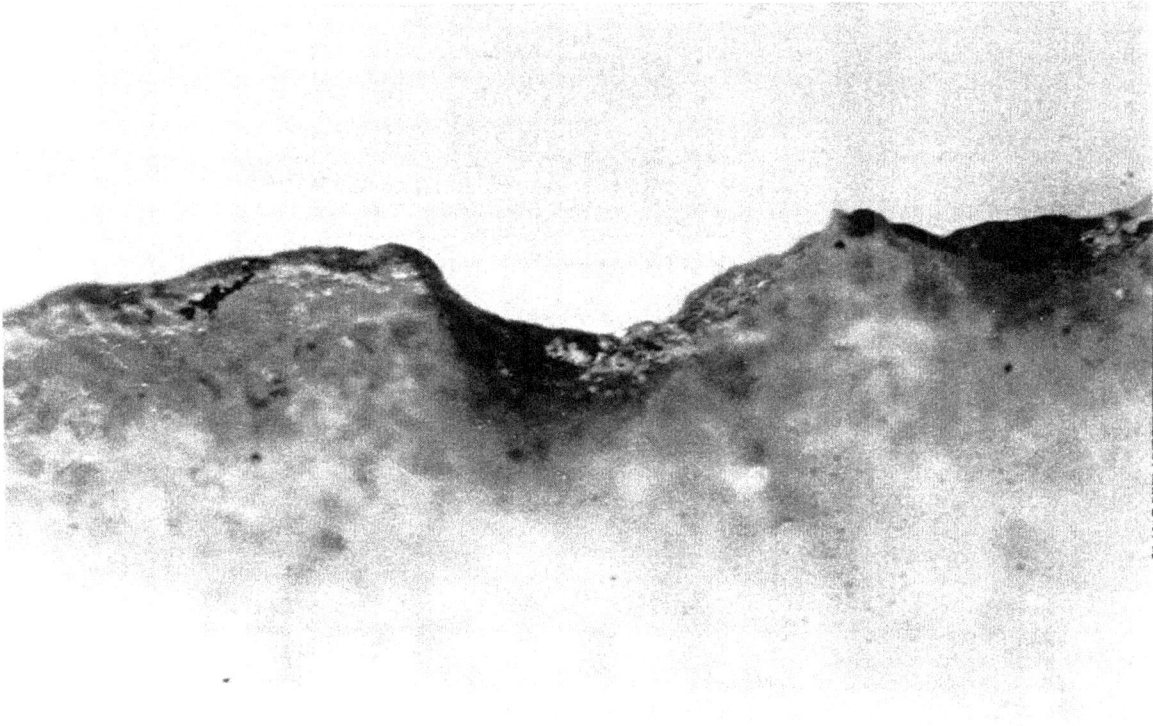

(Tool FOA12 displaying scarring at 120x magnification)

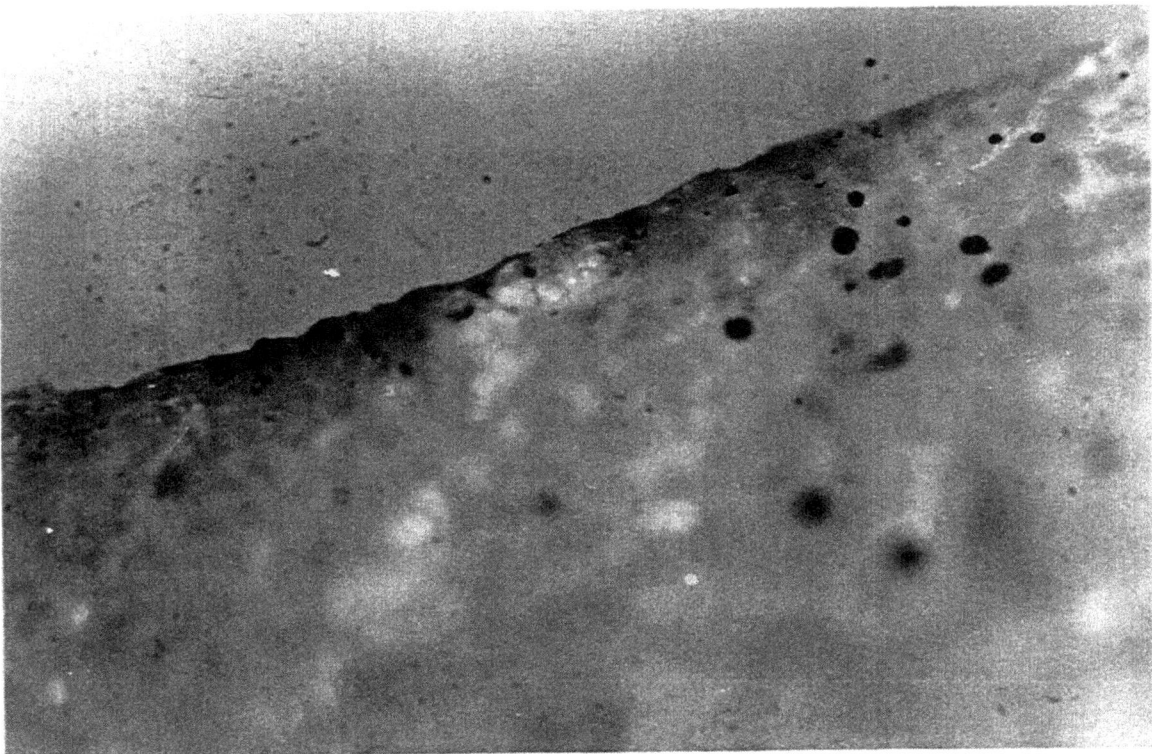

(Tool FO74 displaying edge rounding at 60x magnification)

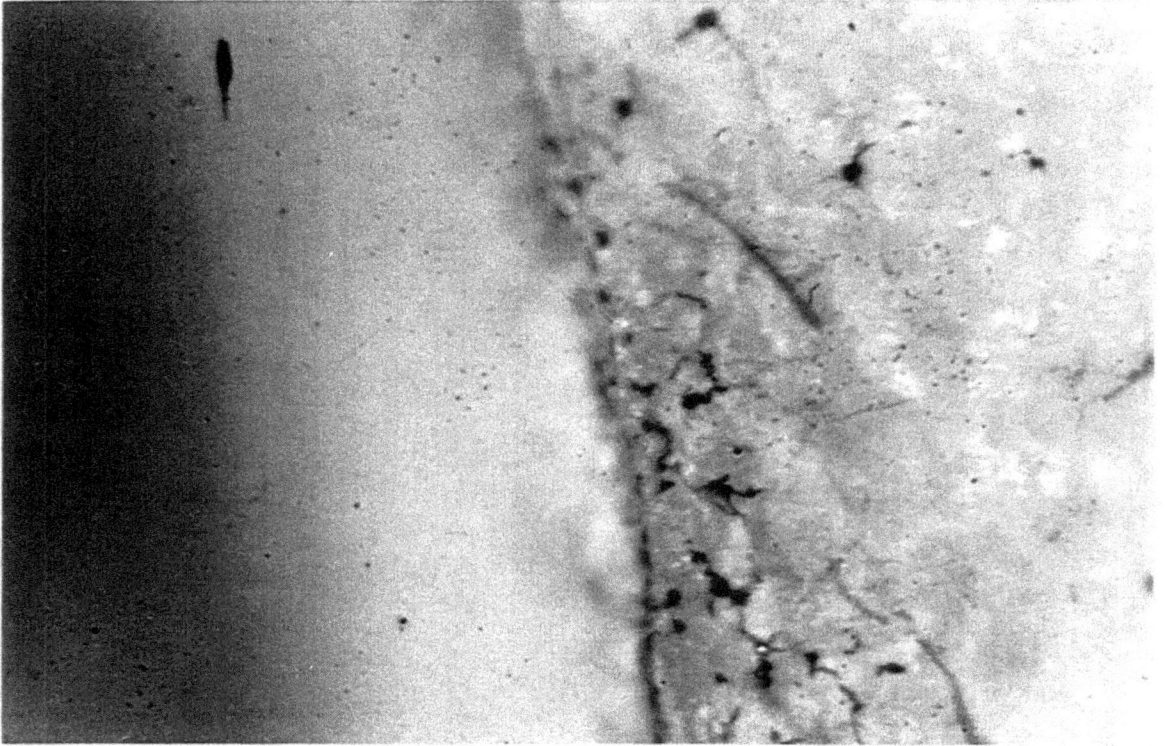

(Tool FOG73 showing smoothed surface at 90x magnification)

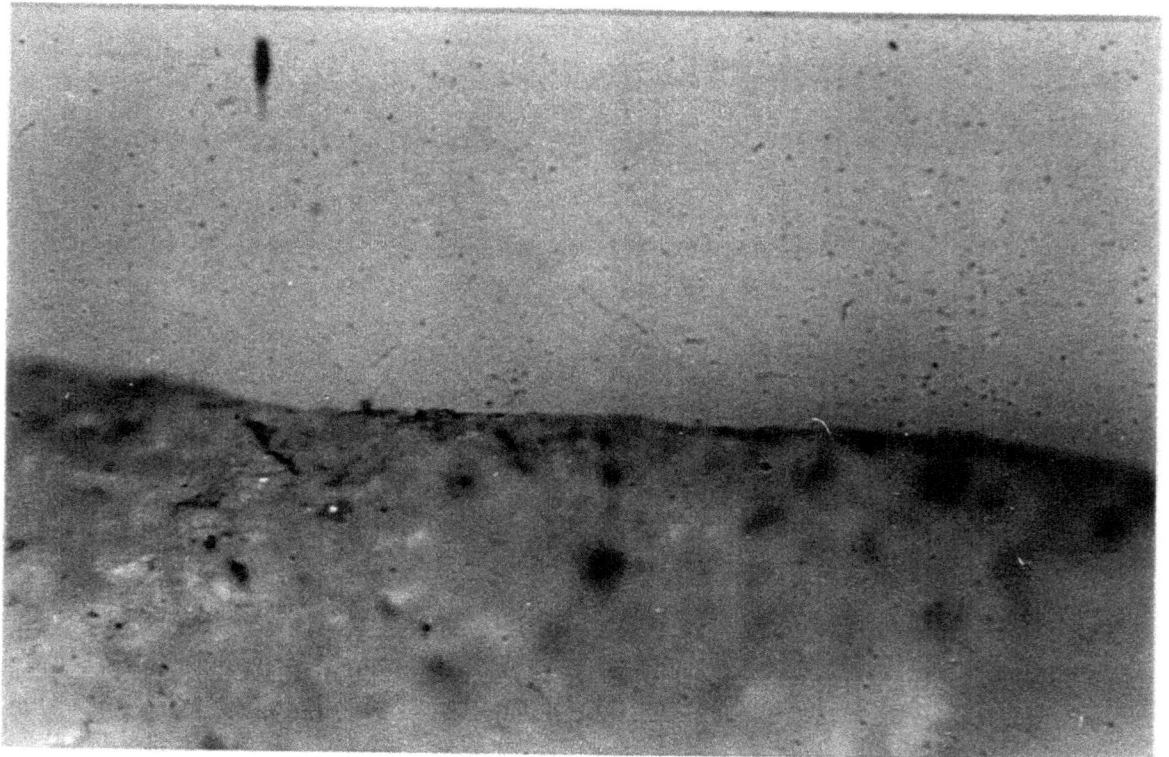

(Tool FOE50 showing polish on dorsal side at 90x magnification)

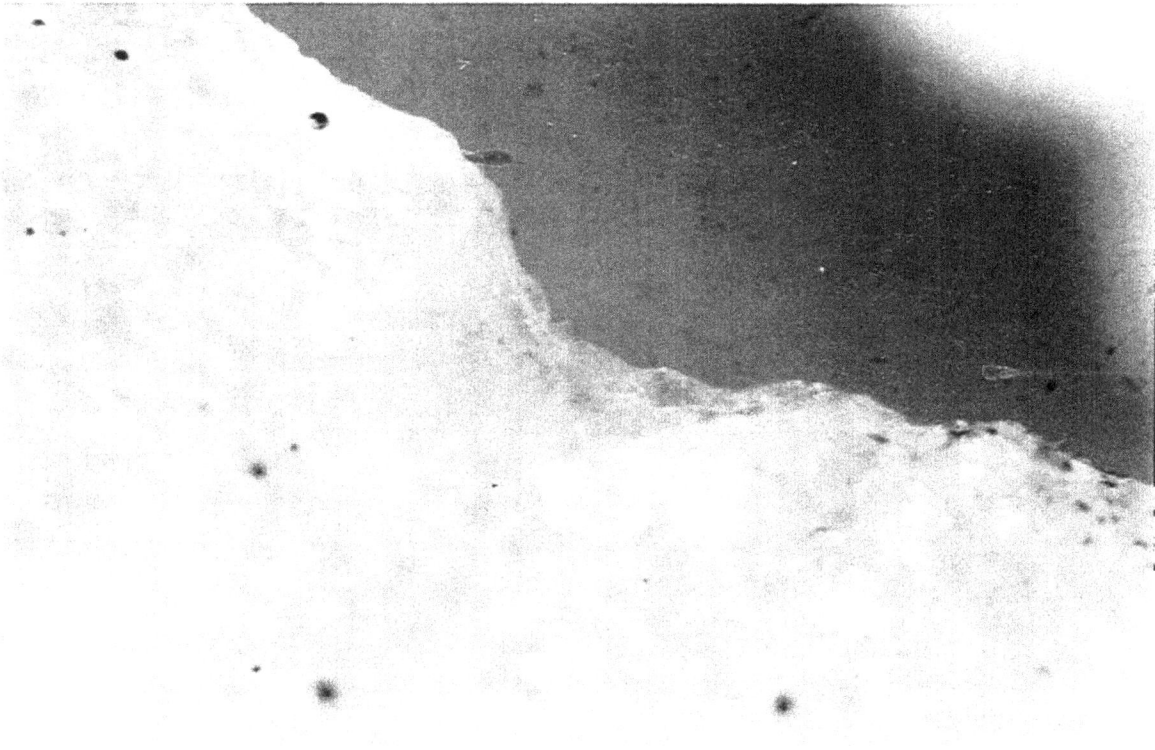

(Tool FOE50 showing retouch at 120x magnification)

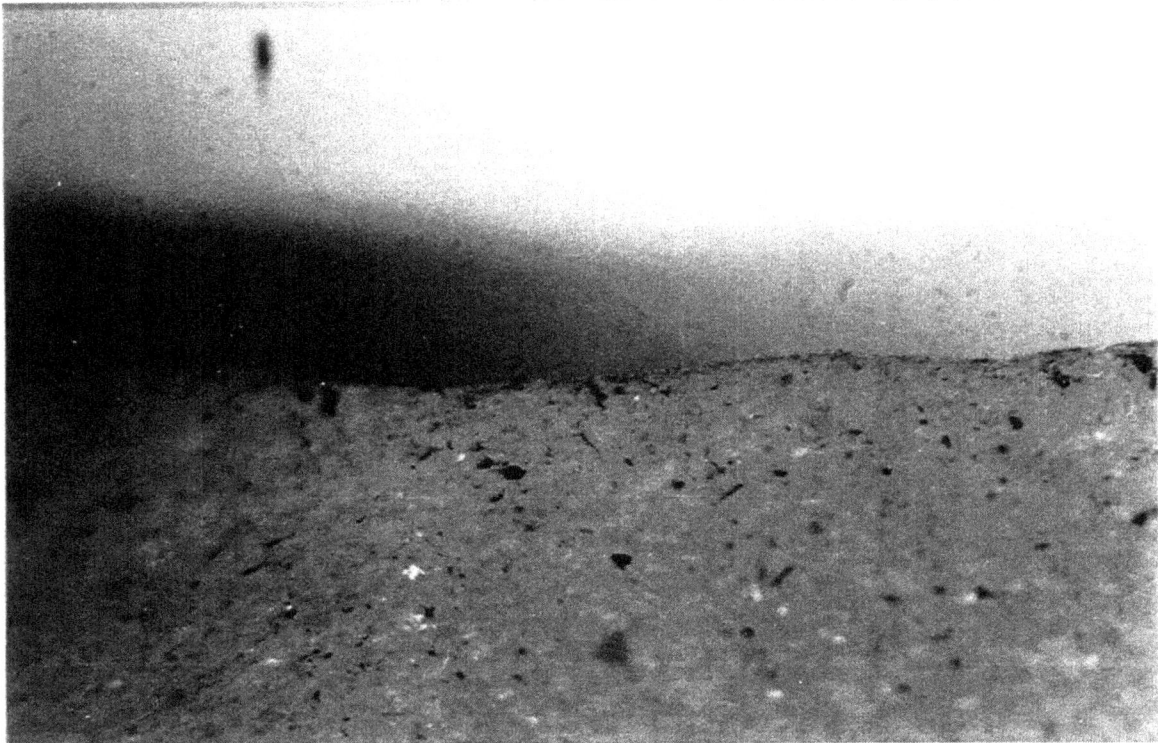

(Tool FOE50 showing edge rounding at 90x magnification)

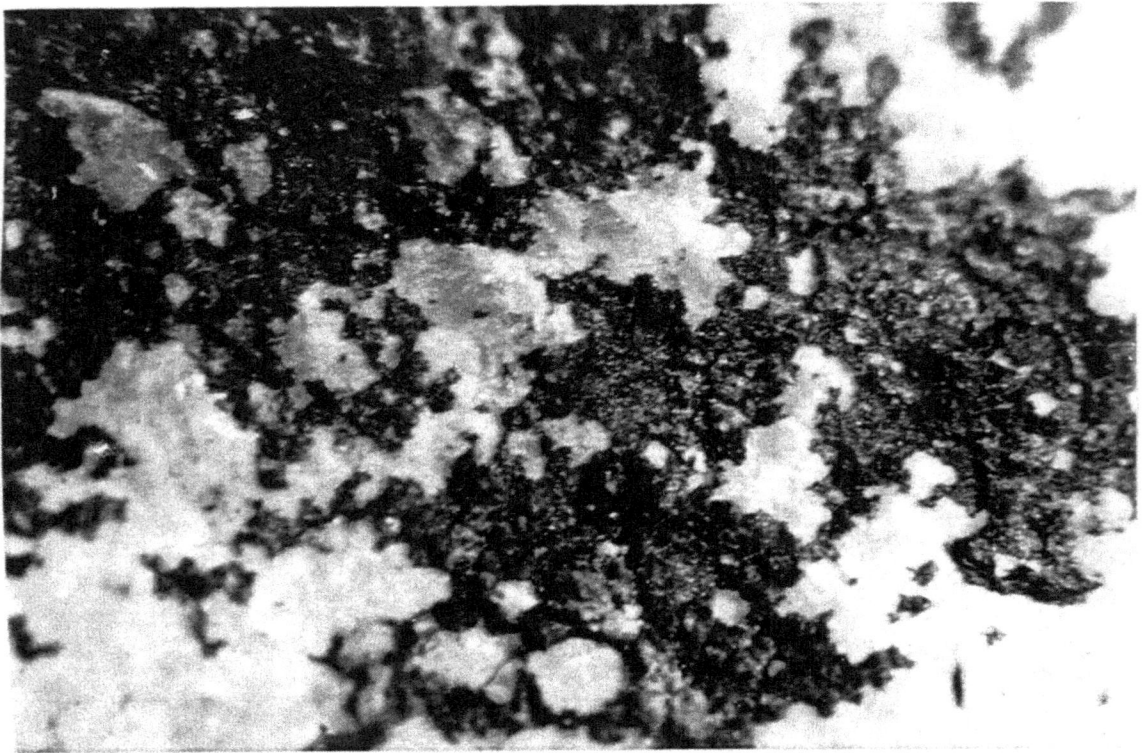

(Tool FO78 covered by thick crust at 120x magnification)

(Tool FO78 after partial removal of crust at 90x magnification)